Editor

Julia Downes is a Research Associate in the School of Applied Social Sciences at Durham University where she is currently working on a longitudinal study into the impact of community domestic violence perpetrator programmes on the safety and freedom of women and children. Julia's ESRC-funded PhD critically examined contemporary queer feminist activist music cultures in the UK including riot grrrl, Ladyfest and grassroots collectives.

She has lectured on popular music and society, feminist cultural activism and queer girl cultures at the University of Leeds, University of Derby, University of Birmingham and Durham University.

Julia has been active in DIY queer feminist cultural activism for over ten years within Manifesta, Ladyfest Leeds, Ladies Rock UK, Star and Shadow Cinema and even clean hands cause damage (http://evencleanhandscausedamage.wordpress.com) and as a drummer in the bands The Holy Terror, Fake Tan, Vile Vile Creatures and the Physicists.

First published in the UK in 2012 by
SUPERNOVA BOOKS
67 Grove Avenue, Twickenham, TW1 4HX
www.supernovabooks.co.uk
www.aurorametro.com

WOMEN MAKE NOISE © 2012 Supernova Books

Series editor: Rebecca Gillieron

With thanks to: Lesley Mackay, Kim Evans, Martin Gilbert, Alex
Chambers, Candida Cruz, Simon Smith, Neil Gregory, Jack Timney,
Richard Turk, Ziallo Gogui, Imogen Facey.

10 9 8 7 6 5 4 3 2 1

Cover design by Hayley Hatton.
Cover images © Rex Features except Tobi Vail and the Sissy Boyz ©
Red Chidgey, Pussy Riot protestor © Lilian Levesque, Trash Kit ©
Ochi Reyes and courtesy of Upset the Rhythm, Gina Birch © Martin
Jenkinson and The Dum Dum Girls © Claire Titley.

Printed by Ashford Colour Press, UK
ISBN: 978-0-956632-91-3

WOMEN MAKE NOISE

Girl bands from Motown to the modern

ed. Julia Downes

SUPERNOVA BOOKS

List of Images

Contents

Introducing the All-Girl Band:
Finding the Comfort in Contradiction

Julia Downes

What is an all-girl band?

'We get compared to those bands [Dum Dum Girls, Vivian Girls and Best Coast] more than we do to the people we know, the people we play shows with on a regular basis, and we affiliate ourselves with, and that comparison is purely based on gender [...] If someone asks me what I do I don't say, "Well I spend a lot of my time being female". Why should that define my music? Our gender influences our perspective and consequentially our creative output, but it isn't the whole of our identity.'[1] *Lillian Maring from Grass Widow*

There is something about being in an all-girl band... It is the place in which I first picked up some drum sticks and as part of a gang of girls created our own interpretation of what music is. With puzzled glances and questions, 'But is that really a song...?', we made our own rules, our own sounds and our own agendas. I started learning about the legacies of feminist punk music and all-girl bands: The Raincoats, Skinned Teen, Erase Errata, The Donnas, The Shaggs, The Shangri-Las, ESG, The

Runaways, Lung Leg, Fifth Column, LiLiPUT/Kleenex, The
Slits, Sleater-Kinney, L7, Frightwig, Babes in Toyland and Slant
6. I became addicted to that girl gang feeling. We figured it out
along the way. From The Holy Terror (who later became The
Ivories), Fake Tan and Vile Vile Creatures to The Physicists,
the all-girl bands I have played in have always felt like home
to me. But my experience in these bands has not been without
awkward attitudes, complications and bad feelings.

All-girl bands occupy a precarious position in local music
scenes and the broader cultural landscape. Like Lillian
Maring, the drummer for all-girl trio Grass Widow, in the
opening quotation, I wondered: Should our gender solely
define our music? Did we get gigs and attention just because
we were an all-girl band? Did putting us on with an otherwise
male line-up mean the problem of women and girls' under-
participation in the local music scene was solved? Was there
only ever enough space for one credible girl band? Would
we always play pretty well... for girls? Did the constant
comparisons, and gigs, with other all-girl bands, who sounded
completely different, marginalise us or offer us community?
Did any attention to what we looked like undermine what
we were doing? Should we dress down or dress up? When
we wrote songs, gave interviews and performed were we
speaking for all girls and women or just ourselves? Were we
defining ourselves as feminists just by getting up and playing?
Was anyone actually listening or interested in why and how we
were making music?

When Supernova Books first sent out a call for contributors
for this book several people emailed me to object to the focus
on all-girl bands. The term in itself had touched a nerve. Here
are a few examples of the kind of emails that hit my inbox:

> 'I have been in bands with men and women. It is way *easier*
> to be in an all-girl band (plus at what point do we get to
> be "women?"). People *love* all-girl bands. There are record

labels, promoters and festivals that will likely be *more interested* in an all-girl band than a female-fronted band.'

'I am a woman fronting a band with men. People (including feminists, band members, the public) often assume I am just a performer and not a creative leader. Men will typically get the credit for my song writing and women have a hard time getting taken seriously by band members, studio people and the music press. It is *much harder* being a woman in a band with men, men stand back and let you fight your own battles or fight against you, you have to work harder to be noticed and be given credit for your work. By focusing on all-girl bands you are *invalidating* my experience and your academic distinctions between female-fronted and all-girl are *trivial*.'

'By focusing on all-girl bands you are excluding some of the most *important* and *groundbreaking* women in music. There have simply not been any *good* all-girl bands. By focusing on all-girl bands you are being *sexist* and *separatist* and *distorting* music history.'

The responses reveal the 'all-girl band' as a contested, ambiguous and controversial term. On one hand all-girl bands are said to have more (possibly undeserved) popular appeal and sit in positions of privilege and opportunity. However, the first responder expresses her frustration at being described as a girl instead of a woman, resisting connotations of being inexperienced, naïve and childlike. (Here I am interested in how the term all-girl band is used, by who and to what effect.) The second respondent argues that life for a woman in a band with men is the most marginalised position in music-making. Interestingly, instead of taking issue with masculine entitlements circulated in music culture (including the behaviour of male bandmates) that construct women's participation in narrow ways, the implication is that this book will reinforce the marginalisation of women with an unfair focus on all-girl bands (who have it much easier). Finally, the last speaker insists that there are no successful all-girl bands to talk about and accuses this book of producing a sexist, separatist and distorted music history. Here I would draw attention to the measures used to assess which musicians are 'good', 'groundbreaking' and 'successful'. Whose standards are these? Are all-girl bands equally able to fulfil the standards to be credible, authentic and original? Is it a coincidence that the women who receive an albeit brief mention in music histories tend to be heterosexual feminine women who have achieved long-standing commercial success often in the more 'conventional' roles as vocalists and singer-songwriters? What is so dangerous or threatening about the legacy of girls and women making music together?

The term all-girl band is full of contradictions. It has been used and abused in so many ways. I would argue that this means we are on the right track. In *Swing Shift*, an excellent oral history of all-girl swing bands of the 1940s, Sherrie Tucker describes the complexity of the all-girl band term that her interviewees used:

> 'The term all-girl bands will resound with historic dissonance – in relation to the women who played in them, the circuits they travelled and the work they performed. The label summons the complexity of working under an umbrella of both opportunity and devaluation, of the easy dismissal from history of the whole category in later years, and of the disparate memories and stakes narrated cross-generationally in the 1990s by women musicians of the 1940s all-girl bands.'[2]

The critical emails I received therefore echo this unease at an exclusive focus on the all-girl band. The all-girl band is always in a precarious position of opportunity, marginalisation, devaluation and erasure from history. We do not yet have any progressive ways to talk about women and girls' collective music participation. As popular music scholar Susan Fast argued:

> '...it is not because they [women] have not participated, but because we choose to think about their contributions in ways that cannot help but marginalise them'.[3]

The inadequacies of language and evaluative frameworks used to marginalise women's music-making have already been highlighted by numerous music journalists and writers[4] (we wouldn't say *male*-fronted, *all-boy* band, *male* singer-songwriter or *men's* music). The all-girl band still remains a paradox in popular music; reliant on narrative strategies that simultaneously marginalise the very all-girl bands being 'rescued' from obscurity.

'Just another book about women in rock?'[5]

Over the past twenty years, interest in women's music-making has increased. Lots of books have been published about women musicians and their struggles within 'male-dominated' music worlds of rock, punk, pop, indie and soul.[6] This 'women in rock' or 'women in music' paradigm has become a well-established corrective strategy that makes women's lives and contributions visible. These accessible biographical summaries of key recordings, performances and live events and/or interviews with women musicians focus on what it is like to be a woman musician in a 'male-dominated' music industry.

Simultaneously, feminist musicologists have undertaken analysis of women's musical contributions including artists like Kate Bush, Madonna, Courtney Love, Tori Amos, PJ Harvey[7] – and, more recently, Amy Winehouse, Adele, Lady Gaga have attracted popular attention. However, the spotlight is on commercially successful, high profile solo performers who are already partially acknowledged in music history and journalism. This tendency to create a separate history of exceptional women musicians leaves women and girls' radical challenges to the dominant values of popular music to be safely contained by authorities and institutions. One common example of this in popular music teaching is the token lecture or module on 'women in music' that provokes negative student reactions and a desire to get back to the 'real' history of music (made and theorised by respectable white men).[8] The popular belief that there are no all-girl bands worthy of attention has suppressed a comprehensive investigation of all-girl bands. All-girl bands remain marginal footnotes in history.

In this context, the critical consideration of all-girl bands and women's grassroots music cultures has barely started. What would happen to dominant music histories if we explored music from the lived experiences of all-girl bands? What if, in particular, we look at all-girl bands that have consciously rejected commercial/music industry routes in order to create radical genders, sexualities and feminisms, to avoid an industry that researchers have convincingly shown to restrain women and girls?[9] What would happen if we moved away from debating the problems of terminology and focused on what all-girl bands actually did with music? What does making music mean for all-girl bands? What choices do all-girl bands make in relation to aesthetics, sounds, song writing, performances and activism? How do they experience the contradictory position of the all-girl band? How does gender (along with other social differences including class, race, sexuality, age) shape music-making in all-girl bands? How do all-girl bands interrupt, resist and reinforce these dominant categories of difference? It is questions like these which have motivated me to accept the invite from Rebecca Gillieron, the series editor, to produce a book which would explore the music of all-girl bands across multiple genres (she plays in one herself – see Wetdog). The resulting volume, *Women Make Noise,* is an important intervention because it provides:

Introducing the All-girl Band

• An overdue celebration of inspirational all-girl bands that dispels the myth that there have been no 'great' all-girl bands. Thinking from the perspective of all-girl bands reveals womens' continuous participation and valuable contributions to popular music.

• A critical take on the idea of an all-girl band as a novelty act or sex object; as untalented, unskilled and inauthentic musicians who are passive in the face of male control. All-girl bands are instead positioned as active, creative, skilled, savvy and politically engaged.

• A fresh assertion of all-girl bands as a powerful force for cultural change. They inspire others. They can and have used music as a tool to provoke social change and justice. (Pussy Riot are the perfect contemporary example – see the epilogue for more on this band.)

But... only so far?

This book has been through a long development process. Rebecca and I decided to circulate an open call for contributors to get the best chance of including diverse viewpoints on the all-girl band from fans, musicians, writers, teachers/lecturers, academics, researchers and journalists. We did not want to hear only from the established 'experts'. The responses led to the development of chapters exploring all-girl bands in relation to questions of creativity, performance, aesthetics and community within different cultural movements. In particular, we wanted contributions that highlighted the use of music by all-girl bands that interacted with wider struggles of social difference (nation, ethnicity, class, sexuality, gender, age and feminism). We looked for contributions that were accessible but went beyond descriptive biographical accounts and looked critically at what all-girl bands did with music

The call was ambitious and we received a lot of submissions to work through. The final collection of essays focuses on western pop and alternative musics, so can unfortunately only scratch the surface of a comprehensive global investigation of the all-girl band. Some chapters just didn't come to fruition, for instance, one submission by Steve Dew-Jones that we pursued focused on Orkideh, the first women's pop band in Iran.[10] Jones highlighted the necessity of the all-girl band and audience due to restrictions on women performing for men in public space. Another contributor found it difficult to use the all-girl band concept in relation to hip hop where women tend to be solo performers. We came to realise that our use of the term 'all-girl band' may not cohere to the ways that *all* women's music collectives and communities work. Once again we come up against language as a classed, racialised and gendered medium. There are also tensions in the use of pre-defined music genres and historical moments used to order the book. These definitions blur and overlap into each other and it is common to see the same bands appear in multiple chapters as these messy creative worlds collided with each other much more often than marketing executives would care to admit. This book aims to provoke more thoughtful consideration of the all-girl band. We could not promise to be a complete, true and comprehensive herstory of every all-girl band but hope to inspire you to question your assumptions and to find out more about the legacy of all-girl bands.

Scratching the surface

The book follows a loosely chronological order to excavate and critically discuss the contributions and legacy of all-girl bands. It starts with Victoria Yeulet's investigation of the all-girl band in US old time and early country music. Elizabeth K. Keenan's essay on girl groups of the 1950s and 1960s discusses

Introducing the All-girl Band

how girl groups emerged within a complicated relationship between performers, songwriters, producers, audiences and wider society. Sini Timonen investigates the all-girl garage rock bands of the 1960s and 1970s who have been buried under the radar of popular consciousness. Jackie Parsons offers a unique chapter on progressive rock music based on first-hand experience of being in the all-girl band Mother Superior. Jane Bradley reflects on her involvement with contemporary punk culture and delves into the stories of radical women and all-girl bands of the 1970s punk movement. Rhian E. Jones looks into the aftermath of punk and the experiences and opportunities for all-girl bands that post-punk and no wave opened up. Deborah M. Withers examines the music-making of women involved in the women's liberation movement in the United Kingdom during the 1970s and 1980s. Bryony Beynon takes issue with histories that have suppressed the matrilineage of global DIY hardcore punk. Val Rauzier explores how all-girl bands of queercore put queer, feminist and postmodern theories into punk action to combat sexism and homophobia. Finally, Sarah Dougher and Elizabeth K. Keenan examine how the all-girl band has changed within feminist musical activism in the 1990s to now, from riot grrrl, to Ladyfest and Rock 'n' Roll Camp for Girls.

Women Make Noise seeks to kick off the process of telling the different and more complicated stories of all-girl bands. It is not enough to counter the marginalisation of all-girl bands, we also need to further investigate the musical processes within all-girl bands. We can reveal more interesting stories of how music has been used by girls and women to open up different ways of exploring and celebrating their gender, undermine dominant categories of social difference and fight for social change. We need to be suspicious of the perpetual year of 'women in rock' and cleverly marketed resurgences of all-girl bands and recognise the continuous participation of musical collectives of women and girls. During my involvement making music and putting on gigs and events that have focused on women, queers and girls a whole world has opened up. I am privileged to have seen and heard numerous all-girl bands form, grow and sometimes collapse over time. Bands like Trash Kit, Mika Miko, Woolf, Muscles of Joy, Wetdog, Grass Widow, Finally Punk, Brilliant Colors, Warpaint, Jesus and His Judgemental Father, Vivian Girls, Household, Explode into Colors, Erase Errata, Tortura, Purple Rhinestone Eagle, Lesbo Pig, Electrelane, Hex on the Beach and La La Vasquez. In closing, to return to Lillian Maring:

> 'We need to shift our attention from "Stop ignoring us!" to "Ok, what do we do now that we have everyone's attention?"'.[11]

It is up to us.

1. Female pioneers in American Old-time and Country

Victoria Yeulet

In the 1920s to 1940s, American roots music was an extremely exciting genre for female musicians. The emergence of the 'modern' woman in popular culture from the flappers through to the Harlem renaissance highlighted multiple forms of female resistance and visibility. Moreover, vaudeville, blues, jazz and country music all provided environments that nurtured female creativity and shared musical experiences.

The history of women's music-making spans innovations in the music industry amidst a changing socio-economic political 'boom and bust' climate from affluence to the depression of the 1930s. However, women's music-making in roots music during this period was largely defined by the public and private spheres within which women existed. The boundaries of these spheres, the points of crossover and the impact of friendship and family networks all affected lyrical content, and shaped the forms of music-making that took place. As women's talents were encouraged to flourish, diverse acts such as The Carter Sisters and The Coon Creek Girls emerged. However, their role in music history still remains unknown to many.

In this chapter, I examine the neglected histories of women musicians in roots music. Casting light on some of those lesser-known artists and, in particular, all-girl bands, I offer a new perspective on the traditional histories of Western rock music.

High impact solo artists and the industry: Mamie Smith, Bessie Smith, Ma Rainey

The beginnings of the recording industry brought huge changes that women musicians in both old-time and country music were key to instigating. Solo artists were the first to hit the public arena and Mamie Smith's 'Crazy Blues' on Okeh records in 1920 broke open the market for 'race records'. These were conceived as a way in which to capitalise on the success of vaudeville and touring musical shows, including the popular medicine shows of the southern states, as well as the city theatre revues. 'Crazy Blues' was immensely popular due to Mamie's charming performance and the vaudevillian 'jazz hounds' backing band, and was the first vocal recording by an African American. The city revues featured many black female performers, primarily from vaudevillian traditions, and after Smith's hit record, they became sought after by record companies hoping to cash in on the new craze for this style of 'blues'.

What followed was a boom of recording and marketing music for use in the home, with labels creating sub-genres including 'hillbilly' to accommodate the musical interests of consumers in both cities and rural areas. The most successful artists from the period were Bessie Smith and Ma Rainey, who catered to both the northern city trend of hot jazz cabaret and the southern tent show circuit. Ma Rainey had been running her own tent show throughout the country for many years before achieving recognition and Bessie had been under her tutorage. Female vocalists and businesswomen such as Rainey at this time were catalysts for this new musical trend. The female-dominated musical environments they provided on their road trips were hotbeds of talent that the labels picked up on fast.

'Hillbilly' women: a new demand

During the 'race record' boom the way in which artists were scouted was influential upon its development. As many of the labels at this time were subsidiaries of companies that made phonograph players, they did not have an established system of artists and repertoire. As a result, the market was very consumer led, with customers requesting artists they had heard at dance parties or seen on the stage, and the labels sending out field recording crews to set up in areas with open auditions. This type of talent scouting became particularly prevalent in southern towns where the most popular male artists such as Blind Lemon Jefferson and Rev. JM Gates were recorded. It also meant that if consumers wanted recordings of female artists, they would be produced.

The demand for white musicians from the south was growing fast as the record companies delved into gospel and blues. So-called 'hillbilly' recordings consisted of white musicians playing string band, 'old-time' and country ballads. The record companies had spotted a market for 'old fashioned tunes' in white record buyers and jumped on it. Although their initial interest was largely commercial – they wanted to sell old-fashioned tunes – what they actually provided was an immensely fertile environment for female musicians to be recorded and even achieve respect for their technical skills; a rarity for any women performer in the 20th century. Female musicians, and their specific environs of mutual tutorage, began to lead the field in terms of popularity and visibility.

Political narratives of resistance: a strong female voice emerges

Running parallel to the commercial recordings of this period were the field recordings being made by folklorists, particularly those searching for Anglo-Irish ballads being sung in Kentucky and the Carolinas. These folklorists had a far more academic approach to the documentation of songs and musicians. In particular, they sought out to preserve the most 'pure' and 'authentic' songs and get as close as possible to folk origins. This tradition continued with fervour in the folk music revival of the 1950s and 60s. These early recordings reveal a powerful history of female innovation that dealt with violent and contentious topics.

For example, the Appalachian folk ballads that have been committed to vinyl are amongst some of the most enduring songs in western music standards. For example 'murder ballads', were frequently written from a female narrator's perspective. The sound of women singing openly violent and brutal songs was juxtaposed with the 'clean cut' image of the simple country female, and added a dimension of darkness to often very upbeat light female vocal performances.

Although distant from small town southern life, the influence of blues, jazz and the modern 'flapper' movement, cannot be underestimated upon the women of this period who were being gradually exposed to news, imagery and sounds of these cultural developments. The performers donned short bob haircuts of the 'modern girl' and openly discussed and politicised their experiences in lyrics of defiance, and opposed subjugation. The political climate for both white and black women in America was significant. The Harlem Renaissance had spawned many of the 'race' record performers and championed the risqué styles and lyrics of the 1920s Blues Queens.

Other examples of confrontational emotional content can be found in the songs of poor white hillbilly women, who now utilised their own methods to speak of their experiences towards liberated living. The legendary Carter Family sang 'Single girl, married girl' released in 1927:

Female pioneers in American Old-time and Country

'Single girl, oh single girl she's going anywhere she please,
married girl married girl, baby's on her knees…
Single girl oh single girl always dressed so fine, married
girl married girl wears just any kind…
Single girl oh single girl goes to the store and buys,
married girl married girl, rocks the cradle and cries.'[1]

Themes of freedom for women included self-respect, individuality, financial autonomy and opposition to the institutionalised ideas of the home-bound wife. The Carter family present revolutionary ideas of opportunity and hope during tough financial times of the depression era.

Many ballads from the period can be seen as early feminist declarations of independence from patriarchal structures and celebrations of female freedom. For instance, aged just fourteen and accompanying herself on guitar in 1925, country singer Roba Stanley also celebrated her status with a song:

'Single life is a happy life,
single life is lovely,
I am single and no man's wife,
and no man shall control me'.[2]

'The Wagoner's Lad', as recorded by the Kossoy Sisters (amongst others) similarly laments the structural confinement of women in the home:

'Hard is the fortune of all womankind,
they're always controlled, they're always confined,
controlled by their parents until they are wives,
then slaves to their husbands the rest of their lives'.[3]

These women were innovators. They used popular music to deliver a political message that challenged the status quo. This feminist, confrontational and ground-breaking song writing tradition influenced future generations of female singer songwriters. From the political ballads of Aunt Molly Jackson, Peggy Seeger, Odetta and Bernice Johnson Reagon in the 1950s and 60s, to Jean Shepard and Loretta Lynn's country feminist anthems 'Two Whoops and a Holler' (1959) and 'The Pill' (1975) – all took their cues from these early trailblazers. In the UK it was the skiffle artists, such as Nancy Whiskey and Shirley Douglas, who took up these traditions within the British folk scene.

In such a turbulent economic era, class resistance also became an issue for women music-makers to give voice to. Poor white women used music to express themselves as active resistors to the patriarchal status quo. Their efforts stand as political landmarks of music and social history, equal to the folk songs of the 'poor white male' expressed by celebrated artists like Woody Guthrie, for example, and equal to the prison songs of resistance sung by artists like Mattie Mae Thomas.

Instrumentation and 'a space to call their own'

It was through instrumentation and technical skill that old-time and country women truly excelled during this period. The significance of the family, and the imagery in rural white America of the mother at the piano, was vital to the way in which female musicianship was normalised and accepted during this period. Although traditionally considered a 'man's' instrument, the banjo was played by many women from the civil war era onwards. The imagery of this 'rustic down home gal' became a stalwart of country music for decades to follow with June Carter and Minnie Pearl being later examples of the 'southern cracker' vaudevillian ideal, 'pickin' on her banjer'.

These vaudevillian touring acts – run in a similar fashion to the blues tents – provided vital inspiration for female audiences who could watch strong women on the public stage command an audience and display musical prowess. This visibility and validation of female players would have been hugely important to other aspiring female artists, as we can see through the communities and networks of female musicians that resulted.

The guitar, piano, autoharp, dulcimer, fiddle, ukulele, mandolin, zither and banjo were all instruments of choice for female musicians of early country music. The emphasis on the family band enabled female musicians to be so frequently recorded and accepted during this period. In looking at the family string bands of the old-time genres it's clear that women and children, including young girls, were seen as part of the family collective of 'work'. In the rural traditions of travelling shows, the entire family would be taken to perform on tour, considered as a unit to have popular appeal and be a viable source of income. For many families who were musically inclined, already performing for friends and locals in their homes or at local events, the recording industry provided a huge opportunity for women and girls. All members of the family were included in the package of making music – and potentially money through performances also.

A 'norm' in the folk scene

The southern gospel tradition was a significant avenue for women in white rural communities to become musicians involved with church music. Some women folklorists interested in popular heritage became involved through the collection and sharing of old folk songs. Although this period has been romanticised (particularly by folklorists), the mutual sharing amongst women of their family and local songs contributed significantly to the lasting legacy of this music. In the 1950s, for example, Alan Lomax and Shirley Collins found artists such as Texas Gladden who had continued such a tradition.

The notion of female musicianship in these environments

was far less of an anomaly. Musicianship was part of everyday life before radio. Families and communities made their own music and girls and women picked up fiddles and guitars far more readily without external judgment. Instruments such as the banjo were seen as less 'ladylike' in some communities and women's public performances may have been frowned upon, and objections to the competition were no doubt rife amongst male musicians who didn't want to be outdone by women's virtuosity. However, this was also a golden period, as girls whose mothers, fathers or grandparents played were almost as likely as boys to pick up and play instruments

For instance, Samantha Bumgardner was a self-taught multi -instrumentalist from such a family, adept at fiddle, guitar and banjo, who produced homemade instruments as a teenager and was one of the first country music recording artists in 1924. Performing with female fiddler Eva Davis, she recorded for Columbia Records, bridging a large gap between the old-time folk ballad tradition and the emerging country music sound.

Glorious duos and all-girl bands

The kind of female creative partnership enjoyed by Bumgardner and Davis was not common. Many of the greatest and most overlooked women musicians of this period were performing in male duos or mixed family bands. However, I believe that to remove their contributions is to negate the environments that were conducive to their talents being recorded, and to reiterate their continual omissions from popular music history.

Until the Carter Family came along, the opportunities for women to record in all-women groups were slight. Hillbilly may have allowed the space for women musicians to perform on an equal footing as their male counterparts, a rarity in the music industry of the day which was focused on solo female vocalists. But there were still few all-women bands being recorded. The family bands, which frequently featured multiple women and young girls displaying their creative musical abilities were pioneers and set a precedent for women musicians to follow.

Women and The Family Band

The idealised notion of the family band served as a promotional tool. The family represented wholesomeness, which in the Christian southern states was highly regarded. One such band was The Tennessee Ramblers featuring Willie Sievers on guitar, along with her father, brother and male cousin. Eck Robertson, regarded as one of the finest fiddlers in old-time music, played with his wife Nettie and daughter Daphne on guitars. Fiddlin' Bob Larkin and his music-makers featured his wife Hattie Larkin on organ, daughter Alice Larkin on guitar along with her brother on piano, and in a revolving family line-up Mildred McRee also joined in on the banjo. Hoyt Ming and his Pep Steppers featured Roselle Ming on guitar and, initially, although not on recordings, her sister on mandolin. Their unique sound was formed largely by her guitar style and the 'pep stepping' name refers to her keeping time with her feet. Taylor-Griggs Louisiana Melody Makers featured Lorean Griggs on mandolin and Ione Griggs on guitar. Ernest Stoneman played with his wife Hattie Stoneman on fiddle and her sister Irma Frost on organ and vocals. The Shelor family: Dad Blackard's Moonshiners featured Clarice Shelor on piano and vocals and Walter Smith played with his young daughters Thelma on guitar and Dorothy on ukulele.

These, heavily overlooked female musicians, including many under the age of twenty, were treated as equal to the male musicians – a ground-breaking and trailblazing occurrence that had an impact on the future of girl bands for all.

'Moonshine Kate' or Rosa Lee Carson Johnson is one of the more significant musicians of the time. Like Roba Stanley she was a rare female solo performer, playing both guitar and banjo. She came to prominence playing with her father Fiddlin' John Carson, whom she also recorded with, in a wise-cracking comedy routine. Her solo recordings show her proficiency as an unusual vocalist and highly skilled guitarist, and she was renowned for her modern sassy attitude. Gospel acts of this period in country gospel traditions also featured female musicians prominently.

Women as partners: male-female duos

In addition to these, the 1920s and 30s saw a number of religious and non-religious male and female duos produce recordings. These included artists such as Fred and Gertrude Gossett, Bill and Belle Reed and Hugh and Mary Cross, and were often husband and wife partnerships – a trend which was to be continued in 1940s and 50s country music. Cleoma Breaux accompanied herself on guitar, with husband Joe Falcon on accordion, to create the first Cajun recording in 1928 and her recordings have styling that pre-dates 1960s psychedelia by almost forty years. Hawaiian music was also popular during the 1920s, with an open-tuned slide guitar sound being extremely influential. Female accompaniment on guitar and ukulele in these groups was common and its influence pervasive on technical innovations in the field of roots music.

Cowgirls play: The Dezurick Sisters, Girls of the Golden West and The Coon Creek Girls

The other notable tradition in early country music was the depression era western or 'cowboy' based song. This sound emanated from the mid-west regions and developed alongside the mainstream popularisation of cowboys, cowgirls, Hollywood film and national radio. Patsy Montana was the most widely known female artist in this tradition. 'I want to be a cowboy's sweetheart' was the first million-selling female country song in 1935. Lulu Belle and Scotty also enjoyed popularity due to the depression era radio barn dances.

The most interesting of these acts comprised Billie Maxwell and two female duos, The Girls of the Golden West and the Dezurick sisters. Both of the duos incorporated yodelling into their vocals, the Dezurick's performed vocal acrobatics with bird imitation sounds and multiple harmonies. The Girls of the Golden West recorded prolifically and featured Dolly on guitar and Millie on duelling vocals. Harmonising in yodels and Hawaiian-style pitches, they wrote many of their own songs. Although far more of a pop act, their musical abilities were daring and the song writing brash, sassy, and certainly bold. They exemplified a real 'cowgirl' pioneering spirit, as did recordings by Kitty Lee with Powder River Jack.

Although these women were situated in a barn dance vaudevillian spirit, the Coon Creek girls, an all-girl string band from the late 1930s, produced some great recordings with harmonising crossed with earlier old-time traditions. As a female-only partnership The Barn Dance Performers were not credited with technical skill or authenticity. However, they made significant strides for women in early country music.

The 'first' Carter Family women: Sara and Maybelle

The role of Sara and Maybelle Carter in changing music as an industry was frankly phenomenal. They started a tradition that would continue through 1940s and 50s hillbilly and country musicians. Not only did they show that female musicians were viable performers that the public would enjoy seeing live, they also proved that female country musicians could produce records that female audiences would go out and buy.

The musical relationships created and nurtured amongst

women playing country in the 20th century are perfectly exemplified by the correlating talents of Carrie Belle Powers and Maybelle Carter. Their relationship was extraordinary not only because of the level of technical skill involved, but also because of the resulting and enduring creativity.

Powers played guitar in her father's band Fiddlin' Powers and Family, and lived locally to the Carters: Sara, Maybelle and AP. Carrie Belle's exceptional playing was key to the band's sound and she shared ideas and time with Maybelle. Additionally to Carrie, her sisters Opha Lou and Ada played mandolin and ukulele in the group. Carrie Belle can be considered as one of the most overlooked guitarists in history, a casualty of traditional music histories.

Sara and Maybelle Carter, although highly revered, created the fundamentals for musicianship, sound and community that can be felt to the present day. Maybelle Carter, a small and unassuming girl, first played on her mother's autoharp, moving onto banjo and winning a local pickin' competition at the age of twelve. Entirely self-taught, she played music by ear and at thirteen picked up a guitar. She began by playing the traditional ballads that she had learnt from her mother, but her instrumentation was to set her apart from the usual old-time musical configuration. Her strong, rhythmic guitar playing style was unlike anything previously heard in the genre, and she developed what became known as the 'Carter Scratch'. Her innovation was entirely instinctual, a natural progression from her adaptation from banjo picking, and came to form a basic template for sound in western music, transforming the landscape of guitar styling.

Sara Carter was an orphaned child, who was taken in and cared for, along with her sister, by Milburn and Melinda Nickels in Rich Valley, Virginia. She had great reserve as an individual, with an imposing demeanour and generally shy character. Sara's physical presence was seen as quite intimidating, she smoked and wore trousers, a very liberated woman, who divorced at a time when marriage failure was a source of much shame for women. She began playing autoharp at around ten years old, and after listening and learning from a neighbour, Ethyl Bush, she soon progressed onto banjo. By the time she was a teenager she had her own girl group with her cousin Madge Addington, comprising of banjo, guitar and autoharp which they would swap around to sing ballads and old-time tunes. Madge came from a musical family, with her mother Margaret playing banjo and autoharp, and even her little sister playing autoharp – her family were the local area's recognised 'musical family' who provided the entertainment for social events.

Alvin Pleasant or A.P. Carter had taken up fiddle playing, but due to his nervousness had to quit. He had a distinct ear for music and developed a strong bass voice, he also began what was to become a significant collection of canvassed folk songs from southern states. He married Sara Dougherty (née Carter) in 1915 when she was seventeen years old.

In 1927 Ralph Peer set up a makeshift recording studio for Victor records in Bristol, Virginia to record local talent, with the help of 'Pop' Stoneman who he had previously recorded in New York. A.P. Carter's complete confidence in Sara and Maybelle's abilities led the Carters, including a heavily pregnant eighteen-year-old Maybelle and a nursing Sara, to Peer's session in Bristol where their lives (and the history of music) were to be changed forever.

Sara and Maybelle's relationship was renowned for its mutual encouragement and understanding. Many found Sara to be quite an aloof and difficult character lacking humour. However, with Maybelle she found the comfort and security of a friendship that allowed her the freedom to be herself. Maybelle's laid-back and well-meaning fun nature, along with her homely attitudes and rebellious streak complimented Sara's shy and unassuming ways. They enjoyed each other's company like sisters, bringing up their families together and engaging them in musical song and dances.

Women Make Noise

As Maybelle's husband Eck worked away from the valley for much of the year, and A.P would also spend much of his time out on song collecting trips, the women forged a friendship and working partnership of legendary communication, intimacy and intuition. Although both A.P. and Eck were extremely supportive of their wives' musical talents, which was rare at this time, the scouting industry was not so convinced. They did not see a market for female lead vocals in white recording artists. However, the exceptional quality of the Carter's sound was so alluring to Ralph Peer that Sara and Maybelle were recording duets on the second day they spent at his studio, without A.P.

Sara's distinct vocal style and delivery, which had a lonesome sound, became a huge hit, especially amongst female listeners. The lyrical focus on loss, worry and dread, with her melancholic stoic delivery, struck a chord with southern music buyers, accustomed to poverty, illness and death, and the southern gospel tradition could be heard throughout their repertoire.

The Camden sessions recorded in May 1928 saw Maybelle expand her styling to include Hawaiian fretting and some slide guitar and Sara's voice soon showed that a white female vocal could be immensely popular amongst a record-buying public. Maybelle's guitar style became imitated throughout American roots music, and soon the two women were pioneering a whole new era for sound and for a changing music industry.

It is interesting to note also the way in which even from this period of time, the industry struggled to market these women. Ralph Peer often told stories of their arrival in Bristol, dressed in rags, describing them as real 'backwoods' hillbillies – despite the fact that they showed up in their Sunday best outfits. They were also photographed for publicity in their hometown against backdrops of specifically and purposefully 'rural' and run down environments to enhance this 'authenticity' and 'rusticity'.

Peer was an agent and a city man, who was a businessman first and foremost and whose vested interest was in selling products back to consumers, via a male-run recording industry.

Although these women did not quite have the 'southern cracker' imagery, they were still subject to systems of discourse that falsified their lives for the general public.

Sara and Maybelle's lives changed rapidly, they swiftly become professional musicians – famous musicians – who made a prosperous living from their recordings and embarked on a touring circuit. Their own disdain for the way in which they were marketed in photographs was evident from their dignified public performance which shied away from any kind of 'hillbilly' or vaudevillian stage antics. They viewed the shows as forms of entertainment, but more closely aligned themselves with a church-like family programme than a revue of any kind.

As recordings of their music continued, they expanded their repertoire to include sacred African-American songs. Maybelle utilised bottleneck-guitar techniques, most often seen amongst black male songsters and gospel artists, and certainly not played by other female musicians at the time.

This was a revolutionary female act. For many shows A.P. took a complete back seat, and the shows really revolved around the musicianship of the women and their daughters. Sara Carter's experience of this changing musical life pre-empts that of many later 20th century and also contemporary female musicians. The pressure to perform and entertain did not sit well with Sara's personality. She wanted to make music without the rigmarole, the publicity or the business side of things. She enjoyed the comforts of home life far more than taking her family out on tour, she had no interest in fame or fortune, and compared to Maybelle's musical fervour and A.P.'s obsession, her interest in music seemed far less significant, and took its toll on their marriage. Sara and A.P. eventually split.

The 'new' Carter Family

Maybelle, keen to reinvigorate their musical performances and maintain the 'Carter' reputation, decided to grab the reins. She created a new family band of women and girls, incorporating her daughters Helen, June and Anita from a young age. Maybelle Carter as a musician, businesswoman and female, single-handedly created new environments for female musicians throughout her life. In the Carter Family, she was known for her business acumen, daredevil antics such as driving her Cadillac through mountain roads at 70 mph on tour, and her ability to adapt readily to situations. Her charm, technical ability and courage within the music industry has received high praise, although primarily within the realms of folk and country music. The significance of her ongoing legacy – she helped form a sound that was to follow through genres from blues, rockabilly and then rock – remains largely un-noted. Without her pioneering styles many artists such as Bob Dylan, who covered the Carter's 'Wayworn traveller' and renamed it 'Paths of Victory' and other key players in the normative histories of musical canon would have no grounding. Indeed Maybelle was Woody Guthrie's favourite guitarist. Doc Watson, Jerry Garcia and many other players cited her as hugely influential in the history of western music[4] and the formation of 'rock' in its forms were indebted and influenced greatly by Maybelle's innovations and experimentations.

The influence of Sara and Maybelle upon the industry became far more prevalent in later country music, where the market for female record buyers went from strength to strength, and Sara and Maybelle pre-empted this with their huge impact in the field and their methods of working, touring and presentation. Maybelle provided business, management and touring models that later musicians such as Patsy Cline would incorporate into their ways of working. Her role as a musical tutor was significant also. She mentored many female musicians such as her own multi-instrumentalist daughters June and Anita, Ruby Parker and Carrie Belle Powers. The ways in which she created environments for female musicianship, not collectives of wives of musicians, was to impact strongly on later communities of country musicians and affect how they supported one another within the music industry.

Ongoing legacies of the sounds

The influence of highly skilled female musicians such as the Carter women in the period of 1920s-1940s American country, folk and roots music deserves to be recognised and needs to be championed. Without these artists, the music we enjoy today may never have been written. Many were included on such historical landmark artefacts as Harry Smith's *Anthology of American Folk Music* (1952), which changed the musical framework of the 1950s and 1960s, but subsequent histories have ignored their contribution.

We know that artists such as Chet Atkins, and contemporary musicians such as Jack White and Gillian Welch openly cite Maybelle Carter as an influence, but how many of the lesser-known female guitarists – Carrie Belle Powers, Willie Sievers, and Roselle Ming – are referenced by musicians? Despite a resurgence of interest in American roots music in the last ten years, how many music fans would reference Hattie Stoneman's fiddle playing or Cleoma Breaux's Cajun guitar freakeries?

Many great writers such as Gayle Ward, Sherrie Tucker and Mary Bulwack have written extensively, yet the vast histories of female musicianship in both populist and specialist musical canons are still slight at best, and often informed by predominantly male 'authority figures' to validate their existence. Some artists, such as Memphis Minnie, have gained more notoriety in previous decades with popular male rock bands covering their songs. Bessie Smith and Ma Rainey are synonymous with the idea of the 'Queens of Blues'. Bob Dylan's mentioning of Sister Rosetta Tharpe on his radio show can be seen to account for much of the more recent popular interest in, and acknowledgement of, her contribution to musical history. The 2011 *Godmother of Rock* documentary, along with Ward's book *Shout Sister Shout!* gave a comprehensive history after the initial Dylan-fuelled surge of YouTube interest.

However, we hear only two or three female names assigned to genres that featured endless female talent. Until Roselle Ming's name is as much a reference to great innovation as Clarence Ashley's, then even historical landmarks such as Harry Smith's *Anthology* are being selectively listened to and chosen from. If 'women in blues' for instance comes to mean solely vocalists, as traditional histories represent, then we overlook the guitar work of Geeshie Wiley or the ground-breaking move from acoustic to electric that Memphis Minnie pre-empted. If The Girls of the Golden West were as well- known as Bob Wills we would have some equal sense of progressive musical history.

Oh Sister, Where Art Thou? Romanticising the 'old-time' music and country story

In the year 2000, the Cohen brothers' film *O Brother, Where art thou?*' raised the profile of old-time music. The alluring sounds of early American folk became suddenly popular and critically acclaimed. In fact, the soundtrack consisted of mainly cover versions by contemporary musicians such as Alison Krauss and Gillian Welch, but the songs romanticised Depression-era America. The poor rural white and black folk music sounds became synonymous with an idealised notion of the American South during the late 1920s and early 1930s.

This served to further mythologise the blues 'crossroads' myth, as well as the 'male rambling troubadour' of romantic music idealisation. The female counterparts to this in the film are represented very wholesomely, closely aligned with the saintly religious Country Gospel traditions, despite the film having a Southern Gothic undertone. The negotiated way in which gendered and classed representations of femininity are played out depict the role of female musicianship and autonomy at the time as marginal. The women are a far cry from the sassy, organised, and politically engaged businesswomen that I have discussed. They are again romanticised into less gaudy versions of the 'Southern Cracker' or the saintly 'Southern Belle', the binaries are defined and structure our knowledge through already existing conceptualisations of the American South.

Through their identification with this film and the artists featured on the soundtrack, some of whom were involved in the emerging 'alt country' movement, we see the continued way in which female musicians served to mask the truth through carefully constructed commentaries. The quasi-authenticity, and 'reclamation' of the role of female old-time musicians, although significant for contemporary female musicianship, is somewhat problematic.

The alt country music movement's revivalist take on country music covered all areas from old-time string band to honky-tonk styles. Musicians credited sound and visual identities to periods of country music's past. The artwork, clothing and lyrical content idealise and romanticise different eras. Masculinities, femininities as well as classed and raced dialogues are played out through representation and 'reclamation'. Contemporary musicians such as Krauss, Welch, Jenny Lewis, Jolie Holland, Blanche, and the Secret Sisters talk of their influence from women of this period and construct visual identities that sit with the alt country vein. Despite its claims to reassess and reappropriate female folk and country music's archetypes, alt-country's repackaged form of female old-time musicians reiterate classed and elitist conceptualisations of music. Whose desires and specialist knowledge really inform these revivalist notions? Which of the romantic notions of the American South and its 'feminised' folk song tradition relates to the actual musicianship of the time, and which can be more closely aligned with the folk collector's often condescending image of purity, authenticity and 'down homeness'?

Interpreting the legacy

Until we acknowledge the talent of the ground-breaking women mentioned in this chapter, we cannot understand the active influence of women musicians on genres such as rockabilly, garage rock, rock, punk, indie and experimental music. Concepts of 'feminisation' as a devaluation, and of private and public spaces, help us to understand the ways in which female musicians have continually stood up for their talents and resisted patriarchal traditions. It wasn't just about the music though. The business structures and communities created by these female artists should be placed in a history of old-time, country and emerging rock genres, paving the way for what became the music 'industry'. Why should women ever be excluded from something they very clearly helped to create?

Contributor biography

Victoria Yeulet is a musician, film-maker and music historian specialising in the history of women in music. As a musician she has performed in The Television Personalities and Congregation, and her filmwork has been shown internationally. Her specialist interest is 1920s-1940s American Roots music. She holds a BA in Media and Communications and an MA in Gender and Culture. She has been involved in much activist and feminist cultural activity since the late 1990s including organising Ladyfest London 2002, Homocrime queer club and Girls Rock Camp UK. She is currently working on a book of oral histories of women musicians and an all-female gospel record. See www.victoriayeulet.com

2. Puppets on a String?
Girl groups of the 50s and 60s

Elizabeth K. Keenan

'If you were looking for rock and roll between Elvis and the Beatles, girl groups gave you the genuine article.'
Rolling Stone Illustrated History of Rock & Roll (1976)

A handful of teenage girls huddle in a school auditorium, watching a group of slightly older guys sing doo-wop. The doo-wop songs captivate the audience with tales of budding romance, aching first love and inevitable heartbreak matched to perfect vocal harmonies. Not one note, not one gesture, is out of place. The girls think they could do the same. They've been singing all their lives, after all. Maybe they could make it big. They practice after school, maybe in breaks at choir practice, maybe in one girl's apartment, always under the supervision of teachers and parents. They audition – for a radio DJ, for a friend's mom, for a famous producer – and, before they know it, they end up in a recording studio, working on their first single.

It's a hit. They don't know what their contract looks like and they don't get much money beyond a *per diem*, but they're famous. They appear on American Bandstand, they hear themselves on the radio, maybe Murray the K's show or, if they're really lucky, Alan 'Moondog' Freed's, where they're sure to get national attention. They go into the studio and record another song. And another. But their producer isn't happy or their record label has moved onto another group of girls. They hear a song announced on the radio. It's their new hit! Only it's not them singing. Their producer tells them not to worry about it. They try to find out who replaced them on the record, only to learn that they don't own their name, or their songs, or anything that will bring future royalties. They might keep performing, or they might just give up. Eventually, they land in court, or, even later, performing on the gruelling oldies circuit.

At the same time the girls are honing their sound in the school gym, a young woman – a teenage bride – sits at a piano in a tiny cubicle in a packed, non-soundproofed building: the Brill Building at 1619 Broadway in New York City. She works with her husband to churn out songs as quickly as possible. They each take turns working on lyrics and song structure. At first, it's an equitable partnership, with their names appearing together on the records. Then, she starts to feel pressure: he wants credit as the producer, or as the sole writer. Or he wants to do all their business dealings. But she's the one doing the majority of the work. The producers want her perspective because it's closer to the girls in the groups, but, for that exact reason, they often dismiss her capabilities. Sometimes they want her to sing on the recordings they put out – the demos are so good there's no reason to spend extra cash to get a group to sing them. But she still doesn't get the recognition. Instead, a dummy group appears on the record and she gets paid a flat fee for her performance. Her marriage breaks up. She finds the style of music she was writing out of style. Maybe she weathers the late 1960s and comes out with a successful solo career. Or maybe she doesn't. Maybe she just ends up with a divorce. Either way, it takes her years to recover.

The stories above are composites, but they're all true to individual women as well as a general experience of the US and UK girl group phenomenon of the 1960s. Almost universally, the singers from the groups – mostly still teenagers, mostly

Puppets on a String? Girl Groups of the 50s and 60s

African-American – became disposable cogs in a hit-making machine. The Chantels, who forged their sound in a Catholic school choir in Harlem and were the second African-American girl group to make it big in the US (after The Bobbettes) never quite found their place after their hit 'Maybe', when their first producer moved onto other things. Ditto with The Shirelles, formed in 1958 in New Jersey, who were cultivated by label owner Florence Greenberg, but were just as quickly abandoned when Greenberg turned her attentions to Dionne Warwick.[1] And, when the Crystals were unavailable to record because they were on tour, Phil Spector replaced the singers with Darlene Love, an easy thing to do when he had control over their name.[2] And, in turn, Darlene Love, who played piano, sang and even wrote her own music, was often overlooked as a soloist and songwriter.[3] NYC's The Ronettes and the Dixie Cups – a band of three sisters with their cousin from New Orleans – both ended up in legal battles with their management and producers.[4] The songwriters, such as Carole King, Ellie Greenwich, and Cynthia Weil, worked with their husbands. Neither King's nor Greenwich's marriages would survive the 1960s. And, while King went on to release *Tapestry*, one of the biggest selling albums of the 1970s, Greenwich's solo career foundered.

The music of the all-girl groups emerges from a complicated network of relationships between the musicians, songwriters and producers, between performer and audience, and between teen girls and society at large. This chapter foregrounds the 'girl' aspect of the girl group phenomenon, examining the ways that the girl groups performed and thus created room for teen girl subjectivities in popular music. Unlike the rest of the chapters in this book, which focus on all-girl bands, the girls in the girl groups rarely played instruments. Their vocals took centre stage. However, rather than treat this as a 'typical' aspect of female performance, it's important to recognise that the girl groups were the first – and only – genre of music at the time to focus on the desires and perspectives of teen girls.

At times, the songs represented the girls' perspectives directly, such as The Chantels' 'The Plea', written by their lead singer, Arlene Smith, or The Bobbettes' 'Mr. Lee', which that group helped compose. At other times, the girls contributed as musicians – though that role was often played down, as was the case for Darlene Love – in ways that shaped the song's meaning and style. But for the most part, the music stressed the voices of the girls in the group, and, consequently, the lyrics. As a result, the songs showcased girls' experiences in a new way that marked them as separate from both the male rock 'n' roll stars that preceded them and the female pop music stars of the time, whose audiences were older. The music, while much more constructed as pop than as the rock 'n' roll of the time, carves out a path for women of later generations, pop and rock and everything in between.

Because many girls and women have taken that path in the decades since, this chapter also explores the legacy of the girl groups in popular culture. At first critically dismissed as factory-made music, girl groups were later embraced in the 1970s in punk and rock culture. In the 1980s and 1990s, the 'girl group formula' – young women, singing pop in harmony – flourished in groups such as Bananarama, En Vogue, the Spice Girls and Destiny's Child. And in the 2000s, Amy Winehouse's soulful *Back to Black*, the Pipettes' playful interpretation of sexuality and NYC's the Vivian Girls' blending of vocal harmonies with fuzzy garage instrumentation offered a wide variety of interpretations of the girl group sound. This chapter ends with an examination of recent performers who find influence in the classic girl groups.

Setting the stage: girl groups in the civil rights, pre-feminist era

Between 1958, the year that The Chantels scored a hit with

Puppets on a String? Girl Groups of the 50s and 60s

'Maybe', and 1964, when the British Invasion supposedly brought an end to the girl group heyday,[5] the USA faced the major tumult of the Civil Rights movement and the beginning of the feminist movement. In 1961, for example, the Freedom Riders rode on buses to the Southern USA, where they confronted segregation and were often violently attacked; in 1962, James Meredith became the first African-American to attend the University of Mississippi; in 1963, Civil Rights activist Medgar Evers was assassinated; and, in 1964, Congress passed the Civil Rights Act, which outlawed segregation.

In the nascent women's movement, Betty Friedan published *The Feminine Mystique* (1963), which addressed the issues of women's dissatisfaction with restrictive roles. Friedan wrote from a white, middle-class, adult perspective that probably wouldn't have recognised the issues of the girl groups or their fans. Teen girls at the time faced numerous new pressures: the 1950s were a decade in which rock 'n' roll encouraged rebellion and freer sexuality (for young men), but expectations for young women to conform increased. A much-cited survey for the *Saturday Evening Post* in 1962 found that ninety percent of women between the age of sixteen and twenty-one wanted to be married by the age of twenty-two.[6] In the 1950s, the median marriage age for women dropped to just twenty years, and women were supposed to go straight from their father's house into their husband's.[7] If they went to college, they were also expected to find a husband by junior year.[8] And, though the birth control pill was approved for contraceptive use in 1960, it was almost impossible for unmarried women to obtain.[9]

The intersection of racial and gender prejudices shaped the music, images and reception of the girl groups. Within this context, girl groups sang about true love, awakening sexuality, bad boys, and 'Goin' to the chapel' where they were 'gonna get married',[10] a collision of topics that reflected a tension between the influence of rock 'n' roll sexuality and the desire to conform to the strictures of pre-feminist femininity. The majority of the girl groups were young women of colour from urban areas: New York City and its suburbs, especially, but also Detroit (The Marvellettes, The Supremes and numerous others on Motown), New Orleans (the Dixie Cups), and Los Angeles (The Blossoms). Racial prejudice affected the music they sang, the ways that these groups were marketed toward white and black audiences and the exploitation they faced at the hands of unscrupulous producers, managers and record companies.

The Brill Building songwriters, unlike folk musicians and many R&B (and later soul) acts, strategically avoided social issues in their attempts to reach the broadest audiences.[11] The few times girl groups addressed these topics, they did so obliquely. For example, in The Crystals' 1962 single 'Uptown,' the protagonist sings of her boyfriend, who works for 'the man' downtown but returns every night to her 'tenement', where he's a 'king'. 'Uptown' signals Spanish Harlem through Spanish guitar playing and castanets, and the lyrics reinforce an idea of a hard-working man of colour who, despite facing discrimination every day, persists in struggling to 'make it' in America. But the song never directly discusses racial injustices, leaving its interpretation open.[12]

In addition, African-American girl groups had to 'cross over' to white pop audiences through musical style cues (such as close vocal harmonies, string sections and elaborate production) that signalled middle-class femininity and blurred assumptions about racialised 'authenticity'. Until the early 1960s, pop music had mostly been associated with white female artists, such as The Chordettes and The McGuire Sisters, who presented a 'young housewife' image and sang sanitised versions of rock 'n' roll songs, while African-American female singers found success only on the R&B charts.[13]

At times, the girls themselves negotiated the process between the demo and final versions of the song in ways that blurred these genre boundaries. Some girl groups took a more active role in the hit-making process. For example, The Shirelles, who sometimes wrote their own songs and often contributed suggestions in their music's production, initially resisted the 'twangy' demo version of 'Will You Love Me Tomorrow?' Describing the songwriting process, Sheila Weller writes:

> '[Florence] Greenberg [owner of The Shirelles' record label] gave it to Luther Dixon [The Shirelles' producer] and he played it for The Shirelles. Beverly Lee recalls, "We looked at each other like, 'Is this a *joke*?'. It sounded like a country-western song, real twangy." The girls' consensus: it was too white. But Dixon, who is black and whom they trusted, said, "You're *gonna* record this song," Beverly says.'[14]

While the original may have sounded country-like, the final version was equally far from R&B. Layered with violins and cellos, the song placed The Shirelles into a more definitively pop space.[15] Additionally, the song's lyrics created an ambiguous situation in which a girl asks herself if a boy will love her tomorrow, implying that she's 'gone all the way' with him. The protagonist isn't a young housewife, but a teenage girl. Musically and lyrically, the song positioned The Shirelles as something new – neither the young housewife nor the experienced R&B singer – and the song's chart success reflected that: with 'Will You Love Me Tomorrow?', The Shirelles became the first African-American all-girl group to reach #1 on the Billboard Hot 100.

Similarly, the ways that girl groups were marketed and the conditions that they faced on tour reflected the fact that much of the United States was segregated. In 1962, The Ronettes were turned away from a hotdog stand in Miami after the server realised that the girls' mothers were black, and the girls were mixed race.[16] Sometimes, the girls encountered more dangerous conditions. The Chantels' lead singer Arlene Smith described the conditions the group faced on an 'Alan Freed' tour:[17]

> 'We got involved in the race riots in Boston, about '57.
> There was a fight, and we had to get out of the theatre.
> I thought it was fun! We did clubs, but we were really
> too young, though we managed a few southern spots.
> During that time, there really were not a lot of places for
> five little girls to work. The real harsh places our parents
> would object to.'[18]

Smith's observations on race and touring conditions
connects with the ways that young women – especially young
African-American women – had to modulate their responses
to violence in the world around them. Smith mitigates the
seriousness of the race riot with a quick aside about how it
was 'fun'. This can be read as having been protected from the
worst of it by her father, the girls' chaperone. But it can also
be read as Smith deliberately ignoring the violence in an effort
to maintain a feminine propriety.[19]

Pulling the strings: supervising respectable femininities

This polite comportment emerged in the ways that African-
American girl groups were marketed to black and white middle-
class audiences of the time. While some later girl groups, such
as The Ronettes and The (white) Shangri-Las, were marketed
as 'bad girls', earlier girl groups emphasised respectability.
The Chantels, who crossed over from the R&B charts to the
pop charts in 1958, were careful to stress parental approval,
in particular. In her interview with Charlotte Greig, Arlene
Smith constantly reiterates the relationship The Chantels had
with authority figures: their singing begins under the tutelage
of a Catholic nun at St. Anthony of Padua school in Harlem;
their parents are in the background when they audition for the
manager of Frankie Lymon and the Teenagers, and when they
receive their contracts; and Smith's father acted as a chaperone

Puppets on a String? Girl Groups of the 50s and 60s

for the group.[20] Finally, while The Chantels didn't receive much publicity, it's also worth mentioning that the group's album had a very different cover in its second edition – rather than The Chantels, the second cover featured a pair of white teenagers, a boy and a girl, choosing a record on a jukebox.

Maintaining proper behaviour and 'ladylike' choreography became the mainstay of girl groups, especially as Motown grew in influence as a record label. In his history of Motown, writer Gerald Early argues that label owner Berry Gordy deliberately cultivated female acts for white audiences:

> 'Gordy … felt that women were less threatening and, in some ways, more comforting to the white public than a black man would be, especially with the intense sexuality and sensuality that the "new" popular music of rhythm and blues and rock and roll suggested.'[21]

This careful crafting was indeed evident while the Detroit-based record label included in its stable The Marvelettes, who achieved the label's first number one song on the Billboard Hot 100 chart with 'Please, Mr. Postman' in 1961, and, later, the Supremes, who would go on to be one of the label's most successful groups. In order to ensure that the girls (and women) maintained proper 'ladylike' behaviour, the label hired choreographer Cholly Atkins to train its girl groups. Atkins, who worked with many girl groups, described the process in his autobiography:

> 'I worked it out, softened them up, The Chantels, The Crystals, The Shirelles – any group I had the chance to work with. See, the girl groups had to be more concerned with what I call physical drama.
>
> Instead of trying to move like the guys, I wanted them to use the kind of body language that was associated with women – using your eyes, hands on the hips and so forth,

> but not in a macho way. They had to really think about
> this approach and keep that uppermost in their minds.'[22]

Drawing on the work of feminist scholar Susan Bordo,[23] Jacqueline Warwick argues that this kind of practiced choreography is a way of disciplining the body, a means of controlling appropriate female behaviour on stage.[24] But, beyond Warwick's generalised view of femininity as control, this retraining was also a specific means of projecting an image of 'proper' African-American femininity. Recalling Berry Gordy's belief that African-American men were too highly sexualised, this restricted femininity reads differently in the face of racist presumptions about African-American sexuality that became visible in the rock 'n' roll era and in the fight for Civil Rights.

Rethinking the bad girl aesthetic: Race, class and 'ladylike' femininities

African-American girl groups negotiated layers of perceived respectability in much more restrictive ways than white acts did, particularly when it came to representation as 'good' or 'bad' girls. The stories of The Ronettes and The Shangri-Las – both groups positioned as 'bad girls' – reflect some of these differences. The Ronnettes, composed of sisters Veronica 'Ronnie' Bennett and Estelle Bennett, along with their cousin Nedra Talley, followed a similar trajectory to The Chantels. They first sang together at home, then – as a trio of underage girls – danced at the popular Peppermint Lounge, performed for radio DJ Murry 'the K' Kaufman, and, eventually, 'accidentally' spoke to Phil Spector on the phone, leading to an audition.[25] The girls in the group were often represented as 'bad girls' from Washington Heights, a working-class neighbourhood in Manhattan, where Latino and African-American residents had begun to mix with the Irish, Jewish, and Greek immigrants who lived there since the early 1900s.

As Jacqueline Warwick notes, the girls' tight dresses, giant, teased beehives, and extensive mascara ran counter to the images of the 'good girls' of the time: 'In a culture in which parents concerned about preserving their daughters' reputations kept them confined at home, The Ronettes' mothers – working-class, mixed-race women who worked as coffee shop waitresses – actually encouraged their girls to venture unchaperoned into the legally off-limits world of nightclubs'. Warwick argues that in her memoir, 'bound by the ideology of respectability and middle-class decency,' Ronnie Spector rationalises the encouragement as efforts 'in the service of the trio's career ambitions,' since the girls dressed identically and stuck together as a trio.[26]

But it is more likely Spector's mother and other adult relatives did not see their style of dress as going against middle-class values; rather, the dresses presented them as feminine. Anthropologist Sherry B. Ortner, in her ethnography of her New Jersey high school class of 1958 notes that the symbols that indicated 'bad girls' to the middle-class members of her high school class read differently among different ethnicities and social classes.[27]

For Ortner's classmates, 'sluttiness was actually a complex idea'.[28] Working-class girls who wore too much makeup, blouses and long, straight skirts most often received the label, Ortner writes, but:

> '...in retrospect I think the style had little or nothing to do with looking sexually provocative. On the contrary, it was meant to be "feminine", even "ladylike", compared with the bobby-soxer style of the middle-class girls'.[29]

The description Ortner offers of the 'sluts' in her school – who were often less sexually active than the 'good girls,' but were usually non-white or 'white ethnics' such as Italians – makes them sound like The Ronettes. From her cultural and class perspective, Spector's mother was *not* putting her and Estelle in outfits that marked her daughters as 'bad girls'; instead, she was ensuring that The Ronettes would be seen as 'ladylike.'

In contrast, as Warwick writes, The Shangri-Las' whiteness 'afforded them greater freedom to play with this version of girl identity than was available to groups like The Ronettes'.[30] NYC's The Shangri-Las – sisters Mary and Elizabeth Weiss, and twins Mary Ann and Marge Ganser – arrived at the tail end of the girl group phenomenon and recorded mostly on Red Bird Records, owned by songwriters Jerry Leiber and Mike Stoller and promoter George Goldner. Their songs and their image often crossed the boundaries between 'good' and 'bad' girl images. While The Ronettes' tight dresses might give a feminine 'bad girl' image to middle-class, white audiences, The Shangri-Las were able to construct a very different kind of 'bad girl'

Instead of the crinolines of The Shirelles, the sparkling evening gowns of The Supremes, or the tight dresses of The Ronettes, The Shangri-Las dressed in fitted black slacks, white shirts, vests, and boots.[31] The tough look went along with their songs, which often valorised bad boys and featured spoken-word sections that emphasized their New York accents.[32] 'Leader of the Pack,' their biggest hit, offers a dialogue between a 'good girl' – sung by Mary Weiss – and her friends. Weiss narrates a tragic story of her love for a boy that others said was 'bad', but she knew was 'sad'. After she breaks up with him at her father's request, the boy dies in a motorcycle accident, which the song details through screeching sound effects. The moral of the story seems to be that if you listen to your parents, your misunderstood, rebel boyfriend will die. But even some Shangri-Las songs reasserted traditional morality. Their melodramatic 'I Can Never Go Home Anymore' created a similar scenario of forbidden love, but when the narrator runs away to be with the boy, she breaks her mother's heart.

She soon forgets the boy, but it's too late. She finds out that her mother is dead, 'the angels took her for their friend'. In their images and songs, The Shangri-Las crossed more lines than their African-American counterparts, but, in the end, they still paid attention to the boundaries of respectability.

Girl group music: subjectivity and sexuality

The late 1950s and early 1960s were the first decades in which the teenager became a category to be marketed to, and the rock 'n' roll explosion played a large part in defining that category. But in the 1950s, though the rock 'n' roll audience included female fans – the girls screaming on the *Ed Sullivan Show* as Elvis swivelled his pelvis – they were always the object of the songs. Girl groups filled a void, giving voice to the experiences of teen girls everywhere, often in call-and-response format that highlighted talk between girls.[33] Songs such as The Shirelles' 'Will You Love Me Tomorrow?' and The Ronettes' 'Be My Baby,' gave audiences of teen girls a new freedom. But other songs, such as The Chantels' 'Maybe' or the Crystals' 'He Hit Me (And It Felt Like a Kiss)' offer restrictive views of gender roles, in which girls pine for lost loves or, even worse, construct happiness via abusive relationships. Though the girl group songs resonated deeply with the audience, many of the girls listening to – and more importantly, buying – the girl groups' records were often white and middle class.[34] While these white, middle-class girl group fans didn't share the racial discrimination that shaped the ways that girl groups were marketed and at times exploited, both groups of women faced restrictive boundaries for acceptable feminine behaviour; yet rock 'n' roll had encouraged rebellion.[35] The music of the girl groups reflects this tension in its conflicting views of girls' agency and self-determination through romance.

Youth as a marketing tool: the girl teen voice

The girl group songs, many written by married couples, such as Carole King and Gerry Goffin, Ellie Greenwich and Jeff Barry, and Cynthia Weil and Barry Mann, often capitalised on the youth of the songwriters, most of whom were barely out of their teens. The songwriters attempted to capture the essence of both the 'girl' and the 'group', even if they weren't specifically written with one particular group in mind. The structure of lead singer and backing vocalists led to what musicologist Barbara Bradby calls a 'divided subject'. In her article 'Do-Talk and Don't Talk: The Division of the Subject in Girl-Group Music' (1988), Bradby argues that most girl group songs can be divided into 'you' songs that directly address a boy and 'he' songs that talk about a boy, often in a group setting among the girls. Through her surface analysis of top-ten girl group songs, Bradby posits that girl group songs are always both for and against romance, often using the chorus as a means to articulate this conflict. The kinds of internal struggle that Bradby outlines are, as well, part of a larger cultural framework in which girls were constantly sent mixed messages about finding and keeping a boyfriend, going steady, and 'going all the way', a euphemism for having sex.

Bradby's overall classifications of 'you' and 'he' songs offer a jumping off point for more in-depth musical analysis of girl group songs.[36] In these songs, the singer's role could range from completely passive to deliberately active. In the case of The Chantel's 'Maybe', the singer pines after her lost love, hoping that if she prays every night, her boyfriend will come back to her. In contrast, The Ronettes' 'Be My Baby,' one of the most enduring and influential songs of the girl group era, suggests a sexually assertive subject position and also exemplifies the girl group's pop-oriented musical sound.[37] Written by Ellie Greenwich and Jeff Barry with producer Phil Spector, the song was intended for Ronnie Bennett (later Spector) from its inception. Beginning with a booming drum pattern, the song layers on percussion (kit drum, castinets, hand-claps) and a bevy of musical instruments (piano, saxophones, a full string section). But soaring above it all is Ronnie's voice, the centrepiece of the song. The singer takes control of the pursuit right away: 'The night we met, I knew I needed you so/and if I had the chance, I'd never let you go.' Throughout the chorus, the singer asks the unidentified 'you' if he will be her baby; the backing group reiterates her question with 'Be my, be my baby'. Even though Ronnie Bennet Spector is asking a question, her confident, assertive alto indicates that she already knows the answer is 'yes', making her the inversion of Shirley Owens's hesitant protagonist of 'Will You Love Me Tomorrow?'.[38]

The song offers an unusual perspective in more than one way. First, girls in the early 1960s were not supposed to pursue boys in a relationship. As Stephanie Coontz cites in her book *Marriage, a History: How Love Conquered Marriage* (2005), only twenty-six percent of girls in high school in 1961 agreed that it would be good if girls could ask boys out on dates.[39] Phoning a boy, Gail Collins points out, was regarded as 'shockingly forward' and left girls' motives open to misinterpretation, even if they called about a school assignment.[40] In this light, the assertive questioning of 'Won't you be my baby?' stands out as much more 'shockingly forward' than a mere phone call, as it stakes a claim on controlling the terms of the relationship. Second, its language – asking the boy to be *her* 'baby' – runs counter to the gendered expectations of the time, in which women were more likely to be called 'baby' in a relationship (or song). Finally, for the female listeners of 'Be My Baby', the song offered an unprecedented surge of freedom. Singing along, they could imagine themselves as full agents in a relationship, capable of asking a boy out. Even if they could not do it in real life, the song at least offered a fantasy where they could approach a boy with confidence and as an equal.

Assertive artists

This kind of confidence spilled over into other songs of the time. The Shangri-Las' 'Give Him a Great Big Kiss', a conversation among a group of girls, highlights the appeal of the forbidden 'bad boy'. The 'bad boy' made frequent appearances in girl group songs, such as the Crystals' 'He's a Rebel' and The Shangri-Las' 'Leader of the Pack' and 'Out in the Streets'. In this song, The Shangri-Las take full advantage of their own bad girl image to create a scenario in which pursuit of the bad boy leads to a 'great big kiss' in public. The song begins with one of The Shangri-Las signature spoken word sections, 'When I say I'm in love, you best believe I'm in love, L-U-V.' Singer Mary Weiss then outlines the reasons that she's in love, describing the physical characteristics of a bad boy. After every verse, spoken interludes with the other Shangri-Las reveal that the protagonist doesn't really know 'her guy' all that well: she doesn't know the colour of his eyes, because 'he's always wearing shades'; he may be tall, because 'she's got to look up'; and, most importantly, she assures her friends that 'he's good bad, but not evil'. The backup singers encourage Weiss throughout, their refrain of 'tell me more, tell me more' after each physical description.[41] By the end of the song, it's clear that the protagonist barely knows her 'bad boy'. He isn't the sad, misunderstood Jimmy of 'Leader of the Pack', nor the dampened, former bad boy of 'Out in the Streets', but a boy who appeals because he merely looks the part.

Unlike many of The Shangri-Las' other songs, which offered dramatic consequences for teenage impulsiveness, 'Give Him a Great Big Kiss' treats the pursuit of a 'bad boy' as a fun excursion with your friends. Beyond the song's lyrics, 'Give Him a Great Big Kiss' creates the atmosphere of a playground game, structured around percussive handclaps and tambourine strikes. In the 'tell me more' sections, the handclaps and tambourine strikes are the only audible accompaniment to the girls' questioning. In some ways, 'Give Him a Great Big Kiss' can also be thought of as a 'crossover song'. Though the Weiss and Ganser sisters were white, the song's structure implies playground hand-clapping games associated with African-American girls.[42] This playful approach to the song suggests less the overt desire of 'Be My Baby' and more a group of girls giggling about a flimsily constructed flirtation, in which the lead singer doesn't really know the object of her affections.

Both 'Be My Baby' and 'Give Him a Great Big Kiss' let girls put themselves in the assertive subject position of the singer. But it is important to keep in mind that other songs of the time reinforced the gender restrictions on girls of the time. Both The Crystals' 'And Then He Kissed Me' and the Dixie Cups' 'Chapel of Love' follow protagonists on their path to matrimony, eliding the teenage girls with the young housewife. And many others, such as The Crystals' 'Da Do Ron Ron' reinforced the notion of traditional courtship, even if they stopped short of marriage. While the songs of the girl groups allowed fans to try on more assertive subject positions, they also let them imagine their assumed future roles, implying that the 'bad boy' was a temporary phase, but the good guys in these songs were for keeps.

Girl groups' legacy

In the late 1960s, as the rock world became more and more associated with masculinity,[44] the harmonies of the girl groups faded. Boy bands such as The Beach Boys and The Beatles who had equally drawn on close harmonies also faced choices: after a few years of experimentation, the Beach Boys drifted into an ever more retro version of themselves, while The Beatles abandoned the harmonies that had infused their earlier music in favour of harder-edged songs. The girl groups, however, largely did not survive the shift toward counter-cultural rock, and the term 'girl group' became something of a joke. In her influential essay 'Why The Shirelles Matter,' Susan Douglas argues that the rock-critic establishment long-dismissed girl groups of the 1960s. She cites author Ed Ward in *Rock of Ages: The Rolling Stone History of Rock & Roll* (1986), who wrote:

> 'The female group of the early 1960s served to drive the concept of art completely away from rock 'n' roll … I feel this genre represents the low point in the history of rock 'n' roll.'[44]

Even The Shangri-Las' lead singer dismissed the term:

> 'Oh, kill me now! Thank you. How do you take an entire sex and dump them into one category? Girl groups, I mean, please! What if we all had penises?'[45]

The treatment of girl groups of the 60s informed pop music scholarship in a number of ways, from the association of women with pop music (and not rock) to a tendency to label any all-girl group as drawing on 'girl group harmonies'. But, even within mainstream criticism, girl groups have had their advocates. In the *Rolling Stone Illustrated History of Rock & Roll* (1976), Greil Marcus writes: 'If you were looking for rock 'n' roll between Elvis and The Beatles, girl groups gave you the genuine article.'[46] Marcus positions girl groups as rock 'n' roll itself, not the nadir between its decline and resurgence. And, perhaps more importantly for 1983, he acknowledges the power differential between the singers and the producers:

> 'Within that listing is emotion of staggering intensity, unforgettable melodies, great humour, a good deal of rage, and a lot more struggle – the struggle, one might think, of the singer – a young, black girl, likely as not – against the domination of her white, male producer.'[47]

Marcus's assessment reinserts girl groups into the critical discourse in a moment that valorised masculine authenticity.

Audible impact

Beyond their critical importance, girl groups have retained a currency in pop culture since the 1960s. While the girls themselves vanished from the airwaves, the songs they sang, the images they produced, and the echoed from all corners of pop music. In 1970, fewer than ten years after she wrote the song for The Shirelles, Carole King included a haunting, minor-key rendition of 'Will You Love Me Tomorrow?' on her album *Tapestry*. Three years later, the New York Dolls referenced The Shangri-La's line, 'When I say I'm in love, you best believe I'm in love, L-U-V' in their song 'Looking for a Kiss', and later they would cover the song itself. In 1975, Bruce Springsteen turned to the 'Wall of Sound' in the production style of his hugely popular release *Born to Run* (1975). The late 1970s only furthered the trend, when punk and new wave bands like the Go-Go's, Blondie and The Damned all covered or referenced girl group songs in their lyrics.[48] Over time, musicians and fans continually reinforced the value of girl groups, whether as a standard for creative vocal harmony, or as evidence of creative songwriting, or, most importantly, the first genre of music to offer a specific, teen, female perspective in the rock 'n' roll era.

Revamping girl power

In the 1980s, the original girl groups went mainstream again, with The Shirelles landing a prominent spot on the soundtrack for the film *Dirty Dancing*. And, in the pop world, a younger generation of women carried the pop tradition of harmonised singing groups, including the UK's Bananarama, as previously mentioned. But it wasn't until the 1990s that girl groups re-emerged with a twist. 'Girl power', whether it was taken from riot grrrl or borrowed from hip-hop acts such as Queen Latifah, became infused with the classic harmonies of the girl groups. In 1992, R&B act En Vogue's album *Funky Divas* produced two songs that bridged the gap between empowerment hip-hop and empowerment girl pop. The first, 'My Lovin' (You're Never Gonna Get It)', uses the girl group tactic of directly addressing a man, but, this time, the singer enumerates all the reasons a strong woman would reject him. The second single, 'Free Your Mind', called for an end to racial prejudice. Both songs set the tone for later girl groups of the 1990s, positioning their singers as strong, opinionated women who drew on the narrative structure and group concept of the girl groups of the 1960s.

Later in the decade, the Spice Girls combined the 'girl power' slogan with the girl groups' group identification. In songs such as 'Wannabe,' the Spice Girls emphasised female friendship over relationships with men, calling on the 'girl talk' of the 1960s but inverting the themes of such songs as 'Don't Say Nothin' Bad about My Baby,' in which the boy can do no wrong. In terms of sexual presentation, though, the Spice Girls occupied a different world than the girl groups of the 1960s. Nicola Dibben writes that, with the Spice Girls:

> '"Girl Power" is a female's right to display her sexuality, to be autonomous and free from dependence on a man, and instead to find empowerment in girl-friendships and group solidarity.'[49]

What differentiated the Spice Girls from other 1990s acts such as En Vogue was their deliberate courting of the youngest members of the pop market. Their songs were aimed not just at teens and adults, but at little girls (via their parents), through merchandise such as lunchboxes, stickers and dolls. In the years since the Spice Girls broke up, groups such as Destiny's Child drew on the ideas of empowerment and a focus on young girls as audience members. Lead singer Beyoncé's solo career similarly calls on empowerment, with songs such as 'Run the World (Girls)'. She has also made a conscious effort to promote female musicians by hiring an all-women backing band, The Suga Mamas (who often go on to play late night improv gigs without her when the main show is over). However, problematically, Beyoncé's song lyrics suggest that girls run the world with their physical attributes. As Rachel Fudge has noted in *Bitch* magazine:

> 'Girl power sounds like it elevates the ladies, but in fact it does the exact opposite of what riot grrrl tried to do: it turns the struggle inward, depoliticises and decontextualises the cultural messages about gender and behaviour. Like the misguided idea that feminism is really only about giving women choices, it turns a collective struggle into a personal decision'.[50]

Most recently, the sound of the girl groups has appeared in acts that draw on not just the harmonies but the subject matter and images of the 1960s. Amy Winehouse's 2006 album *Back to Black*, for example, meticulously recreated the production sound of Motown and Stax recording labels, while the singer's dishevelled beehive and exaggerated eyeliner recalled The Ronettes. Winehouse's obituary in the *New York Times* referenced her love for girl groups, quoting the singer:

> "'I didn't want to just wake up drinking, and crying, and listening to The Shangri-Las, and go to sleep, and wake up drinking, and listening to The Shangri-Las," she said. "So I turned it into songs, and that's how I got through it.'[51]

During her career, Winehouse covered such girl group staples as 'Will You Love Me Tomorrow?' and Leslie Gore's 'It's My Party'. Later, Ronnie Spector acknowledged that she saw herself in Winehouse, telling *Rolling Stone*'s Matthew Perpetua:

> 'Every time I looked at her, it was like I was looking at myself. She had my beehive, my eyeliner, my attitude. She had such a great soul in her voice and her lyrics were so amazing that I couldn't help but sing one of her songs. I was so happy to see an artist like Amy, because she reminded me of my youth. And she loved girl groups.'[52]

In the same article, Spector drew parallels between her experience of alcoholism in her twenties and what she saw with Winehouse. Winehouse's death in 2011 demonstrated a similar kind of exploitation to what some of the women in girl groups experienced: her handlers were often willing to overlook problems as long as she produced good music.

Though Winehouse's tribute to girl groups was directly on the surface, other groups have incorporated girl group sounds and images in ways that incorporate irony and fuse the genre with other musical styles. Indie rock artists such as the aforementioned Vivian Girls, and The Pipettes as well as groups like Cults (New York), Best Coast (Los Angeles), and The Dum Dum Girls (Los Angeles) have drawn on girl group sounds in ways that comment on the gender and power dynamics of today's pop music. The Pipettes, who describe themselves as a manufactured band,[54] replicated the girl group style visually, with the women singers dressing alike in 60s-style polka-dot dresses and performing choreographed dance moves, and the male backing musicians wearing coordinated shirts and ties. The group's songs replicate the girl group sound, though they are much more directly sexual: 'Sex' opens with the same drum pattern as The Ronettes' 'Be My Baby,' while songs like 'School Uniform' and 'Judy' use the sound to flirt with bisexuality. And, like the original girl groups, the Pipettes have had a number of line-up changes, with original members RiotBecki[54] and Rosay leaving after the first album.

According to the band's singer Gwenno Saunders, the intentional resemblance to the girl groups allows for parallels, but also demonstrates the differences wrought by the feminist movement:

> 'I think the big difference is who has creative control. We enjoyed the parallels between what we were doing and the original groups, we are a manufactured band and proud of that, but the one thing that is very different is the distribution of power between the sexes that were involved, and that was always equal. Really, that couldn't have happened without everything that's gone on in the feminist movement since the original girl groups were first popular. I'd say the dynamic has evolved over the years, there's been a lot of personnel changes, but I do think that our sense of democracy within the band has remained.'[55]

Saunders' description of the band points directly to feminism, a difference that marks her generation. As someone who grew up with feminism, Saunders is aware of how the girl groups had fewer chances to exert a direct influence over their music than she does.

In the 2000s, along with The Pipettes and solo artists such as Amy Winehouse, numerous all-girl bands also embraced the girl group sound. Indie rock group The Vivian Girls combine girl group harmonies with other elements of the 1960s, such as garage, as well as later sounds, like 1980s hardcore punk. This synthesis of musical styles reflects both the musical trends of the 2000s – mash-ups and retro sounds – but also gives evidence to the important precedent that the girl groups set for offering a place for women's subjectivities. In an email interview for this book, Vivian Girls' guitarist and songwriter Cassie Ramone contrasted girl group songs with those of today:

'Today every song on the radio is like, the same boring chord progression, no nuance in phrasing, the exact same structure, etc. I also love the themes of the lyrics: they are sharp and well written, but also relatable. They tell a story that you can easily put yourself into. The songs radiate innocence and purity in a way that's not forced or cloying. I love that the music can be fun and heartbreaking at the same time. […] I identify with girl group lyrics more often than not. I have a very old-fashioned idea of romance, and I can relate a lot more to the stories told in girl group songs than I can to current love songs.'

Ramone went on to say that her connection to the girl groups influenced her own lyric writing, noting that:

'As much as I sometimes wish that my writing gave off more of a "Who needs guys? I'm an independent woman" vibe, that isn't true to me and I find it impossible to write something decent that doesn't come from a very genuine place.'

While as a self-identified feminist – Ramone felt she came up short on independence sometimes – she nonetheless wanted to stay true to her experiences. This ties back to the idea of a female subjectivity that the girl groups first carved out: it may not be ideal, but it offers a perspective often lost in popular music, especially in the indie rock genre from which the Vivian Girls emerged.

Girl groups in control

The legacy of the girl groups runs throughout popular music, from the tendency to label female vocal harmonies as a 'girl group sound' to the idea of female subjectivity as important and valid within popular music. But perhaps the most important legacy of the girl groups lies in their 'group' status. The songs didn't just feature vocal harmonies; they didn't just sing about romance – they used those harmonies to talk to each other, about boys, about their mothers, about their friends. The Vivian Girls' Ramone also noted that, even when girl groups became obsessed with boys, they still had each other:

> 'More importantly, girl groups in their songs solidify the idea of sisterhood. In so many of the songs, you will find the girls have each other's backs and that friendship matters more than a dumb guy'.

This idea of sisterhood has influenced girl bands across the spectrum of popular music and stands at the core of the 'girl band' itself. The girl groups' solidarity sets up the idea of girls banding together – if not yet a 'girl band'.

Contributor biography

Elizabeth K. Keenan (co-author of chapter 10 also) completed her doctorate in ethnomusicology at Columbia University in 2008 and is a lecturer at Fordham University. She is working on her first book, *Independent Women? Popular Music, Cultural Politics and the Third Wave Feminist Public*, which investigates the intertwining of cultural politics and identity-based movements in the United States since 1990. In 2008, she won the Wong Tolbert Prize from the SEM Section on the Status of Women, and in 2007, she won the Lise Waxer Prize of the Popular Music Section of SEM. She has published in *Women and Music*, the *Journal of Popular Music Studies* and *Current Musicology* and has presented her research at a variety of conferences, including the Society for Ethnomusicology, Society for American Music, the Experience Music Project Pop Conference, and Feminist Theory and Music 9 and 10.

3. Truth Gotta Stand:
60s Garage, Beat and 70s Rock

Sini Timonen

This chapter focuses on some of the many great bands associated with the genres of garage rock, beat and 70s rock. Whereas previous discussions have concentrated on the more high profile acts, I wish to give prominence to bands that are rarely acknowledged within this framework, that didn't quite 'make it' on a national or international scale, but nevertheless achieved some eminence on the live music circuit and provided us with some classic recordings. Like the majority of garage and beat groups of the 1960s (usually teenagers with little musical training), all-girl bands like The Pleasure Seekers and The Liverbirds were not inspiring because they were technically accomplished, but because of their energetic performances, enthusiasm and – as *Ugly Things'* editor Mike Stax puts it – 'the perfection of imperfection'. These bands released records that met with little success in their time, but many have received recognition since and some have become collectors' items.

Placing their music in context, this chapter celebrates these teenage traditions in rock and explores all-girl bands' contributions to 1960s US garage music and the UK beat phenomenon. It will then look at more prominent bands of the 1970s, exploring the legacy of these genres the world over.

Catalytic social context

In the early 1960s, both in the United States and in the United Kingdom, men and women were expected to fill different societal roles and often occupied separate spheres of existence. In this framework, forming and being part of an all-girl band in the 1960s – and even in the 1970s – may have been considered a radical pursuit whether or not the band members would associate themselves with the emerging Women's Movement, which was making advances to secure equal rights for women.

Certainly in rock, 'the band' was traditionally viewed (and still is by many) as a masculine arena that offered limited possibilities for girls and women, and frequently positioned them in supportive roles. Even today, although the women's liberation movement taught women to pursue 'non-feminine' activities if they so desired, while boys in their teens quite 'naturally' end up forming bands, the situation is different for girls. When investigating teenage rock bands of the early 1990s, sociologist Mary Ann Clawson found girls often lacked 'the cultural authority to initiate band formation'.[1] If this was the case in the time frame of Clawson's study, it's easy to imagine how much worse the situation may have been in the 1960s, when suitable roles for girls were much more rigid. Moreover, at that time aspiring female instrumentalists barely had any female role models to look up to; although a few gained some popularity (e.g. Honey Lantree of The Honeycombs, Megan Davies of The Applejacks), most women in bands were picked for their vocal ability – too often coupled with their looks – and resigned to the songstress mould.

To some extent, the all-girl bands that did emerge in the 1960s were already radical just by *being there and doing it*: their very existence was an indication of the expanding role of girls and women at a time when they were gaining more rights and fleeing domestic drudgery. Therefore it's time we celebrated those early all-girl bands that, against all odds, infiltrated this arena of adolescent male bonding. It's also time we reconsidered the typically masculine focus of 1960s American garage rock, which has largely operated to the exclusion of all-girl bands.[2]

In the garage

Popular music researcher Paul Kauppila has defined 1960s American garage rock as a 'musically simple, blues-based form of popular music influenced most heavily by the British Invasion bands of the mid-1960s'.[3] Another scholar Seth Bovey – when examining the more punk-oriented groups within the garage canon – has added that the genre came into being when American youngsters 'mimicked the sound of British R&B and the attitudes of British rockers, but ended up creating a cruder, snottier, and more urgent sound that expressed their own concerns and views of life'.[4] While the British Invasion started the garage band 'boom' in the true sense of the word, the style had in fact been evolving within regional US scenes since the late 1950s. Influenced by genres such as rock 'n' roll, surf rock and R&B, several garage bands (The Kingsmen from Portland, The Trashmen from Minneapolis and Boise, Idaho's Paul Revere and The Raiders) had enjoyed hits in the US national charts in 1963. Hence there had been a garage band scene of sorts before the Invasion, but the landmark appearance of The Beatles on *The Ed Sullivan Show* in February 1964 – and the subsequent, unparalleled success of British popular music in the US – yielded a huge increase in the number of these bands. Overall, while there is certainly a stereotypical 'garage sound', the genre is diverse in character and often refers to a set of aesthetic rules rather than to a musical style.[5]

The archetypal garage band comprised amateurish yet exuberant youngsters who rehearsed in their parents' garage (hence the term). While some of the better-known garage combos eventually ended up sounding as competent as their

British role models, the garage rockers' initial do-it-yourself attitude towards music-making anticipated the aesthetics of 1970s punk: anyone could play an instrument, and even more significantly, anyone could form a band. Undoubtedly, this DIY ideal predominantly inspired teenage *boys* to pick up instruments and thereby attempt world domination; the number of all-girl garage bands active in the 1960s, compared to that of all-male bands, was ridiculously modest. Nevertheless, there *were* a number of all-girl garage bands that frequently became sought-after live acts within, and occasionally beyond, their local scenes (e.g. The Luv'd Ones, The Pleasure Seekers). In stereotypical garage band style, despite their regional popularity, recordings by these groups are few and difficult to find. Considering the genre's later popularity it is also striking that tracks by these all-girl bands are rarely featured on garage compilations. A good example of this exclusion can be found on Rhino's 1998 box set *Nuggets: Original Artyfacts from the First Psychedelic Era 1965-1968,*[6] which has served as an introduction to garage music for many fans. Although a staggering 118 tracks are included on the compilation, not one of them is by an all-girl band.

The Luv'd Ones – sound and style

Michigan's The Luv'd Ones – originally called The Tremolons – were one of the most accomplished all-girl garage bands of the 1960s. Active between the years of 1964 and 1969, the band featured the talents of Char Vinnedge (vocals, lead guitar), her sister Chris Vinnedge (bass), Mary Gallagher (rhythm guitar) and Faith Orem (drums). Char Vinnedge was the undisputed leader of the group; not only did she sing lead vocals, play lead guitar and write the original songs, but she also took care of their equipment, bookings and artwork, and even drove the van when required.[7] The Luv'd Ones were signed to Chicago-based Dunwich Records, but they only succeeded in releasing a small number of 45s in the 1960s, and were reportedly neglected by their label in favour of Dunwich's star group The Shadows of Knight,[8] who had a national hit with their version of Them's 'Gloria' in 1966. In line with most garage bands of the period, The Luv'd Ones' repertoire consisted of covers of popular songs with some originals added to the mix. What set them apart from other groups – aside from the obvious – were Char Vinnedge's moody and dark, but melodic originals. From the Beatlesque 'Yeah, I'm Feelin' Fine' to the bittersweet 'Dance Kid Dance', The Luv'd Ones boasted a unique sound that was instantly recognisable. In contrast with an abundance of garage music from the period which often celebrated directionless teenage angst or partying, The Luv'd Ones sounded rather grown-up. Indeed, Char Vinnedge did not fit into the stereotype of an incapable adolescent garage performer: she had started playing the piano as a child, but switched to the guitar and formed The Luv'd Ones in her early twenties.[9] The group also benefitted from the fact that Vinnedge became an accomplished guitar player – with a preference for fuzz – at a time when female lead guitarists were rare. In fact, after The Luv'd Ones disbanded, she went on to play with Billy Cox (of Band of Gypsys fame) on his 1971 solo album *Nitro Function*.

The Pleasure Seekers

While The Luv'd Ones evaded garage stereotypes, The Pleasure Seekers from Detroit – best remembered for being Suzi Quatro's first band – started out as a teenage garage band. According to Quatro's autobiography, she was inspired to form an all-girl band with her sister Patti after seeing The Beatles on *The Ed Sullivan Show* at the age of fourteen.[10] The group became a more professional act by the late 1960s, but garage devotees chiefly endorse the group for their first single, 'Never Thought You'd Leave Me'/ 'What a Way to Die', which was released by local label Hideout Records in 1965. The A-side, 'Never Thought You'd Leave Me', was a driving but melodic – and hence fairly typical – girl garage number, but the B-side's 'What a Way to Die' was something more extraordinary. Whereas female-led garage songs from the 1960s were frequently stylistically somewhere between garage rock and the girl group idiom and dealt with boys, dating and the unpreventable heartbreak, 'What a Way to Die' was, quite simply, a song about heavy drinking (which might ultimately result in the narrator's death). While Quatro's snarling, attitude-filled vocal delivery already set the song apart, it was chiefly the lyrics that made the track controversial within its contemporary context. In addition to the death theme, the narrator boasts that she is more interested in drinking beer than in her boyfriend, although he does have a body that makes her 'come alive'. All this was rather risqué for a group of American teenage girls in the mid-1960s and therefore it was hardly a surprise that the single was not met with nationwide success. Of course, Quatro went on to achieve icon status as the leather-clad frontwoman of her own band (she was the only female in this case) signed to RAK records from the UK. British producer Mickie Most had spotted her playing in Detroit and helped launch her in England and around the world; albeit she was less successful in the US until appearing in the TV show *Happy Days*. Astride her bass guitar, with an army of followers who copied her haircut and feisty attitude Quatro's girl band beginnings spawned one of rock's first female stars.

The Debutantes, The Co-ets and more...

The Debutantes' beginnings were very similar to those of The Pleasure Seekers: they also hailed from Detroit and, like the Quatro sisters, lead guitarist and vocalist Jan McClellan reportedly decided to form the band after seeing The Beatles' *Ed Sullivan Show* appearance. The group toured extensively in the 1960s, including entertaining US troops in Germany and in a number of countries in the Far East.[11] Other lesser-known garage groups included The Continental Co-ets, an all-girl teenage band from Fulda, Minnesota who specialised in instrumentals. Interestingly, The Co-ets reportedly played 'battle of the sexes' concerts – a reference to 'battle of the bands' competitions which were hugely popular during the garage band era – against a male band called The Vultures.[12] The Daughters of Eve, meanwhile, hailed from Chicago and were originally put together by Carl Bonafede who also managed The Buckinghams[13] (known for their 1967 hit 'Kind of a Drag'). The Eves released eight tracks – a significant number by garage band standards – between 1966 and 1968, of which 'Don't Waste My Time' is arguably the best-known

Another garage band, The Girls, were a quartet of sisters (Rosemary, Diane, Sylvia and Margaret Sandoval) from Los Angeles whose version of Mann and Weill's 'Chico's Girl' has been featured on several compilations. The Girls recorded two singles for major label Capitol Records and as a result these recordings sound considerably more polished than those of most garage bands of the era who tended to record for small local labels. The Heart Beats, from Lubbock, Texas, similarly featured a pair of sisters (Linda and Debbie Sanders). The group benefitted from promotion provided by the sisters' mother, and even had some nationwide exposure when they won a battle of the bands contest on Dick Clark's TV show *Happening '68*.[14]

Other notable all-girl garage bands include The Pandoras who became popular in the New England area and recorded for Liberty Records,[15] with 1967's '(I Could Write a Book) About My Baby' being their most notable offering. The Belles from Miami boasted a fairly harsh garage band sound and are best known for their 1966 cover of the aforementioned garage standard 'Gloria', reworked as 'Melvin'. Meanwhile, She (previously called Hairem) were an all-girl group from Sacramento who were predominantly active in the late 1960s and recorded their psychedelic garage anthem 'Outta Reach' in 1970. The Feminine Complex from Nashville were an extraordinary all-girl garage band in the sense that they released an album, *Livin' Love*, in 1969. However, the group's instrumentalists were replaced by session musicians on the album, and therefore the results could hardly be placed in the garage rock category.

In addition, there were a small number of other US-based all-girl bands that did quite not fit into the ethos of garage rock, but have occasionally been characterised as garage bands. These include, for instance, The Ace of Cups who were more closely associated with the San Francisco scene of the late 1960s,[16] and New Hampshire's infamous The Shaggs, whom researcher Steven Hamelman has quite accurately described as 'fantastically good at being spellbindingly bad'.[17] While sometimes referred to as a garage band, The Shaggs' 1969 album *Philosophy of the World* demonstrates that the group eluded generic classification, at least until the 1990s when Irwin Chusid launched his term 'outsider music'.[18]

Common ground

On the whole, it appears that there were a number of similarities between these groups. Adhering to garage stereotypes, the band members were commonly in their teens when the groups were formed, and their careers turned out to be relatively short. Interestingly, the bands were often family affairs; as noted, a large number featured sisters. Whereas it was not uncommon for male garage bands to include brothers in their line-ups,[19] this appears to have been a more significant pattern with all-girl bands. Adding to the family theme, some of the groups were chaperoned by parents on tours, as reportedly, were aforementioned The Continental Co-ets and The Daughters of Eve.[20] It appears that all-girl groups were frequently viewed as being in need of protection: whereas the age of the band members was certainly an issue, their gender surely played a part in this perception too. While the garage band era took place during a time when women were gaining more independence – including governance over their sexuality – one may envisage that, at least in the context of regional teenage scenes, young women musicians were not granted as much freedom as their male counterparts.

Gender also regularly determined how these groups were received, and although they rarely had trouble getting bookings – featuring an all-girl line-up was a great selling point, which frequently placed these groups (and their management) in a commercially advantageous position – discussion on gender and visual attributes frequently eclipsed discussion on their music. For instance, Suzi Quatro's description of The Pleasure Seekers' drummer Nancy Ball exhibits this in colourful terms:

> 'Every town has its local beauty, and she was ours: five foot one, long blonde hair, small slanting blue eyes, full lips, breasts to die for (...) There was never anything more sexy as she beat her drums, swaying back and forth, whispering the words like pillow talk, and all this without a bra!'[21]

In addition, as indicated above in discussion of The Continental Co-ets and The Vultures, it was not uncommon for an all-girl garage band to be considered *in relation* to a local male band (either as a 'sister band' or a female competitor), rather than as a musical force in their own right.

Garage rock gets a label

In 1972, US label Elektra Records released the original *Nuggets* as a 2-LP set with liner notes by rock critic Lenny Kaye (later of Patti Smith Group fame). This set the ball rolling and consequently, many more compilations and series followed – *Pebbles*, *Back from the Grave* and *Highs in the Mid-Sixties* to name a few – with the result that 'garage rock' became a recognised genre and its canon began to develop. Included in this canon were (and are) a number of loud and snotty bands that, more often than not, did not make an impact on the national charts: in general, these groups would rarely be considered significant in the context of the more general canon of rock. To provide an example of which bands are included, in his influential *The Sound of the City* (3rd edition 1996) Charlie Gillett discussed a number of garage combos including Question Mark and the Mysterians from Michigan, The 13th Floor Elevators from Texas and The Music Machine, The Standells and Love from California.[22] As acknowledged, all-girl bands have not been duly recognised in this canon; indeed, these groups are still today a rarity on garage compilations, with the main exceptions of US-based Romulan Records' *Girls in the Garage* series and a small number of compilations by the UK reissue label Ace Records (e.g. *Girls with Guitars* and *Destroy That Boy! More Girls with Guitars*). As in many genres of rock, all-girl garage bands are frequently deemed to be separate from the canon – hence the compilations dedicated to female acts – or at best, a minority within it.

Where are the women?

There are many possible reasons behind the exclusion of women from garage rock compilations, with the most obvious one being that the number of all-girl garage bands was very small compared to male bands, and they did not release a large number of records for future generations to rediscover. Another possible explanation is the genre's association with male-vocalised lyrics and aggressive vocal style. Indeed, in his article 'From Garahge to Garidge', Eugene Montague went as far as to state that 'the sound of the female voice was almost completely absent from the genre'.[23] While the female voice *was certainly not* absent in 1960s American garage rock, it may not be the voice one first associates with the style. Seth Bovey has indicated this when examining the more punk-oriented groups of the genre, emphasising the aggressive masculinity required in a garage vocal performance: 'the vocalist must be able to sing with a snarl in his voice and a sneer on his lips'.[24] On the whole, the music of 1960s all-girl garage bands tended to lean towards the more melodic and pop-oriented side of the garage spectrum, building a bridge between early 1960s girl groups and garage music.[25] However, who is to say that their approach was somehow inferior to the more contentious style commonly associated with garage rock?

The canonical exclusion may have an ideological (as opposed to stylistic) base given that many commentators have viewed garage music as a particularly masculine arena. For instance Michael Hicks – author of *Sixties Rock: Garage, Psychedelic, and Other Satisfactions* – has remarked that 'while pop groups oozed with the bliss of love, garage bands bristled with the energy of contempt', noting in addition that the target of this anger was usually a woman.[26] Undoubtedly, 1960s garage rock recurrently reflected the outlooks and frustrations of adolescent males, resulting in put-down songs that were habitually (albeit not always) directed at 'no-good' girls, with the numerous anti-heroines of these songs criticised for being unfaithful, dull or aloof.

Popular music scholar Marion Leonard has asked 'in what way do written accounts (such as press coverage and rock histories) produce a gendered rock discourse?'[27] In garage rock histories, the genre has commonly been positioned as masculine; this involves an erasure of girls' contributions and the endorsement of a clumsy, adolescent and white masculinity so often associated with the style. Again, *Nuggets* – or more accurately, the booklet that accompanied the 1998 box set – offers us several examples of the gendered nature of garage histories. For instance, the cross-cultural developments in garage music from the 1980s backwards are described as follows: '80s white Italian boys copying 80s white American boys copying 60s white American boys copying 60s white English boys copying 50s black American men',[28] while another essay celebrates playing in a garage band as a way of attracting girls: 'every band scrambled to reinvent themselves into a form that would inspire the Beatles-crazed gals to spare a glance'.[29] Whereas neither of these claims is inaccurate they, together with the fact that the compilation does not feature any all-girl bands, paint a fairly bleak picture of how girls' contribution to the 1960s garage phenomenon is viewed.

However, one may argue that garage rock as a genre was no more masculine than most genres in rock; in fact, with its 'anyone can do it' ethos, garage music may indeed have been more welcoming for women than many other styles of rock. Given that it appears that girls were rarely encouraged to learn to play rock instruments in the 1960s,[30] garage rock certainly would have been more inviting than, for instance, subsequent styles of progressive rock and heavy metal which embraced virtuosity and required years of practice.

All-girl beat: Gingerbreads and Liverbirds

Goldie and The Gingerbreads provide us with a link between US all-girl garage bands and their UK counterparts. While The Gingerbreads emerged from New York, they could not be placed into the garage category musically and, in addition, they achieved more success in the UK than in their home country. Arguably the best known all-girl band of the 1960s, the classic line-up comprised Genya Zelkowitz (later Ravan; vocals, harmonica), Ginger Bianco (drums), Margo Lewis (organ) and Carol MacDonald (guitar). The group met members of The Animals in New York in 1964 and they were subsequently brought to the UK where they became a popular live attraction, touring with likes of The Rolling Stones and The Kinks. In addition to their popularity as a live act, The Gingerbreads were signed to Atlantic Records in the US and recorded for Decca in Britain, and had a UK hit single in 1965. It also appears that the group were held in high regard by the British beat fraternity, as The Small Faces' Ian McLagan reminisced in his autobiography *All the Rage* (2000):

> 'Although they were seen as a novelty and only had one hit in the U.K., "Can't You Hear My Heartbeat", they were a really good band, and Margo Lewis played the Hammond B3 organ like she was on fire'.[31]

Conversely, in her autobiography *Lollipop Lounge: Memoirs of a Rock and Roll Refugee* (2004), vocalist Genya Ravan asserted that the group took full advantage of the all-girl novelty upon which McLagan remarked:

> 'We were chicks, and we got paid more just because we were chicks. So the fact that we were working in a male-dominated, chauvinistic industry in fact profited us... and we were smart enough to know it'.[32]

The Gingerbreads were a very professional act both in terms of music and image; they were habitually praised for their musical competence (although the 'good for a girl' school of thought was surely in attendance here) and they rarely looked anything other than glamorous. They were also remarkably successful compared to most all-girl bands in the 1960s. However, within the general context of beat music they remained very much a footnote.

Liverpool's The Liverbirds inhabited a somewhat similar position within beat music as Goldie and The Gingerbreads: while they were probably the UK's best-known girl band of the 1960s, The Liverbirds are not properly acknowledged in the beat canon. Nevertheless, these two bands differed in many ways. Whereas The Gingerbreads were a very polished act, The Liverbirds would have indubitably fitted into the garage band aesthetic, had they been American (for instance, The Gingerbreads could be pictured in dazzling matching mini-dresses, but the promotional pictures of The Liverbirds mirrored those of all-male beat groups). Also, the repertoire of The Liverbirds set them apart from most all-girl bands of the 1960s and also from other bands associated with Merseybeat. Whilst generally placed in the beat group category, they predominantly chose to play versions of R&B songs made famous by male African-American performers such as Bo Diddley and Chuck Berry. Comprising Pamela Birch (vocals, guitar), Valerie Gell (guitar, backing vocals), Mary McGlory (bass, backing vocals) and Sylvia Saunders (drums), the group did not find much success either in their home city or the UK in general, but became a popular act at Hamburg's renowned Star-Club. Their two LPs, *Star-Club Show 4* and *More of the Liverbirds*, released on Star-Club's own label, are not necessarily aimed at those who endorse musical sophistication; nevertheless, their music has an exciting rawness that extends beyond their position as a minority interest in the beat phenomenon.

Mandy and the Girlfriends, Beat Chics, Alleycats and Fabs

Hull's Mandy and The Girlfriends were a teenage beat group in the same vein as their garage equivalents in the US. The band was popular on the live circuit in Germany and frequently performed for the American troops stationed in the country; The Girlfriends also recorded an album which was chiefly sold to the forces. Other all-girl beat groups included The Beat Chics[33] whose claim to fame was supporting The Beatles in Spain, and Sally and The Alleycats who were an off-shoot from Ivy Benson's orchestra. To my knowledge, both of these groups released only one single each (both in 1964): The Beat Chics on Decca and Sally and The Alleycats on Parlophone. Another UK group, The Fabs were a Welsh all-girl beat combo that appears to have comprehensively faded into obscurity; however, it is known that they released an album called *The Fabulous Fabs* in the late 1960s. What is striking about all these groups, including The Liverbirds, is that they appear to have been more popular abroad than in their own country. In particular, British all-girl beat groups frequently found work in the US air bases in Germany.[34]

Escape from the garage: Fanny and Birtha

Whereas all-girl bands of the 1960s were predominantly live acts that achieved little national or international success, in the 1970s a couple of girl combos succeeded in infiltrating the world of mainstream rock. Fanny and The Runaways might not have been topping the US charts, but they nonetheless released a number of albums and reached a considerably wider audience than their 1960s counterparts. Fanny's driving force were sisters June and Jean Millington (guitar and bass respectively, and vocals) and their original line-up was completed by Nickey Barclay (keyboards, vocals) and Alice de Buhr (drums, vocals). The group was signed to Reprise Records and released its first, self-titled LP in 1970. Originally called 'Wild Honey', the band decided to change its name to

'Fanny' prior to the release of the album. While the members reportedly did not realise that their new name might turn out to be controversial their record company took full advantage of it by, for instance, giving out bumper stickers with the slogan 'Get behind Fanny'.[35]

Dubious promotion aside, Fanny was a musical force in its own right. Its members were experienced musicians who wrote their own material; and even when they tackled a cover song, they portrayed a considerable level of confidence, as demonstrated, for instance, by the inclusion of Cream's 'Badge' (written by Eric Clapton and George Harrison) on their first album. The band released five studio albums in the 1970s, but was hindered by several personnel changes, and disbanded midway through the decade.[36] Birtha were another early to mid-1970s all-girl band that recorded two LPs for Dunhill Records. While they boasted a heavier sound than that of Fanny and were at least as musically proficient, they appear to have been overshadowed by their better-known rival.

The Runaways

Whereas Fanny and Birtha had demonstrated that all-girl bands could indeed compete with male bands in terms of musical aptitude, The Runaways were a teen rock combo in the vein of 1960s garage groups. While frequently dismissed as Hollywood rock hustler Kim Fowley's creation, the band inaugurated the careers of Joan Jett and Lita Ford, both of whom eventually became more prominent in the 1980s. The classic Runaways line-up consisted of Jett (rhythm guitar and vocals), Ford (lead guitar), Cherrie Currie (lead vocals), Sandy West (drums) and Jackie Fox (bass). Active between the years of 1975 and 1979, the group received a fair amount of attention, but this did not result in chart success or critical approval. Indeed, The Runaways' 'girls gone bad' image –

highlighted in songs such as 'Neon Angels on the Road to Ruin' and 'Born to Be Bad' – proved to be controversial in the 1970s. The group had the advantage of being young, good-looking and musically up-to-date, but whereas the audiences and critics were used to sexually assertive performances from male rock stars, they were not accustomed to teenage girls behaving in this manner. Hence much of contemporary writing on The Runaways belittled or ignored the band's musical output, but journalists were more than happy to write about the musicians' personal lives, reckless behaviour and, above all, the sexy image of the band. This was demonstrated by, for instance, a lengthy article in *Crawdaddy* in 1976 which introduced the band members accompanied by sexist remarks throughout, with the piece eventually culminating in the inclusion of the members' measurements.[37] However, while the world may have not been ready for The Runaways in their time, later decades have viewed the band more favourably and songs such as 'Cherry Bomb' and 'Queens of Noise' have achieved a near-classic status amongst those who like their 1970s rock loud and undisciplined.[38]

What makes a band 'garage'? Contemporary perspectives

Since the 1970s, a large number of performers have been directly influenced by the traditions discussed in this chapter; in particular 1960s garage has been favoured in this context. For instance, inspired by the compilation LPs of 1960s obscurities, plenty of neo-garage bands came into existence in the 1980s.[39] The early years of the 2000s witnessed the latest 'garage rock revival', endorsed by the indie rock press, with acts such as The White Stripes, The Hives and The Von Bondies associated with the genre.

Whereas this revival has now subsided, PJ Crittenden – co-founder of London's much-missed Dirty Water Club[40] –

acknowledged its importance in that there now are more fans of garage music than there were prior to the revival, whilst also adding that 'those who were just into it because it was briefly fashionable have moved on to the next fad'.[41] Indeed, today's global garage scene comprises relatively small regional and national scenes in different parts of the world,[42] with fans connected by various internet sites and forums,[43] as well as festivals that attract people the world over.[44]

In the all-girl framework, The Pandoras[45] were the best-known all-girl band of the 1980s revival and since then a number of groups have followed suit by embracing the garage aesthetic. For instance, bands such as Gore Gore Girls and The Donnas (both from the US),[46] The 5.6.7.8's (Japan), Thee Ultra Bimboos (Finland) and The Boonaraaas (Germany) emerged in the 1990s.[47] Furthermore, the 2000s have brought bands such as The Vivian Girls, The Like, Dum Dum Girls, The Ettes (all from the US), Las Robertas (Costa Rica), The Nuns (the UK) and The Micragirls (Finland) who have made use of garage sounds and images – albeit some more than others – with many of them gaining popularity either in the garage subculture or in the world of indie rock.

What makes a contemporary band a 'garage band', what are the criteria? In an interview for this book (and all quotes hereafter), PJ Crittenden discussed the issue:

> 'It's something I feel more than can explain in mere words. But for me the band has to have the basic set up of guitar, bass and drums (and can also have an organ – not a modern style keyboard) and be influenced primarily by rock 'n' roll music of the 1950s and 60s.
>
> Bands can incorporate a good amount of blues, vintage soul, and 70s punk rock, for example. But many other styles of music are out of bounds – try to mix in some reggae or funk for instance and, in my eyes, you're no longer a garage band'.

Meanwhile Cassie Ramone, vocalist-guitarist of New York's The Vivian Girls[48], listed the requirements in an interview for this book (and all quotes hereafter):

> 'Guitar-based, generally short songs, got the spirit of rock 'n' roll, somewhat debaucherous, extensive knowledge of older garage music and/or related genres like punk, power pop, rockabilly etc'.

What is evident in these descriptions is that garage bands are expected to wear their influences on their sleeves, and that these influences are fairly clearly defined. Garage musicians are envisaged to embrace and know a lot about certain vintage rock sounds and genres, with the displays of this appreciation ranging from overt to more elusive.[49] Also indicated in the narratives is an emotional, rather than purely rational approach to the question posed and towards garage rock in general. For many fans the genre represents return to 'real' music, with the garage band signifying a platform of resistance against commercial considerations so often linked with popular music of our day.

When asked whether she would describe The Vivian Girls as a garage band, Cassie Ramone stated:

> 'I definitely wouldn't say we're a 60s revival act of any sort, but if you wanted to describe it in the simplest terms, "garage" is adequate enough.'

Debbie Smith, meanwhile, plays with The Nuns who are a London based all-girl Monks tribute band[50] and thus, already by definition, closely linked with the tradition of garage rock. Smith reflected on why her group chose to pay homage to The Monks in particular:

Truth Gotta Stand: 60s Garage, Beat and 70s Rock

'They were unique and actually played a pretty big part in musical history – they kinda invented punk with songs like "Shut Up" and "I Hate You" (...) they had a strong image and a completely different sound.'

Smith also acknowledged that part of the reason why they formed the band was that they 'wanted people to hear these tremendous songs',[51] linking The Nuns to numerous other garage bands who wish to introduce repertoire from the original era to new audiences (perhaps even the verb 'educate' may be accurate here). While inspired by a variety of genres, both Ramone and Smith affirmed that they had been influenced by female musicians associated with garage music[52] and by the aforementioned *Girls in the Garage* compilations. They also acknowledged the influence of female rockers from other genres in their formative years as, for example, Ramone asserted:

'Bands with strong front women like No Doubt, Garbage and Hole were very inspirational when we were young girls, and riot grrrl bands like Bikini Kill inspired us to start making music in the first place, but weren't necessarily an influence on our music.'

So, why is garage rock important in its contemporary context? While Debbie Smith responded that 'because when it's good, it's exciting and raw – that's what rock music is all about,' PJ Crittenden elaborated on the sentiment:

'It takes music back to the basics, it shows people that you can learn an instrument without being a virtuoso and have fun being in a band. At a time when mass-produced music-as-product is forced upon the public and promoted to them by big business and their dubious TV talent contests, it is more important than ever that

> people realise that music is fun, that it can (and should)
> be something enjoyable to participate in rather than
> a career, and that anyone with enough enthusiasm can
> have a go at it and enjoy it for what it is.'

This inspired amateurism so aptly described by Crittenden has always been at the core of garage music, and continues to provide us with an example of how, drawing on the ideals of the genre, anyone with a bit of interest and ardour can make music with little or no previous experience. In our contemporary society, these ideals may offer young girls a supportive framework to get together and play music for the first time as demonstrated by, for instance, the popularity of the Rock 'n' Roll Camp for Girls which started in Portland, Oregon in the early 2000s (see chapter 10), and has since then helped girls learn instruments and form bands. Also, we hope that the music and stories of the pioneering all-girl bands discussed in this chapter will inspire at least some aspiring female musicians who like their rock vintage and amplifiers turned up loud.

Contributor biography

Sini Timonen is a PhD student in Music at City University London, working on an AHRC-funded research project on women musicians' contribution to popular music in England between the years of 1962 and 1971. She is active as a seminar speaker and guest lecturer at various universities in the UK, and she was awarded an MA by Research degree for her thesis 'Girls in the Garage: Gender and Tradition in Garage Rock' at Kingston University in 2008. She also plays in a band and runs a monthly 1960s club night in central London.

4. Prog Rock:
A Fortress they call The Industry

Jackie Parsons

Progressive rock or 'prog rock' (as it is otherwise known), was an extension of the LSD-fuelled psychedelic rock of the late 60s that included the UK underground bands Pink Floyd, Soft Machine and King Crimson. The move away from the restrictive line-up of guitar, bass and drums allowed the inclusion of expanded instrumental solos along with more involved, inspirational and often fantasy based lyrics, in preference to those that dealt with teenage romance or new dance crazes, like the Twist or the Mashed Potato. These bands and their music continued to develop, dispensing with the limitations of the repetitious verse chorus structure and the need to play in 4/4. By the time the likes of Yes, Jethro Tull and Genesis entered the mix, a new genre had been created and the name 'progressive rock', was coined. Everything was pushed to the extreme – technical ability, musical complexity, and artwork: the covers for so-called 'concept albums' could be spectacular pieces of art, like *Tales from Topographic Oceans* by Yes (1973) designed by Roger Dean.

This chapter begins in 1973, when Britain is in the middle of the cod wars with Iceland, the IRA has brought the fight to the mainland, Edward Heath's Conservative government instigates the three-day-week and freezing cold winter weather combined with the depressingly regular power cuts leads to women being allowed to wear trousers in the workplace.[1] Sadly, I miss this thrilling moment as I have already left my job at the University of London library to become a self-employed dressmaker and can work in my pyjamas and slippers if I feel like it.

Music had long been a big part of my life, usually involving live band performances from the likes of Captain Beefheart, Frank Zappa, Sharks or Dr. John, but until this point I had only been on the receiving end; now I was in the process of turning that around by adding bass playing to my skills and getting involved in music-making myself (see http://jackiebadgersblog.blogspot.com for more information).[2]

The following year (1974), Jackie Crew (drums/vocals), Lesley Sly (keyboards/lead vocals), Audrey Swinburne (guitar/lead vocals) and myself (bass/vocals) (then called Jackie Badger) formed a band called Mother Superior – some of our recollections and still vivid memories of that period are included here. Deirdre Cartwright recalls her time with the band Tour de Force and Judy Costello comments on the attitude towards her as the drummer in the Australian all-girl band Garbo. We will use these experiences and those of other female musicians to examine the way the music industry treated women who had chosen to play electronic instruments with particular emphasis on those who were part of the prog rock scene during the 70s. A male point of view is provided by my old boss Snips and colleague Simon Etchell.

Later in the chapter, we discover those who are often underappreciated and unmentioned, the ones who make it possible for the gigs and recordings to happen – roadies and sound engineers like Boden Sandstrom and Fran Rayner. We look at the marvel that is Kate Bush and as progressive rock in its original guise is forced into retirement, we search out the all-girl bands and instrumentalists who inhabit the many and varied sub-genres it spawned. This includes The Holy Sisters of the Gaga Dada, who valiantly carried the torch in the mid 80s and the bands drawing on prog rock's legacy in the present day, meeting Verity Susman of Electrelane, sound engineer Elli Dorman and Maggie Vail from the Kill Rock Stars (KRS) label, and more along the way.

This journey began whilst archiving material and creating the Mother Superior website,[3] with help from Jackie and Lesley. During the interviewing process, it became jaw-droppingly clear that four decades later women playing rock music are still hitting the same obstacles. And while this has been an opportunity to make a short guilt-free visit to the past, and speak to friends and colleagues from that time, I can see a similar chapter being written in 2050, unless there is a genuine desire to transform the perception and credibility of women as rock musicians working within any of its genres. Only with belief and backing from all aspects of the music industry, including the musicians themselves, will public opinion (without whose support you will be unable to make this a career) be fundamentally changed.

But right now we are travelling back in time to the era of long hair, perms, flares, tank tops, satin, velvet and platform shoes (all non-gender specific) to experience the challenges that faced women in rock and see how they managed to create opportunities within this notoriously male-dominated environment.

Leaping hurdles to get started

Technology

The immediate stumbling block for many women who had chosen to play electric instruments was their lack of technical knowledge. A budding guitarist or keyboard player needed to understand the basic workings of their equipment and keep it well maintained as most of it was second hand. At this time girls were not routinely taught metal work, wood work or basic electronics in school or at home, just as boys did not learn to knit, sew or cook, so when you needed to change plugs, replace valves and speakers or fix a broken jack plug it was a major problem.

This was a world without CDs, videos, fax machines, computers or mobiles – technology was still quite basic and information was hard to come by. Prog rock exacerbated the problem, as the keyboards and early synthesizers, which played an integral part (like Hammonds, Mellotrons, Moogs and Oberheims), required significant technical expertise and although this was never reason enough to stop us, it was one more obstacle littering an uneven path. We had to learn how to work these instruments on the job, either by trial and error or occasionally from men who already knew how.

The classifieds and band auditions

Reaching the point where you were looking to join a band, in a pre-internet era where online social networking did not exist, meant checking the classifieds in the back pages of *Melody Maker*. For me and many other women, the first step seemed to be to reply to those ads specifically asking for female musicians. When I decided to change this approach and answer ads that were purely for bassists, rather than female bassists, I knew I was often asked along out of curiosity, but I opted to play the game and see where it took me. Deirdre Cartwright, guitarist with Jam Today, Tour de Force and Rock School, amongst others, who now performs under her own name recalled that:

> 'In the 70s, you had to be tough and determined to overcome the prejudice. I was always going to play the guitar and nothing would get in my way.'[4]

Prog Rock: A Fortress they call The Industry

If auditions weren't daunting enough, turning up to a hall full of male bass guitarists and being the only female was one hell of an experience. The other applicants were convinced that if I got the gig it was because I was a girl; I chose not to care. All I wanted was the opportunity to play, but this new enlightened music genre calling itself progressive, had omitted to open its doors to female musicians. It was a white male enclave and intentionally or not, a microcosm of the difficulties that women were experiencing within an industry that had no idea how to market them and saw them as a threat to their stronghold.

While female lead singers were acceptable, like Sonja Kristina from UK prog rock pioneers Curved Air and Jane Relf and Annie Haslam in Renaissance (formed by ex Yardbirds), and the occasional acoustic instrument woman player was permissible; as soon as a woman got in arm's length of an electric guitar, they found the doors of the music business were locked, barred and bolted.

A personal case study: Mother Superior emerges

In the summer of 1974, when Audrey, Jackie and I decided to form a new band from the ashes of a previous all-girl band – Cosmetix, that Jackie, Audrey, Gaynor Woolford (guitar/lead vocals) and Jackie Carter (bass/vocals) had started at school in South London, the first thing we did was to advertise in *Melody Maker* for a keyboard player. Lesley answered the ad and together as Mother Superior we wrote our own music, sang our own songs and played our own instruments.

Blissfully unaware that we were everything the music business did not want, presented in one neat package, we embarked on the road to oblivion. I can guarantee you never heard of us even though we played over 200 gigs during the next two years, released an album and were on radio and TV.[5] The initial interest sparked because we were an all-girl band, dissipated quickly – we were not mainstream, our songs could easily last five minutes or more, some compositions were instrumental and we were quite capable of playing solos. Audiences were loyal and growing but it was not enough to convince any record company to consider us a viable signing.

An A&R man from Sony turned up for our set at a packed venue in Fulham. We came off stage after several encores to be told that he was unable to see an audience for us because girls would not like us and they would not want their boyfriends to like us either. Leslie Sly continues the conversation:

> 'I said "Who have we just been playing to? Wasn't that an audience? A room packed with men and women who kept wanting more." He couldn't relate to that. The problem was that we could play quite well and that was somehow not sexy. Our original songs were too long to be singles and the biggest sin of all, we didn't want to be a pop band. Countless all-boy bands at this time could play quite well and didn't do singles, that was perfectly acceptable.'[6]

The man from Artistes and Repertoire was mistaken, we always attracted a mixed audience. But they often found us intimidating and seemed to have a problem knowing how to react to us personally. Rarely did members of either sex come and speak to us after the gig and when they did they appeared quite nervous. What was the protocol? The traditional sex and rock 'n' roll combination made it a tricky path to tread. Should they tell us we looked good or played well or maybe both? How would we respond? We were an unknown quantity.

There were plenty who found it difficult, if not impossible, to accept the idea that women could actually play an electric instrument with enough skill for an audience to take seriously, even though we were doing just that, right there in front of them. We were in challenging territory to say the least. They may well enjoy the spectacle but could not believe what they were seeing. As guitarist Deirdre Cartwright experienced:

> 'After a gig at the Camden Palace with Tour de Force a man said to me "I've never seen a woman play guitar like that. You must be taking lots of drugs." I told him I wasn't – he was stunned that a woman could play that fast.'[7]

And Judy Costello, the drummer from Garbo, an Australian all-girl band formed in 1975, recalled men in the audience coming up and actually asking to feel the muscles in her arms as they could not believe that a girl could hit the drums so hard. Another female guitarist, who prefers to remain anonymous, was asked who wrote her guitar parts.[8]

For me, the only way forward at that time was to get out there and do it. We were among a growing number of females with musical knowledge and ability, who wanted to play in a band without having to be a sexual stereotype. The fact that this equated with being uncommercial was limited short term thinking at its best on the part of the industry. No one was asking for a free pass to success just because they turned up, but having the door slammed in your face because you did not fit the 'women in rock' template was not acceptable either.

Why is being 'all-girl' political?

Keyboard player and singer Lesley Sly agrees that the prejudice against all-girl bands still continues, four decades later.

> 'A problem then, and still, with all-girl bands is that the choice to be an all-girl band is regarded first as a political statement. Boys who choose to have all-boy bands don't have that problem. Then, and still in commercial music, boys could dress as weirdly as they liked, but if girls didn't dress in ultra femme style, they were automatically

assumed to be lesbian man-haters, and this upped the ante of political statement. If you could play pretty well, if your guitarist didn't wear and play guitar like it was a fashion accessory, this reinforced it further. Women fronting bands of boys had a lot more latitude than women in all-girl bands.'[9]

The sight of women on stage, playing with the command and power audiences were used to seeing delivered by men, was a worrying prospect for many. If our music could be accepted for what it was and, not just tolerated because we were pleasing on the eye, we were seen to be sending out a genital shrinking 'we can do this without men' declaration.

Prog rock a no-go: the Mother Superior story

These reactionary attitudes towards girl bands dogged Mother Superior. We constantly frustrated managers and agents with our stance and when record companies heard what kind of music we had recorded there was a collective and resounding 'no thanks'. Male prog rock bands could make the choices we did and get signed to album deals with no demands for hit singles or a revealing dress code; why not us, Tour de Force or Garbo? All we wanted was a chance, all they saw was a chance being squandered. Prog rock females were not on the menu, they were not commercial nor apparently, were they sexy.

Our first manager signed us to a three-year deal in March 1975, but by April 1976 he'd had enough; we were not raking it in, there had been no overnight success and the album had not taken off – hardly surprising as it was only available in Scandinavia. Promoters loved us, we could have worked day and night, but to earn enough money to live on, you needed a bona fide record deal. Our relationship with him was at an all-time low; the lack of money caused many problems, keeping a band on the road is not cheap whichever gender you are, even at micro-budget levels. The vehicles were worse than useless and the accommodation usually dire (except for the marvellous B&B run by Barbara in Nottingham, who made great breakfast, didn't use nylon sheets and never complained when we came in after midnight!)

Breaking point came during a tour of Sweden and Denmark, promoting our album *Lady Madonna*, when the van came to an abrupt and unequivocal end in deep snow, in the middle of the night. After being rescued from certain hypothermia by a delivery man who drove us to a hotel, we began a series of desperate phone calls to our manager in the UK. We needed a vehicle to complete the tour and one to collect us and our equipment from the ferry. There were no days off, we were playing every night, this needed to be resolved fast and we felt he was not on the ball or even bothered by our plight. He was so sick of our calls he left the phone off the hook. The tipping point came when we convinced the operator to sound a klaxon down the line to attract his attention. He sold us on while we were still away and SMA, the Swedish record company who had released our album, reluctantly provided transport.

On our return, we were met on the dock at Harwich by our new manager, who drove us and our gear back to London. Still with stars in his eyes he purchased a Mercedes truck and joined us as driver/manager on our eighteen-day tour of Finland in May 1976. His desire to get up close and personal was not reciprocated and on our return to England we were told that unless we started writing hits and dressing sexy his management company would take our instruments (instruments that we owned) and make sure that we never worked again.

This threat certainly had a dramatic effect – Lesley and Audrey left the band within a few weeks of each other. Jackie Crew and I were asked to find replacements by our agent, to tour the UK in October. In August while we were still auditioning, the manager who was now determined to claw back some of his investment drove off with the Mercedes containing most of our equipment – Jackie's entire drum kit, the PA and my bass amp and speakers – to be held hostage until we signed a document confirming we would repay the money he decided we owed him, within one year. We had to sue him to get our gear back. He relented on the day before the tour was to start.

End of the all-girl set up

Ludicrous and heavy-handed though this whole experience was, it summed up the feeling of the music business in general, except that no one had the balls to say it. Why couldn't we just be frothy, sexy and write pop songs? Answer: that wasn't who we were. Did anyone ever ask Yes to write pop music?

Mother Superior was never an all-girl band again, a fact that was described as unfortunate, disappointing and a pity by agents and reviewers – so many confusing messages. We became a five piece, joined by American singer Kate Buddeke, Simon Etchell on keyboards, guitarist Janis Sharp who was later replaced by Pete Chapman and finally came to an end in 1977, at the point when we were most successful financially but unable to see any future. (No one guessed our album would be available on CD in the 21st century.)[10]

Meanwhile Lesley Sly had joined Judy Costello in the previously mentioned Australian all-girl band Garbo, as keyboard player and singer alongside Kelly (piano/vocals), Faye Reid (bass) and Veda Meneghetti (guitar/vocals/congas). But they unfortunately headed straight down the same cul-de-sac as Mother Superior. Lesley Sly said:

> 'The band (Garbo 1975-81) played original material and some rearranged covers – I would describe the music as alternative rock with progressive leanings. We were professional, lived off touring alone, wrote our own press releases, printed the band T-shirts and did our own

accounts. With sponsorship from Electrovoice we had a
large PA, permanent road crew of two guys and lots of
keyboards, but couldn't continue without a deal.'[11]

With the demise of Mother Superior, Jackie Crew replaced
Val Lloyd as the drummer in Tour de Force. This band was
formed in 1977 by Deirdre Cartwright and her sister Bernice
Cartwright on bass, with singer Viv Corringham on board also.
(Deirdre Cartwright had decided to leave covers band Painted
Lady after their change to more mainstream heavy rock and
just prior to them morphing into Girlschool.)[12]

Deirdre Cartwright reflected on the significance of sound
and skill for the wider acceptance of all-girl bands:

> 'The music biz was not interested in Tour de Force until
> we became more poppy. The problem that women playing
> in bands experienced, was that if they can play quite well
> it was too much for some people to accept. The more skill
> you presented the more difficult it was for them.'[13]

There was no way to win: if you couldn't play well you were
derided for being a female musician and if you could play well
you were, even worse, disliked and ignored. The complete
refusal to acknowledge excellent female musicianship within
the industry (acoustic guitarists and piano players aside perhaps)
remains a real core problem. It helps limit the numbers of
women who are prepared to put in the hard work and make the
sacrifices it takes to be professional rock musicians, progressive
or mainstream, as they know their fate is decided almost before
they begin. In turn, this prevents some of those women who
may have great talent, skill or genius from being recognised. In
the vast forest of male guitarists, how many trees would you
have to walk into before you found Jimi Hendrix or Jeff Beck?

Being able to demonstrate that they are more than capable
of acquiring the equivalent skill and technique possessed by

their male counterparts is not enough to secure them a chance, let alone a decent career within the music industry. The result of this restrictive attitude is that only the occasional talented female musician breaks through, creating little change in the long term. It is far too easy for them to be seen as the exception that proves the ongoing misapprehension, that rock music is best created by men. As women's rights campaigner Huda Shaarawi points out: 'Men have singled out women of outstanding merit and put them on a pedestal to avoid recognising the capabillities of women.'[14]

To catch the public's attention and ensure you and your music are a long term success is no mean feat, but if you are attempting this within the genre of progressive music you are pushing your luck to the limit. Bands like Pink Floyd and Genesis have achieved it, but there has only been one woman to reach this level...

Kate Bush: a unique voice within the field

Another proud moment in the annals of the British music industry, akin to Decca turning down The Beatles, has to be the one that involved the incredibly gifted composer, vocalist and musician, Kate Bush. One of the most talented and successful artists, male or female, to come from the progressive rock genre, she uses synthesizers, unrestricted arrangements, inspirational and fantasy based lyrics in the experimental pop music she continues to make. I would have thought that being the female lead singer with a male backing band she would have walked straight into a deal, but until Pink Floyd's Dave Gilmour 'recommended' that EMI take her seriously, she was turned down by all the usual suspects, whose A&R departments should have known better. Perhaps she was too unique to be an obvious sell. EMI signed her in 1975 when she was sixteen years old and waited a further three years for her to be ready to launch her first single 'Wuthering Heights'. We (Mother

Superior) were aware of her EMI deal and saw her perform a few times in South London during that three year period, as we were acquainted with the band Conkers, who in part would become the KT Bush Band – Brian Bath, Del Palmer and Vic King. Initially, she was promoted like any stereotypical nineteen-year-old singer but Kate Bush would show what she was capable of, writing almost everything she has ever recorded in her remarkable and ongoing catalogue, including the album *Never for Ever* (1980) which entered the charts at No.1 and the unforgettable classic *Hounds of Love* (1985).

Women in music 'off stage', tech and equipment

The male bias of the music business was not limited to record companies: it was everywhere – management, agents, studios, crew, people selling instruments and equipment... Having played bass guitar in bands from 1973 onwards, the first time I met a female roadie was seven years later, in December 1980, while touring in Canada. This was a woman called Mikki, who had worked with Martha and the Muffins (a band from Toronto, formed in 1977, who had a hit with 'Echo Beach'),[15] and ended up working as a roadie for us. She attracted a fair amount of interest and disbelief from anyone who saw her at work – she drove the van, carried our equipment, tuned the guitars and fought it out with a promoter who insisted we should perform, after Mikki discovered the electricity supply was not earthed and could have fried any one of us. (The promoter finally admitted defeat and called out an electrician.)

Of course, women have been and still are, working long, hard and successfully in all the above categories, it is just that they are very thin on the ground. Daphne Oram was one such example. One of the founders of the BBC Radiophonic Workshop and creator of the Oramic Machine (an experimental synthesizer), in the 1940s she was an early proponent of synthetic music and continued to play, construct and compose well into the 90s. As a pioneer of electronic music in general, she was the first woman to set up a personal studio and the first woman to design and construct an electronic instrument.[16] Or Boden Sandstrom who, as well as being a producer and lecturer at the University of Maryland, as a sound engineer started a company in 1975 with singer Casse Culver, called 'Woman Sound', touring with artistes like Cris Williamson and Lily Tomlin. Boden also produced the 2002 documentary film *Radical Harmonies* exploring in great depth the gender barriers faced by many women in music (directed by Dee Mosbacher).[17]

In the late 70s, Fran Rayner was the only female sound engineer I knew of, apart from myself. Fran had studied electronics. She not only looked after the live sound for Jam Today and Tour de Force when they were performing, she also had the invaluable technical knowledge to keep them on the road; if anything broke Fran would be there to fix it.

During the same period, my friend Pete Chapman and I branched out into PA hire, as over the years, we had acquired most of the gear necessary. We worked for all sorts: Adam and the Ants, The Bodysnatchers, the South African sax player Dudu Pukwana, a whole lot of reggae, although we had to cut back on the punk band bookings because of the grotesque amount of gob you had to remove from your equipment afterwards. Sharing all the various tasks, the fact that I could use the controls on a mixing desk usually came as a surprise to bands and they could get a bit twitchy if a man was not working the desk. Being on one end of a bass bin was a bit strenuous, but it did not mean my ears were not fully functional.

If you were doing live sound, you learned in the field. Most live sound engineers came either from road crew or from bands, like me and Pete. In the late 60s and early 70s the standard PA (the equipment needed for a live show) in small venues, consisted of a pair of speaker columns (usually Vox or Sound City), which you stood either side of the stage, along with an amp with about four channels for the mics (usually the very hardwearing Shure Unidyne Bs), all this controllable by the band or their roadie, which is what Mother Superior started with. The need for improved sound quality came with the changes in music and equipment – mixing desks, bass bins, mid range horns etc. were added and the live sound engineer's job was born which included the ability to hold forth on the finer points of JBL, Altec Lansing, Soundcraft or any other well-known brand.

All of the musicians I've contacted recently have said how they would love to see more women working in this area, either in studios or on the road. So I was lucky to be able to speak to Elli Dorman who, after studying French horn at Trinity College (London) and getting a BMus (Hons) from City University, has been a live sound engineer for over five years. Elli has worked with electronic indie bands such as Crystal Fighters, Bear in Heaven, Cibelle, Drums of Death, The Golden Filter and We Have Band. I asked her if the traditional attitudes towards women working as sound engineers had improved and whether their numbers had increased. Elli thought that although women are much less deterred from considering it as a career and on the whole male colleagues have been fair and good to work with, a few of the old prejudices still exist. The supposition that men have a superior understanding of sound and what it takes to get a good mix, seems to be a difficult one to quash. Some female artistes, tired of this over bearing attitude from their crew, have realised the advantage of employing women in this position.[18] The fact that Boden Sandstrom's company, Woman Sound, first saw life back in the mid 70s, only accentuates what a painfully long time it takes for the message to get through.

The music shop experience too, was mentioned by several of the women I have spoken to and it is predominantly not a positive one. Although the male clientele do not get off scot-free when browsing for a new guitar, replacement drum heads or whatever, women come in for an extra helping of ridicule. If

I entered the 'hallowed ground' of a music shop I was usually ignored by the men working there, who appeared to think I had either entered the premises by mistake or that my boyfriend must be in there somewhere. When they realised I had actually gone in to buy something, they spoke to me as though I could not possibly understand what I was talking about.

Jackie Crew made a recent visit to look at drums in the music shops around Charing Cross Road and Denmark Street in Central London, only to encounter the same condescending, or just plain rude attitudes as before, although she did note that women assistants had started to make the odd appearance.[19]

And a few months ago, guitarist Tedra Jeffries from the band Murder Act, was on the receiving end of some classic 'music shop treatment' – while trying out a guitar an assistant took the instrument from her hands, to show her how it's done.[20] Unbelievable...

Playing an instrument

As already mentioned, a female singer fronting a band of male musicians could be an asset, but if that lone female is playing an instrument the industry alarm bells go off. In late 1977 while considering what to do after Mother Superior, I auditioned for a band called Snips and the Video Kings. The fact that they were men was of no significance to me. I was looking for a job and here was a vacancy.

I wasn't aware at the time but Snips told me recently that the management company had been dead set against a woman joining this group of overloaded male egos (his words, not mine), because it would be a hassle, a possibly divisive element they didn't need and more importantly, an extra expense on tour – having to provide a separate room for me.[21]

Despite their reservations, I was offered – and accepted – the fairly unusual position back then of being the only woman musician in a band who wasn't someone's sister or partner. I was aware that at least one band member was not keen on the choice of bass player and I felt there was an ongoing concern that I was going to spoil the boys' party, a spy in the camp, reporting back to their girlfriends on any shenanigans.

The job was quite stressful with a lot of pressure (mostly from myself it has to be said). NYC's Talking Heads with the great bassist, Tina Weymouth had released 'Psycho Killer' and were big news. I was very relieved to get good feedback and not judged to have been hired as the token female. The management needn't have worried. I do not think I was personally responsible for the lack of record sales, which brought the band to an end the following year.

On the plus side: being a woman in rock

Regardless of what I have said above, being a female musician was by no means all doom and gloom, there was unsurprisingly loads of fun to be had, travelling the world, playing, composing, recording and the novelty value did have its plus side. The media interest in Talking Heads and particularly Tina Weymouth may well have pushed Snips into auditioning a female bass player. I would not have been hired if I couldn't do the job, but maybe the fact that I was a woman meant I got a second look.

In early 1974 when I was working with the Californian drummer Holly Vincent (this was a few years before she formed Holly and the Italians in LA), we advertised ourselves in *Melody Maker* as a female rhythm section looking for musicians to form a band. The phone never stopped ringing, there were so many replies, including Mark Knopfler, we didn't know which way to go. It did lead to our first recording session – at Sarm Studios in Whitechapel, East London with a band called Amazin. We also joined guitarist/singer Mike Corby (The Baby's) in a heavy rock three piece called Tintagel, for a few months. Sadly as far as I am aware there is no audio or visual record of these projects.

Creative teamwork

Bands playing original music create in different ways, largely dependent upon who is doing the composing. Some, including Electrelane,[22] will jam for hours, recording everything they play, listen to it back, keep the bits they like and turn those into songs or instrumentals. Others might have one writer who turns up with songs fully completed and tells the other group members what their parts should be.

In Mother Superior, and as is the case for many bands, ideas for original compositions were brought into rehearsals to be thrashed into the finished article, with contribution from everyone. Being part of this band was something of a joint voyage of discovery, we were a very egalitarian group who encouraged each other's creativity. Everyone's suggestions for covers were given equal consideration and while this inevitably led to a 'pick and mix' collection of songs, it was a true reflection of all four of us.

Like a lot of bands in the 70s, we did not stay strictly within one category, we meandered around straight rock, progressive rock, blues and anything else that might take our fancy. We felt we had that freedom, whether this was due to gender, the times or our personalities, I honestly don't know, but I do know that I didn't experience it again. None of this altered with the changes in line-up. As far as I was concerned Lesley Sly's replacement, Simon Etchell, who at eighteen years old and in 1976 as the lone male in an otherwise female band on a UK tour, was a 'natural' part of the Mother Superior line-up. The band ethic remained the same. We were musicians with the same goal and gender did not seem relevant – we shared the same dressing room, if there was one, and accommodation. Our band enjoyed equality on all fronts (and if you've ever carried a Hammond organ to the gig Upstairs at Ronnie Scott's you'll know what I mean). I asked Simon what he thought:

Prog Rock: A Fortress they call The Industry

For me it was always about the music, I just answered an ad for a keyboard player, most of my male friends were musicians and they didn't have a problem with it, neither did my girlfriend.'[23]

I found the reaction from male musicians varied, some were so dead set against the idea, that it did not matter how good you may or may not be, they couldn't deal with it; others were so shocked that you could play at all, they would stand there open mouthed and some, like Simon, were happy just to accept you as another musician.

The demise of prog rock

Prog rock struggled over the coming years; technique won out over content to no great effect. It became pompous, overbearing and something of a joke. Begging to be put out of its misery, with rare impeccable timing, punk came along to deliver the *coup de grâce*.

Ubiquitous though punk rock was, it was not the only music on offer; the prog rock subgenres – alternative, experimental, art rock, avant garde, electronic and others, found there was still an audience out there, and among those musicians performing it were The Holy Sisters of the Gaga Dada, a US female alternative rock band, using synth sounds and lyrics very reminiscent of early progressive rock. Formed in Santa Cruz, California in the early 80s, the line-up included Jill Fido (bass, vocals), Wild Kim Sockit (guitar, percussion, vocals), Mary Jean Shaffer (keyboards, vocals) and Zero Jessephski Jr (drums, percussion). *LA Times* described them as the sweethearts of the underground in February '86.[24] Their album *Let's Get Acquainted* was released on Bomp! Records in the same year.[25] If the internet is anything to go by they are still much missed.[26] [27]

Prog rock and the industry today: where are the women?

Back here in the present day, changes in the music business have been wide ranging. The making and selling of records or CDs is no longer the big money spinner it was, nor does it reside solely in the hands of the record companies, major or independent. The internet and digital distribution have altered the whole industry. Profit, if that's what you're looking for, lies in touring, festivals, merchandising and sponsorship.

Perhaps the search for potentially big selling acts of previous decades, like The Beatles, Led Zeppelin and Pink Floyd will diminish and the playing field can level out to encompass all. It's good to see that all-girl bands are currently playing in the areas that back in the 70s would have been called progressive and have been able to find the time and space to be themselves.

In the summer of 2005, Purple Rhinestone Eagle formed in West Philadelphia, an all-girl band comprising Andrea Genevieve (lead vocals/guitar), Morgan Ray Denning (bass/backing vocals) and Ashley Spungin (drums/backing vocals), their six track demo recorded at Radio Sloan's Haunted Mansion studio in Oregon. Their album (2009) *Amorum Tali* on Eolian Records had reviewers lauding their mastery of 70s heavy, psychedelic, fuzzed out blues rock and describing them as post-Haight throwback with exhilarating doom.[28]

From California, Warpaint with their soft vocals and distinctive art rock style, include King Crimson and Yes amongst their musical influences.[29] Emily Kokal (vocals/guitar), Theresa Wayman (vocals/guitar), Jenny Lee Lindberg (bass/vocals) and Stella Mozgawa (drums/keyboards/vocals) have been going since 2004 with a couple of changes of personnel. They were nominated for the BBC Sounds of 2011, the EP *Exquisite Corpse* and album *The Fool* are available on Rough Trade. With a 2011 summer tour in the UK and

Prog Rock: A Fortress they call The Industry

Europe, including Glastonbury, Coachella back in March and even *Later with Jools Holland*, things look good for Warpaint.[30]

I recently met with Verity Susman, a talented musician whose influences include the 70s German band Neu!, Stereolab and John Coltrane. She is a member of Electrelane, started by four friends in Brighton in 1998, an all-girl alternative rock band whose material mostly comes through improvisation. The track 'Bells' from the album *Axes* among many of their compositions clearly highlights their progressive connections. They toured Japan, Australia, Europe, UK, USA and Russia promoting their four albums,[31] achieving notable success and impressive sales until they split in 2007. The group, although now living on different continents, reformed to play festivals in 2011 with Verity (vocals/keyboards/guitar/saxophone), Mia Clarke (guitar/vocals), Ros Murray (bass/vocals) and Emma Gaze (drums). Verity is also working on her solo project Vera November.

We discussed the influence that feminist, punk and riot grrrl genres may have had on increasing the numbers of women playing instruments. She felt there had been a very real change in recent years due in most part to the achievements of riot grrrl and thought that when Electrelane began in the late 90s attitudes had already begun to improve. They were not coerced into recording anything or appearing in any way they weren't happy with. Although disappointed that the notion still existed, their experience was that if there was a male in the band, audiences would assume he was the composer and probably in control. She notes the regular appearance of women in bands is making it more routine and less of a novelty, but realises that the music industry and the media in general tend not to pay much attention to older women making alternative music so, unless you search these women out, they are not part of your general cultural landscape when you're growing up.[32]

The women band members from the 70s and 80s may well help to solve this problem, as Maggie Vail from the label Kill

Rock Stars mentioned when I asked her opinion on the dearth of older female musicians:

> 'There are soon going to be lots of amazing punk role models around. There are The Raincoats and LiLiPUT all in their 50s, the riot grrls are in their late 30s / early 40s. Wild Flag, an all female powerhouse band of Carrie and Janet from Sleater-Kinney, Mary Timony, and Rebecca Cole, are about to take the world by storm.'[33]

Perhaps Wild Flag will do something to alter the minds of the majority of the music buying public that find it impossible to accept the fact that a woman is capable of playing a guitar solo. This point of view seems to be written in stone and will take some shifting. And as Maggie Vail (KRS) points out, in the past it might have felt like a missed opportunity when you had female guitarists/singers fronting successful bands, who choose not to include an occasional solo.

> 'I loved The Pretenders and Joan Jett and the Blackhearts growing up but always felt let down that there wasn't another woman in the band or that neither ladies solo'ed.'[34]

Fortunately there are a handful of current guitarists happy to prove otherwise: Mary Timony, a guitarist and vocalist from Washington, has played with several bands including the alternative rock band Helium from 1992-1998, Autoclave and her own Mary Timony Band. A self-proclaimed progressive rock fan, one of her favourite albums is *Fragile* by Yes and she names her ultimate guitar hero as Jimi Hendrix. The band Wild Flag sees her continuing to perform in this genre.[35]

Also from the US is another guitarist/singer, Marnie Stern, whose music has been linked to the prog rock genre by reviewers like Sasha Frere-Jones in an article in the *New Yorker*.

Prog Rock: A Fortress they call The Industry

'Stern's music is part of a continuum that began in the late sixties with progressive-rock bands like King Crimson.'[36]

Her first CD *In Advance of the Broken Arm* was released in 2007 by Kill Rock Stars, the label that launched The Gossip. Maggie Vail from KRS says:

'Poor Marnie. I feel like everything about her is about her gender ... It's all about the novelty of being a female shredder ... most of the writing/discussion around her involves that. It doesn't involve that she has a truly unique and amazing songwriting voice.'[37]

It seems that the same preconceptions and attitudes exist as before and each time a female comes to the forefront, they are met with disbelief and have to prove that women can play, all over again. Talking about this with Tedra Jeffries, a guitarist with a career spanning twenty years, she told me that, playing with her current band (Murder Act) is the first time she has noticed a drop in the number of derogatory comments she has received as a female playing an electric guitar.[38] Discussing the same topic while drinking coffee at the Bar Italia in Soho, Central London, with my long time friend Jackie Crew, drummer with Cosmetix, Mother Superior, Jam Today, Tour de Force, Dangerous Designs and Ponytails, her view was:

'There may be more women in numbers in the music industry but the idea that they can occupy the same space as men is still as unlikely as it ever was.'[39]

(As we were finishing our drinks Jackie reminded me of a gig we played in Yorkshire in the 70s, where only men could be served at the bar and we went on just before the stripper (female). Neither of us could remember the name of the venue so I am unable to confirm if this still goes on.)

Women Make Noise

Maggie Vail from the label Kill Rock Stars (KRS) offered a glimmer of hope when I asked her opinion.

> 'It is still difficult for a woman to be taken seriously as a musician. I am certain it is better than it was, but I don't believe the change moves very fast. Our culture is so intensely patriarchal that it is a struggle to make real change. My real hopes lie with the rock 'n' roll camps for girls that have sprouted up all over America.
>
> For these young girls there is nothing strange about picking up the instrument and writing a song. They are being given easy access to the tools and encouragement that most of us couldn't get. I love it that Beyoncé's touring band is all women.'[40]

If women are going to be customarily accepted as valid and serious musicians, the need to change the mindset of the music industry and the public is essential. Working on the inside is as critical and valid as building your forces on the outside, whether it be increasing the numbers of women in the pool of mainstream musicians for hire, like Gail Ann Dorsey (bassist David Bowie, Gwen Stefani), Orianthi Panagaris (guitarist, Carlos Santana, Michael Jackson's last tour) and Tal Wilkenfeld (bassist Jeff Beck, Herbie Hancock); making your career as a session musician such as the legendary bassist/guitarist Carol Kaye; or being part of the vital, uncompromising feminist movement/riot grrrls like Bikini Kill, Sleater-Kinney, Tribe 8 and Le Tigre (see chapters 9 and 10).

Maggie Vail told me:

> 'I have never wanted to be part of the mainstream music business neither as an artist nor as a label person. It holds zero appeal to me. It's way more sexist, way more corrupt and way less interesting to me than punk/ underground music.'[41]

Prog Rock: A Fortress they call The Industry

For there to be a lasting and positive effect on the perception of women as serious rock musicians, there has to be a sustained increase in the numbers of those who can play with skill and confidence and their appearance on the public stage must be continuous. Change will occur when there are more women who are able to inspire the following generations and convince audiences, both male and female, that not only can they do it, there is no reason they can't be exceptional too.

DARE TO BE BRILLIANT.

Contributor biography

Jackie Parsons played, sang and composed with several bands during the 70s and 80s, including Mother Superior and Snips and the Video Kings, touring the UK, Europe and USA and supporting The Ramones on their 1978 UK tour. She also looked after live sound in clubs and ran Bonny Street Studios in Camden. Together with her husband Stephen Parsons she went into the production of music for TV, film and commercials, which ultimately led to them making their own movies – *Wishbaby* and *Rough Magik*. She currently has a music publishing company, is writing songs and singing with the North London Community Choir. For further reading visit her blog: http://jackiebadgersblog.blogspot.co.uk

Jackie would like to thank: 'Audrey Swinburne, Deirdre Cartwright, Elli Dorman, Ingrid Schroeder, Jackie Crew, Judy Costello, Lesley Sly, Maggie Vail, Rosie Parsons, Simon Etchell, Snips, Tedra Jeffries and Verity Susman for their time, input and assistance and all the women who continue to work so hard to maintain a strong presence in the music industry.'

5. Feminist Musical Resistance in the 70s and 80s

Deborah M. Withers

Women's Liberationists wanted more than just changes in the law. They wanted to redefine what it *meant* to be a woman and through this, transform the whole of culture and society. They set up women's centres and safe houses for women and children who experienced domestic abuse. They published books, magazines, newspapers, pamphlets and newsletters. They held art exhibitions, reading and discussion groups. They learnt manual trades. They set up cab driving companies and other business ventures. They organised protests and huge conferences. They experimented with sexuality. They created agitprop theatre collectives, established community nurseries and free schools. And, of course, they used music as a tool to raise consciousness and help women find their political voice.

The music-making legacies of the UK's Women Liberation Movement (WLM) have been largely untouched by historians, commentators and academic researchers.[1] There is a reasonable amount of documentation of the 'Women's Music' scene in the USA that inspired some of the strategies UK feminist music-makers used.[2] This included setting up all-women record companies, organising 'womyn' only festivals and empowering women to try sound engineering, to name a few.

Feminist Musical Resistance in the 70s and 80s

This chapter looks at some of the feminist music-makers who shook things up in the UK context. It uses the stories of three very different feminist bands – Jam Today, Ova and The Fabulous Dirt Sisters – to understand how women used music in a feminist way. It draws on research from the Women's Liberation Music Archive, an online blog archive that aims to map the music-making communities of the UK WLM from 1970-1989. The archive includes information about over 100 all-women acts and is growing all the time. It is a project that I started with Frankie Green, who was the drummer in Jam Today 1, in September 2010. The archive is very much a starting point and aims to create a legacy for present day audiences.

My own interest in sharing this obscured part of women's music heritage is to ensure these histories are not lost. I want people of all genders to have the opportunity to engage with the music and the stories of what women did to claim space in a cultural arena dominated by men. Many commentators note a resurgence of feminist activism in the UK today.[3] The histories and strategies presented below offer one way to make connections with the creative ways women have used music to protest social injustice in the past. With artists such as PJ Harvey winning awards for an album of songs that protest the futility of war and violence, *Let England Shake* (2011), it indicates that oppositional music made by women has a 'platform to be heard'[4] today. So who were these women and what is their legacy?

Jam Today (1976-1984)

'We want freedom, changes, power.' *Jam Today theme tune*

Jam Today's line-up and musical style evolved over the band's lifetime. There were three different versions of the group (distinguished now as Jam Today 1 (1976-1978], 2 [1979-1980] and 3 [1980-1984]). Jam Today 1 was one of the flagship bands for the WLM. Like other bands, such as the

Northern Women's Rock Band (1974-1976), the Mistakes (1978-1982) and the Stepney Sisters (1974-1976), they often provided dance music for events and actions. Many people who featured prominently in Women's Liberation music-making communities were one-time members of Jam Today. This included Teresa Hunt, Deirdre Cartwright, Alison Rayner, Barbara Stretch and Jackie Crew.[5]

Jam Today 1's drummer Frankie Green remembers how the band formed:

> 'Through a notice in the London WLM workshop newsletter in spring 1976. Women turned up at a flat I rented in Peckham and a line-up emerged: Terry Hunt the guitarist, who knew Deidre Cartwright, Alison Rayner who decided to take up the bass, Angele Veltmeijer on sax/flute, Josie Mitten on keyboards, Corrine Liensol with her trumpet and Fran Rayner who became our sound engineer. A singer we liked, Joey, parted company with us...she didn't support abortion rights, and Josefina Cupido was our vocalist and percussionist for a while. Diana Wood joined us... and when the Women's Film Group asked us to provide music for "Rapunzel" we met Laka Daisical, who sang with us sometimes, and Sarah Greaves, another sound engineer.'[6]

Across all three generations of the band the *Stereotyping* EP (1981) remains the only studio recordings of Jam Today to be 'properly' released. It was done so as part of Stroppy Cow Records, a feminist Do-it-Yourself (DIY) label set up by Alison Rayner and Terry Hunt. The DIY ethos that was burgeoning in the late 1970s offered artists full control of their creative output. It fitted in well with the feminist politics of Stroppy Cow. These were anti-commercial yet had the 'aim to make [a] living as musicians rather than profit as a business.'[7] There are some recordedings of Jam Today 1 and 2. Jam Today 1 recorded a number of songs in a studio, but plans for the full album never materialised. These songs became part of the soundtrack for the film *Rapunzel, Let Down Your Hair,* made by the London Women's Film Group. There are a number of recordings of Jam Today 2's rehearsals, but nothing 'finished'.

Jam Today 3 did not record as much as they would have liked, largely because of a lack of money. Recording music in studios was very expensive, and recording music at home did not always produce the best quality, unlike today. However, Jam Today 3's work is documented in other ways. There is a collection of live performances on Jam Today 3's You Tube channel.[8] Jam Today 3 were also interviewed and performed on television on three occasions, including an Open University programme called *Women in Rock* made by Mavis Bayton, that featured Tour de Force and The Raincoats. Many of the song lyrics are collected on the Jam Today song sheets. These were handed out at shows so women could understand the feminist words that could easily be lost because of poor quality PA systems or bad live mixes. The song sheets also provided an opportunity for audiences to join in if they wanted to.

Over an eight-year period, Jam Today changed its members and styles more than any other band in the WLM. As Jam Today 3 they were the first British feminist act to practically realise the political ideals of female musical autonomy combined with commitment to professionalism. Creating Stroppy Cow, and having their own PA and group van, they set an example of independence that many of their contemporaries followed.

Ova (1976-1989)

> 'Do what you have to do but don't sit back and let the world die.' *'Granny Song', Ova*

Jam Today's label mates (and later owners of Stroppy Cow) Ova were another important UK feminist band in the 1970s and 1980s. Formed by Rosemary Schonfeld and Jane (later Jana) Runnalls in 1976, Ova were one of the most productive feminist bands of the period. In the thirteen years the duo played together they recorded and released four albums: *Ova* (1979); *Out of Bounds* (1981); *Possibilities* (1984) and *Who Gave Birth To the Universe* (1988). They played regularly in Europe, with particular popularity in Germany. They were also a hit in the United States, doing one three-month coast-to-coast tour of the country and played the famous Michigan Womyn's Music Festival three times.

Ova were originally called the Lupin Sisters. As the Lupin Sisters they recorded a cassette album on a 2-track reel-to-reel recorder called *Women Everywhere This Is For You*. Each cassette had a different cover, hand-drawn by their friends. Copies were replicated individually on Jana's brother's tape recorder. Created in 1976, this album is a very early example of the DIY ethic in music production and distribution that was to seize the cultural zeitgeist a few years later. After flirting with various members, including Maggie Nicols from the Feminist Improvising Group, The Lupin Sisters became a duo. Now called Ova, a name suggested by Sally Beautista, they fully declared their feminist intent.

In 1986 Ova set up the Ova Music Studio, a Greater London Council (GLC) funded resource for girls and women. The studio provided facilities where women of all ages could try out recording music and rehearse. It aimed to create a space where women could build their confidence as musicians and people in what they described as a 'non-oppressive environment.'[9] Voice workshops, run by Jana, allowed women to gain the vital self-assurance needed to speak in public, as well as exploring the 'magic of singing in an all-women environment.'[10] Drumming workshops, run by Rosemary, allowed women to find their own rhythms.

Ova went their separate ways in 1989. They achieved a tremendous amount during the time they worked together. In the hundreds of workshops they conducted they had a positive impact on many women. The four records they created make their work one of the most well-documented of the era. Ova lived their politics through music and 'challenged everything.'[11]

The Fabulous Dirt Sisters (1981-1989)

'War time, peace time, never our time. Ask your sisters, ask your Mum, when will our time come?' *'Street Song', The Fabulous Dirt Sisters*

The Fabulous Dirt Sisters were a music collective based in Nottingham, England. They played together throughout the 1980s. Like Jam Today and Ova, they set up their own record company, Spinaround Records, to distribute their music. On this they released two albums, *Flapping Out* (1986) and *Five Strong Swimmers* (1988). They performed regularly throughout the UK and often played what they described as 'World Tours' on the streets of Europe. Throughout their career they were predominantly a four-piece, consisting of Deb Mawby (saxophones/ vocals), Dorry Lake (now Karunavaca), (accordion, piano, vocals), Kaffy[12] Matthews (bass guitar, percussion, fiddle, vocals) and Stella Patella (violin, trombone, vocals). Jane Griffiths joined the band to play double bass in 1987. Karunavaca (née Dory Lake) explained their approach:

'The Dirt Sisters' music was never in one style. We don't play rock, we don't play funk, we don't play folk – we play music that we write ourselves – Dirt Sister music. We're playing women's music – its very celebratory.'[13]

She also commented that:

'We didn't want to make music like everyone else. We just invented it from what was in our heads.'[14]

The Fabulous Dirt Sisters played gigs indoors in venues such as art centres, pubs, theatres and festivals. They were also street musicians. Inspired by their antecedents The York Street Band (1978-1982), they claimed public space for women in entertaining and creative ways. The Dirt Sisters enjoyed almost a decade of making people smile with their music. As well as their albums and live performances, they featured prominently in Penny Florence's 1986 film *Silk Sow's Ear* that creatively documented women's music-making in the 1980s. The Dirt Sisters split up in 1989. Kaffe Matthews went on to have a successful career as a sound artist while Karunavaca, Deb and Stella still play together in the band Salmagundi.

Capitalism, creativity and survival

'We totally reject the values of commercialism and the profit making of the music business. We are working towards setting up alternative ways of sharing music.'[15]
The Women's Liberation Music Project

There are a number of ways in which women in bands made their music 'feminist'. The way bands dealt with their finances, for example, was often used to make a political statement about female oppression. Women's Liberation music-makers made a strong connection between capitalism and patriarchy. In other words, they wanted to challenge economic and gendered exploitation of women in the music industry and wider society. One of their answers was to be self-sufficient and work 'outside the system'. But was this really possible and how successful were they? What did they do to realise their aims? How did they remain committed to music-making when working on a small budget, or worse, persistently being out-of-pocket?

Like it or not, money was a crucial influence on the musical careers of Jam Today, Ova and The Fabulous Dirt Sisters. It affected what they did, how they did it and for how long. Let's take the issue of financial survival to start with. After a year and a half of being in the group, Jam Today 1 was forced to organise a benefit gig for themselves. This reveals much about the practical financial difficulties women had in sustaining musical ventures within the WLM. The band was very open about their finances with other women in the movement, distributing newsletters that included a full breakdown of their costs. These revealed that:

> 'Apart from Fran, our roadie, the other seven of us pay £160.71 (around £852 in today's money) on average per year to be in the band. And none of us have another job.'[16]

At times it was even a struggle for Women's Liberation bands to get paid for their work. This was partly because of the types of gigs they played. Bands were booked for benefit events where the purpose, of course, is to raise money for *other people*. This would usually mean forgoing wages in order to 'support the cause'. Jam Today, for example, played benefit gigs for different types of Women's Liberation initiatives such as *Spare Rib*, WIRES and Women's Aid. They also supported specific campaigns, such as the Grunwick strikers.[17]

Strong political ideologies within the movement questioned whether musicians were entitled to get paid for their work. 'The whole discussion that if women are paid it creates a division between performers/non-performers,'[18] meant that 'sometimes we've had to argue with women about being paid,'[19] Frankie and Terry from Jam Today remember, respectively. Sometimes the creative contributions were not always recognised by other feminists in the movement as sufficiently 'political'. Rosemary remembers:

> 'One of the debates was: is it entertainment or is it political activism? That used to annoy me because I felt what we were doing had a lot of relevance *and* it was a

form of activism. We were not entertainment! We were challenging roles, singing about issues and empowering women in a creative way.'[20]

Ova also struggled to survive financially. Their first album was partly funded by friends and a grant from the Gulbenkian Foundation. Well-paid tours overseas (in Germany, for example) helped to pay their way over the financial year. This included the cost of printing records. British shows were always less well paid than those on the continent. Although funded by the Greater London Council, the work done for the Ova Music Studio was poorly paid.

The Fabulous Dirt Sisters would also benfit from time-limited public funds. During the mid-80s the band was awarded a grant and they set themselves up as the Catflap Music Collective. The Dirt Sisters also talked about being permanently out of pocket, despite working on the project full-time. 'It would be lovely to earn some money from it – we don't earn anything now,'[21] they lamented in 1986. Their statement on the record sleeve for *Flapping Out* is telling: 'We have borrowed money to make this recording so please do not copy.' It reveals how fortunate we are to be able to listen to the album today, and that acquiring funds to record music involved personal financial risk.

Feminist autonomy – record labels

Monetary limitation was a very significant issue for many feminist bands, and the challenge of maintaining creative and political independence was hard work. Yet being independent was an important way feminists challenged commercial music-making. Women's Liberation bands maintained their independence by having their own record labels, enabling them to take complete control over the recording, production and distribution of their music. Stroppy Cow was set up by

Teresa Hunt and Alison Rayner to do precisely this. The name came from a tirade of sexist comments directed at Jam Today sound engineer Sarah (Greaves) Baker from a man working at the Barge Recording Studio in London. Sarah's work with women musicians threatened him. Stroppy Cow later released feminist acts Ova and the theatre group Siren.

The label's policy was to 'encourage women to define their own musical output and to be involved in every stage of production.'[22] The creation of Stroppy Cow was a logical conclusion to the politicisation of musical activity in the WLM. The ethos of these communities was 'a total reject[ion of] the values of commercialism and the profit-making of the music business.'[23] In the mid-80s Stroppy Cow was passed to Ova. Throughout Ova's career, like many other Women's Liberation bands, they operated as a collective. Livvy Elliott, a sound engineer and Jenny Gibbs, the group's administrator, joined Jana and Rosemary to help realise Ova's plans for a grassroots 'cultural revolution.'[24] Stroppy Cow was later passed on to the Women's Revolution Per Minute (WRPM) distribution service, run by Caroline Hutton.

Subversions of the public: radio, the street and women's social space

An important aspect of Women's Liberation music-making was the type of performance spaces women created and, sometimes, reclaimed. Women were faced with an interesting political problem: how do you totally reject the mainstream while spreading the feminist message far and wide? There were many different ways bands dealt with this issue. 'Working towards making our own music and playing to as many women as possible'[25] was one the specific aims of Jam Today 1. They decided to perform at a variety of venues such as colleges, community festivals and playgroup benefits to achieve this.

Bands did not completely reject mainstream media channels. Jam Today 3 appeared on television and Ova appeared on radio several times which provided them with an opportunity to discuss the politics behind the band. One radio commentator described their music as 'dangerous'[26] because of its lesbian content and proceeded to have a discussion with Jana and Rosemary about the place of lesbians within society. The challenging interview, that included excerpts of Ova's music, was broadcast into the homophobic climate of Thatcher's Britain on a Saturday morning! This is just one example of how Ova, and other WLM music-makers, used popular media forums to subvert and reclaim public space.

Another way was playing on the street. The Fabulous Dirt Sisters did this to great effect. Playing on the street was another way of making their music accessible to audiences. They didn't want to 'hide behind a barrage of equipment and cool.'[27] Street performances were an opportunity for chance encounters. It was about 'the unexpected. There was no set script. We were trying to be a breath of fresh air by surprising people who passed by,'[28] Stella reflected. This kind of spontaneity meant that you could just 'appear and play anywhere without having to be booked for gigs.'[29] It was a way of shirking mainstream approval, retaining creative autonomy but still being visible. The Dirt Sisters had a separate repertoire for the street. These were instrumental because vocals could not be heard so easily over general street noise or the sound of instruments. They captured audiences by playing 'high energy, jolly numbers,'[30] and wearing bright coloured, circus-like clothes. For women in particular, claiming public space of course has its own political resonance. Jam Today 1 similarly performed on the street. One memorable occasion was at a pro-choice march organised by the National Abortion Campaign. Women danced in 'long loose lines around the float carrying Jam Today, an all-women rock band.'[31] It is an image that evokes the energy and dynamic creativity of Women's Liberation protests.

As well as reaching out to wider publics, a significant part of WLM music-making was organising independent social spaces. Rosemary Schonfeld remembers: 'we had to create everything. There were no spaces for us. It really started from scratch. There started to be a few more women's spaces, upstairs in pubs, one night a week, women-only performances. Because of squatting there were a lot of spaces available.'[32] Within the spaces there were attempts to explore ways of making the music more accessible. One example of this is to break down the hierarchical relationship between audience and performers. There were plans to keep lights on at gigs and abandon stages, although this was not always successful, as Alison Rayner reflects:

> 'We generally preferred to play on stages – practical and better for our own space and safety. I think we generally reached some sort of compromise with a softer lighting all round.'[33]

It was not always easy to reach compromises within feminist music-making because everything was up for discussion.

Professional or amateur?

A key debate that circulated among WLM music-makers explored the relationship between professionalism and amateurism. Should women reproduce male musical prowess or should they deconstruct it? Is being musically proficient elitist or, worse, patriarchal? How can women be empowered to try out musical instruments in ways that are empowering and accessible? Of course, these political questions were interpreted and explored differently by women throughout the movement.

It is important to remember that Jam Today, Ova and The Fabulous Dirt Sisters made music as a full time venture. It was not something done in their 'spare time,' although this was not the same for all music-makers. A lot of time and energy was committed to making music. While bands were not professional in a profit-driven, fame seeking sense, they certainly took their job very seriously. Jam Today 1, for example, practiced three times a week. Often long, emotionally intense meetings in which 'we discussed the politics of everything constantly'[34] happened afterwards. The Dirt Sisters also combined practices with meetings. Practices would take place two times a week from 10am-4pm in a small room in Dorry's house. Kaffe remembers that in meetings 'we would talk a lot … sometimes the politics was more important than the music.'[35]

One way that many Women's Liberation bands sought to make music-making accessible and 'feminist' was by running skill-sharing workshops. Playing a gig *and* running a music workshop was a regular occurrence for WLM bands. It was a concrete way music-making was demystified, as workshop spaces helped women find their political-personal voice in creative ways. Music workshops provided informal environments where women could 'try out instruments [and] find out about setting up equipment,'[36] an experience often denied to women growing up in a male dominated society at that time. Ova of course took the political commitment of Women's Liberationists to 'make music and music-making an accessible, demystified activity available to women as an empowering tool for social change'[37] one step further by opening the Ova Music Studio.

Debates over the feminist credentials of taking a professional or amateur approach to music-making sometimes became contentious. Jam Today 1, for example, were criticised for their professionalism by other women in the movement. This was a source of frustration for Angele: 'We're just as involved in the musical side as the political – the music's got to be challenging for us as well'.[38] Different levels of musical skill also created different expectations within Jam Today 1. 'It did become increasingly relevant and, in fact, eventually led to the break up of that particular generation of the band,' Teresa Hunt reflected in 1986.[39]

The Fabulous Dirt Sisters were keen to try out different instruments and styles. They wanted to eschew being slick, professional and technically proficient. Karunavaca commented at the time:

> 'I want women's things to sound different – as well as being "as good as" or "better than." Wanting to be technically amazing can be a bit of a red herring. You can get so lost in being slick […] that you lose that energy and the ability to communicate.'[40]

As with many aspects of Women's Liberation music-making, bands interpreted the political ideas in different ways.

Controlling sound

Challenging sexism in music-making applied to all aspects of the process, from learning instruments and writing songs to grappling with mixing desks. Providing a space for women to learn sound engineering was important given how male-dominated music technology was in the late 1970s, as Jackie Parson's chapter in this book demonstrates. Often gigs would be women only, a fact that necessitated women learning sound engineering. Taking control of sound was a feminist act. Jam Today 1 had their own PA system that was inherited by later generations of the band. They took the system to gigs and hired it out to other women's collectives to help finance their activities. Feminist bands often had their own sound engineer who knew how best to mix them in a live context.

Recording studios could often be unfamiliar places for women. This inexperience could sometimes affect the finished recorded product. For example, when you listen to the Fabulous Dirt Sisters' first album *Flapping Out* (1986), the changes between songs can sound awkward. This had a lot to do with the male sound engineer who recorded the band. He made them play to a metronome, a device that helps musicians play to a set time. Kaffe Matthews remembers.

> 'The engineer was really weak. He'd never done anything like us. He put down a click track and we should *never* have played to a click. For us to record we needed to go into a studio and play live. We were totally naïve and didn't have a clue about recording, and we didn't have a producer. Basically the guy who engineered it suggested we did it like that and we were like "oh all right then."'[41]

Kaffe's comment highlights how crucial the work of the Ova collective was in helping demystify sound recording and technical equipment for women in the 1980s. As a consequence of the lack of confidence they had to assert themselves in a male-dominated recording context, The Dirt Sisters today do not see *Flapping Out* as a true reflection of the vitality of their sound. Livvy Elliott who had previously worked with Ova engineered their next album, *Five Strong Swimmers* (1988).

What makes a song 'feminist'?

This was a common question that came up among Women's Liberation music-makers. It was debated passionately at meetings and explored within skills-sharing workshops. Was it the sound? Lyrics? Genre? Song structure? Instruments used? Jam Today, Ova and The Fabulous Dirt Sisters all offered different interpretations. The music-makers connected to the WLM were unique because of their musical diversity. Many rejected the machismo of punk rock because of its aggression. Music had to be suitable for 'benefit bops' and women's socials. Aside from that it was in a constant state of (sometimes amateurish) experimentation.

The musical style of Jam Today evolved across the different generations of the group. Jam Today 1 is described by lifetime member and principal songwriter Teresa Hunt as having a 'big sound that was anarchic and fun.'[42] Their sound 'involved a wide variety of music – rock, reggae, blues and funk, and some slightly jazzy material.'[43] Lyrics expressed feminist ideas about freedom and empowerment. Jam Today 2 offer a high-jazz take on feminism. Joined by Raincoat-to-be Vicky Aspinall on violin, Jam Today 2 favoured songs that revelled in exploratory, often instrumental, musical journeys. Jam Today 3 marked yet another change in the band's style. This time the band adopted a slick, tight, rhythmical arrangement that equally fused pop, rock and jazz elements. Throughout the musical evolution of the group, the strong commitment to feminist principles undoubtedly remained, most clearly demonstrated through the lyrics on the *Stereotyping* EP (1981).

The *Stereotyping* EP contains 'Friend in You' and 'Song about Myself' that embody the anti-romance philosophy of feminism of the late 1970s. Romantic love was seen as an ideological block to women's self-empowerment: 'Love, I think you control our lives too much and in a negative way,' the lyrics of 'Friend in You' state. 'Stereotyping' satirises the endless stereotypes that afflict women in two and half minutes of feminist jazz-pop joy. 'She's a lousy drama, a frigid frump, she's a bitch, a butch, a useless lump, she wants a prick,' Barbara Stretch sings decisively. Julia Dawkins's elegant saxophone and flute playing perfectly complement the musical unit of Alison Rayner (bass), Terry Hunt (guitar) and Jackie Crew (drums) throughout the EP.

Ova offered another take on feminist music, an eclectic mixture of pop, rock and folk. The duo was committed to a non-hierarchical approach to music-making, as many Women's Liberation groups were. As Jana explained in 1983:

'Our music is radical because we don't have a standard
line-up. We don't have a lead singer for example; both of
us are lead singers.'[44]

Ova used a range of instruments in their recordings and live
performances. This included state of the art drum machines and
synthesizers played alongside acoustic and electric instruments.
These helped articulate an uncompromising and fierce anti-
capitalist, eco-leaning lesbian feminism. The unforgettable
'Self-Defence', for example, is a tale of a universal woman who
fights back after sustaining years of male violence. The refrain
of 'One day I'm gonna kill a man in self-defence,' sung on top
of a drum duet between Jana and Rosemary on the African
djembe and South African Log drum respectively, aimed to
encourage women to separate from abusive partners. The
statement: 'every time you rape a woman, you rape me, you
hurt me' is an undeniable declaration of female solidarity.

Songs like 'Nuclear Madness', inspired by reading Mary Daly's
1978 eco-feminist tract *Gyn/Ecology*, articulates the burgeoning
feminist politics of the early 1980s that saw the destruction
of (Mother) Earth and women as intimately connected. The
urgent anti-nuclear demand, sung by Jana, for an end to nuclear
weapons 'Today not tomorrow! Today…' is contrasted with
a chaotic synthesiser solo in the song's finale that conjures
the illogical toxicity of the Cold War. Many of Ova's songs
celebrate lesbian relationships and desire, a brave political act
in itself within the sexist and homophobic climate of the late
70s and early 80s. Songs such as 'Far Beyond the Dawn' are a
brazen declaration of lesbian sexuality. 'I want her to stay the
night / I want her to be my delight' is the song's rousing chorus,
delivered with Rosemary's emphatic, bodily huskiness.

The Fabulous Dirt Sisters' sound, described affectionately
by Kaffe Matthews as 'home-made',[45] is one example of
musically realising the Women's Liberation aim to 'do things
differently.' Songs were ambitious structurally, adopting the

political commitment of feminists to re-order society in ways that did not replicate hierarchy or male tradition. The time signatures of songs undermine the standard marching rhythm of much Western music.

The feminist peace movement also had a massive influence on the aesthetics of The Fabulous Dirt Sisters. Their music avoided aggression and confrontation to make its political point. Karunavaca recalls, 'we wanted to be subversive but not in a violent way. Instead, we wanted to do it by clowning about.'[46] All feminist bands adopted strategies for their audiences to hear what they were saying, and the Dirt Sisters were no different. Their music was often slow-paced, which allows listeners to connect with the language and storytelling of the songs.

Much of the music on their first album *Flapping Out* invokes being at Greenham Common. Greenham Common was the site of the iconic women's peace camp that protested the presence of nuclear weapons that were housed there. It began in 1981 and officially ended in 2000. 'Wood Song', for example, celebrates the act of making a fire at the camp.

> 'Just the time of day I like, the best
> Light fading
> Finding sticks to make the fire
> feeling for damp wood my back turns towards the wire.'

The song describes the architecture of the camp, of tents gathering for night watch under the searchlight of the authorities and the sound of 'generator humming.' It invokes the experience of Greenham for the listener, as the lyrics, delivered in Dorry's deep, emotional voice, are draped between a sparse accompaniment of violin, bass and saxophone. It is minimal, moving, intimate and evocative.

Other songs, such as 'Army Song,' joyfully articulate the pacifist feminist politics that were developed around Greenham. The song pokes fun at the authorities by highlighting the illogical nature of the military venture:

> 'The army is always on the move, convoys always going
> Where? Why? We don't know!
> Ask the boys in the uniform
> What do they know
> Don't worry, someone must know!'.

The song acts as a non-violent 'rescue operation' whose aim is to dismantle the 'male cosmology of separation and fear.' The power of the imagination is invoked by asking 'How many ways can you find to say no?'

'Tree Planting' is another song that resonates with the eco-feminist politics of Greenham. This time the commitment to planting trees is a spiritual act, 'an act of faith' for a better future. The song meditates on the dependency of humans on trees: 'sometimes you need to breathe in times like these.' The song contrasts the nurturing of acts of women, 'under the moon, under the sun, the work that women have always done,' with the destructive acts of men, 'under the sun, under a gun, oh what a world these men have won.' Instead it is the 'love of the women' that can help ease the threats of patriarchal-militarism to life itself.

Women's Liberation Music – an open and complicated legacy

From this brief foray into the history of music-making in the UK WLM, it is clear that women did many things to make music 'feminist.' No blueprint was developed for feminist musical style, and bands interpreted the challenge of creating non-sexist music in different ways. Sometimes they passionately disagreed, creating spaces of heated conflict and discussion. Often political idealism was undermined by the practical challenge of financial survival. This in turn has affected the way we can encounter the Women's Liberation's musical past today: through 'unfinished' recordings and incomplete back catalogues. Yet it is important to remember the dynamic and questioning quality of these musical histories. The challenge to know what feminist music 'is' remains open.

Feminist musicians of the 1970s and 1980s battled long and hard for their grassroots non-violent cultural revolution. They played a major part in developing the field of 'women's music', providing practical and creative inspiration for women that came after. As women not afraid to plug in electrical instruments, sit behind drum kits or work the PA, they were pioneers and challenged head-on cultural stereotypes about women's place within music.

The bravery of such acts cannot be forgotten. Many of these women faced physical violence from men who were genuinely threatened by women playing music. Music can after all be a 'useful and dangerous'[47] force for change. Against many odds they have left activist musical legacy of invention, revolutionary interventions, manifestos, meeting notes and incomplete back catalogues. Such a legacy demands that the history of music achievement be reconsidered to include the unfinished work, the song-sheet and the skill-sharing workshop. It invites us to work harder at listening to the past so it can be connected to a more varied musical present where women are not always stereotyped or invisible.

Contributor biography

Deborah Withers is a researcher, writer and curator who lives in Bristol. She is the author of *Adventures in Kate Bush and Theory* and several academic articles. She is the curator of two exhibitions about feminist cultural history, Sistershow Revisited in 2011, and Music & Liberation, 2012. She is a co-curator of the online

Women Make Noise

Women's Liberation Music Archive. For more information about her projects please visit: www.debi-rah.net

Deborah would like to thank: 'All members of Jam Today, Ova and The Fabulous Dirt Sisters for their feedback on this article, and for the music they made. Particular thanks to Frankie Green for her attention to detail and for the hard work she has done on the Women's Liberation Music Archive. This article is dedicated to her.'

The Carter Family women in full swing

The fabulous Ronettes on stage in the 60s

The Shangri Las: 60s publicity shot

US 60s garage band Goldie and the Gingerbreads

70s rock with Fanny and their guitars

Mother Superior hanging out in the 70s

Suzi Quatro plays the bass guitar

Kate Bush – icon of female creativity –
making music since the 70s

Fran Rayner looked after live sound in the 70s and 80s

All-girl drumming workshop of that era

Ova playing live in Covent Garden in the 80s

The Slits in 1988

The Raincoats breaking boundaries in the 80s

Post-punkers Ut guitars and vox

Hysterics live and kicking in the 90s

Adrienne Droogas of Spitboy performs in the 90s

90s hardcore heroines: Brasphmears live and group shot

Guitarist Bibi McGill from Beyoncé's
all-female backing band The Suga Mamas

PJ Harvey continues the protest song tradition
performing her 2011 album *Let England Shake*

Girl bands of the 21st century: Secret Trial Five

Wetdog in the studio 2011

Beth Ditto from The Gossip: often cited as
part of the dream Ladyfest line-up

The Dum Dum Girls on stage 2010

Warpaint at Primavera Sound festival 2011

The Vivian Girls on a US tour in 2010

Trash Kit at London club Upset the Rhythm

Sissy Boyz getting into the spirit of Ladyfest Manchester

Hello Cuca – regulars on the European Ladyfest circuit

Rock camp USA: Beth Ditto with The Gossip

Rock camp USA: girls play guitars

Pussy Riot in their trademark balaclavas

'We Are All Pussy Riot' protestor 2012

5. You Create, We Destroy: Punk Women

Jane Bradley

Introducing a loud noise

> 'Punk was the first sub-cultural story that *could* be told entirely through the creative lens of all the women musicians, journalists, photographers and managers, with no mention of men at all! The work place in which punk was enacted was male dominated, but a critical mass of liberated women began entering it and changing forever the gender structure of society.' *Caroline Coon*[1]

In March 2011, the so-called 'godmother of punk',[2] Dame Vivienne Westwood, released a series of T-shirts to be sold in aid of UK charity Comic Relief. It was all fairly simple: recognisable images were printed in black and white, with the quirky addition of the famous Comic Relief Red Nose, digitally placed upon the subjects' faces. It was interesting to note that amongst the imagery used by Westwood, which included images of Edmund and Queenie from the popular comedy television series *Blackadder*, and Hogarth's classic etching 'The Laughing Audience', was one T-shirt entitled simply 'Punk Girl'. On 'Punk Girl' an anonymous woman snarls at the camera. Her short hair is spiked and her eyes are circled heavily in kohl. The standard external signifiers of being 'punk' are all there: studs, chains and dark clothing, not to mention the dismissive, hostile attitude.

This was classic self-referential humour on Westwood's part (she is after all, rightly or wrongly, one of the women most closely associated with punk), I couldn't help but contemplate the significance of this in relation to a subculture that I consider myself to be part of. It was meant, I think, to be a light-hearted contradiction. 'An angry punk girl with a funny red nose? Imagine!' Only, all I could think of was how, still, thirty-five years after punk became a recognisable subculture, the 'punk woman' continues to be something of a social anomaly – a figure of fun that has become society's shorthand for everything ugly, unfeminine and unnatural, or considered by many as the epitome of the 'groupie slut'. It reminded me of those old London 'punk' picture postcards,[3] where fresh-faced youngsters were paid to spike their hair, don a bike chain necklace and growl for the camera, as a representation of the London punks. In other words, it seems nothing more than a worn cliché that bares little relevance to, and tells nothing of, the truth of what it means to identify yourself as punk and as a woman. That, to me, is grossly short-changing one of the most dramatic, liberating and culturally significant youth movements of all times, which still manages to resonate as loudly and as fiercely today as it did back in the mid-1970s.

More importantly, from the perspective of this book, the punk movement was arguably one of the most inclusive genres of music in terms of gender equality. The DIY ethos inspired women to get involved in the making of the music, rather than being decorative accessories, with guts and attitude often taking precedence over musicianship. I do not support the common misconceptions that a) punks couldn't play their own instruments or b) that women aren't proficient musicians. On the contrary. However, punk demanded that its followers created their own culture, rather than blindly copying that of others, and this is precisely what many women did.

How punk got me going

My contribution to this book comes from an almost life-long interest in punk and the ever-evolving subculture that sprung up around it. Through fronting bands The Magic Finger, The Radical Possibilities of Pleasure and Late Night Dog Fight and organising gigs in West Yorkshire under the 'Armley of Darkness' (as well as being an avid consumer of other people's music and zines) I have, over time, completely re-evaluated my view of what punk is and what it means to be a woman involved in punk. I have had my eyes opened time and time again to new interpretations and representations of the movement and have been captivated throughout. It is a culture that is now, horrific caricatures aside, almost completely hidden from mainstream view, but that nonetheless manages again and again to grip a fresh batch of pissed-off kids, who swear their lives have been changed forever because of it and with each one holding a varying interpretation of what it means to be, or be interested in, punk.

Understandably, punk is often described in volatile terms; its inception often referred to an 'explosion', because of its brief, unforgettable time in the mainstream (from 1976-78) which had a strong and enduring impact upon popular music, fashion and its fans and critics alike. Classic punk rock imagery has become firmly embedded into conventional fashion, as pink skull-and-crossbones hair bobbles and cute safety-pin earrings are repackaged as standard-issue accoutrements for your rebellion-by-numbers pre-teen. However, for many, the punk scene is also synonymous with genuine violence and rage. This is in part due to the extreme political slant of some aspects of the movement, but also because of the unpredictable nature of the performances of many punk artists and bands. Further to that, 'rebellion' is another keyword often used when discussing original era (old school) punk rock and certainly much thought has gone in from fans, academics and cultural commentators alike, about what precisely this rebellion was against, how it was manifested and who it impacted upon.

Much of the discussion implies that it was/is largely white, working class males at the heart of the action, with women chiefly side-lined into decorative supporting roles, providing amusement and disgust in equal measures[4]. However, many commentators and authors who will appear later in this chapter, including Helen Reddington, Zillah Minx, Caroline Coon, Cazz Blasé and Maria Raha, have made an overt attempt to redress the balance by shedding some much-needed light on the contributions that women (specifically those playing in all-girl bands) made in shaping the punk scene.

In this chapter, I will build on the contributions of the aforementioned, by focusing on the all-girl bands who contributed to the conception and development of punk in the 1970s, looking closely at the various experiences, challenges and opportunities that they encountered when making music and art. I will analyse how women and girls used aesthetics, sexuality, performance, lyrics and politics as tools of resistance and social commentary. Finally, I aim to discuss the effect that punk's brief period of mainstream popularity had on the genre and on its female participants, as well as explore the legacy that these women carved out for those women and girls who consider themselves part of the punk scene today.

How I, eventually, got punk...

Like a lot of teens, I spent far too long contemplating issues of identity, fashion and culture whilst trying to work out where the hell I was meant to fit in this crazy world. I had already isolated myself from my peer group somewhat, when I wore my first pair of Doctor Martens to Brownie Guides aged seven, so the hippy braids and accompanying feathers in Year Six had my stall well and truly laid out for all to see (…and point and stare). Perhaps it was not so surprising – certainly my parents couldn't even muster a raised eyebrow when I took down my beloved Take That posters, pierced my nose and bought a studded dog collar. After all, my brother and sister, at eleven and twelve years my senior, had previously provided sterling examples of teen rebellion via sartorial choices. My brother was on the receiving end of regular lectures about clouding up his miniscule box-room with hairspray, in order to cement his psychobilly-inspired quiff into position. And I have photographic evidence of my sister's fondness for black mesh tops and hair crimping, during her rather unfortunate goth phase.

Punk then, was something that I grew up assuming I understood. The Sex Pistols. The Clash. The Ramones. They were the classic and familiar punk bands. Punk was those men in the torn jeans who lay on the grass in our village square nursing cans of cider. Punk was spiky. Punk was loud. There was even the family anecdote about the time I had innocently mixed up 'clowns' with 'punks' and got really excited, thinking the guy with the pillar box red hair checking out the make-up in our local chemist was actually a jolly children's entertainer.

But I digress. Fast forward to 1996. Punk is suddenly taking on a different meaning to the fifteen-year-old me; actually surprised to find out such a thing still exists. I dress in the baggiest skater jeans I can find and spend my time listening to mix-tapes of Fat Wreck bands, drinking copious quantities of low-quality cider and black on the beach, or in my friend Phil's mam's garage. This is punk, right? We yell along to songs by angry men who seem to get dumped by their girlfriends at least once every verse. We go to gigs where north eastern accents take on a distinctly Californian twang and rowdy boys shove each other for fun. We certainly feel very little affinity with the leather-jacketed, mohawked crew who we occasionally see loitering at the bar, looking weather-beaten and more than a little disgusted at, we arrogantly presume, our American band T-shirts, our clean hair and our youth.

And then, in 1999, I began a degree in Media Studies and Print Journalism at the University of Huddersfield, where I was surprised to learn professionals actually spent time breaking down and analysing youth cultures and that, actually, there was a whole field of sociological research dedicated to the topic. In lectures, I discovered words like '*semiotics*', '*homology*' and '*cultural artefacts*', as we looked at case studies where white, working class males shaved their hair and ripped their clothes in order to challenge the dominant culture of the time.

Then, eventually, it clicked… *The women were almost invisible!* Sure, there were some girls at the gigs I attended. There were a couple of female-fronted bands wedged awkwardly onto the pop punk compilation CDs I played to death. There might even have been one or two punky looking women hanging around with the men in the square. But, for the most part, it was perfectly possible to be a consumer of punk music and a student of punk history, without having to give much thought to where the girls were when all this was actually going on. So what happened? Were women and girls really just decorative adornments used to brighten up dingy pub back rooms with their day-glo make-up and exposed flesh, whilst the boys got on with the real business of kick-starting a cultural revolution?

Punk and the lack of gender politics

Gender, it seems, was the unspoken factor that the majority seem to overlook when discussing the development of youth subcultures as tools of resistance. The women who were involved from the beginning can and should be regarded as true pioneers. In her paper 'The Sound of Women Musicians in the

Punk Era', delivered during a one-day conference on 'Music, Politics and Agency' at the University of East London, Dr Helen Reddington (AKA Helen McCookerybook, bassist and singer in Brighton-based punk band the Chefs) talked about the so-called 'silences' that ensure women's contributions to punk have been largely 'lost' from official male histories of the period.[5] She pointed out that whilst the shock tactics employed by many male musicians were widely celebrated (and yes, in certain circles, vilified) as radical, punk women's contributions were trivialised, viewed as nothing more than a side dish, existing merely to compliment the main course.

Whether you regard punk as something totally devoid of any kind of theoretical underpinning, simply as an outward demonstration of a state of deviancy or, alternatively, as a movement with a clear moral code, there is no doubt that gender politics are still surprisingly way down the chain of interest for the average consumer. Though my formative experiences of punk placed men right at the beating heart of the scene, with the occasional brassy bird loitering moodily in the background playing the part of girlfriend/slut with aplomb, it didn't take me long to find out that this was not the whole picture and women were definitely not the passive outsiders riding on the coattails of their boyfriends. Far from it…

In the beginning

It can be difficult to truly comprehend, particularly for those born in the 1980s and beyond, the changes that have had to occur in popular music to get to where we are now, where women may be regarded as the stronger, more bankable performers – at least in mainstream pop. However, in the 1970s, with rock music at its sexualised and utterly masculinised peak, women were confined to the role of the adoring screaming fan, worshipping their heroes from afar.

Certainly, to get close to the action, it was in the role of the groupie that was deemed most appropriate. As rock journalist and author Maria Raha puts it in *Cinderella's Big Score (2004)*, her celebration of women of the underground and indie music scene: 'Cock rock made it clear to most women that being *near* the rock star was as good as it gets.'[6]

The liberal free-love message of the 1960s had promised a new dawn of independence for women. Freer than ever before, many women became disenchanted when, ultimately, they continued to fall into the patterns of their mothers and grandmothers – raising families and sacrificing their own needs and desires for those of their husbands and children. By the dawn of the 1970s, the music charts of the US and UK were heavy with saccharine sweet pop tunes, that provided sharp contrast with (and perhaps a distraction from) the turbulent political landscape of the time.[7] Over both sides of the Atlantic there were fierce ongoing struggles to promote (or suppress) racial equality, women's liberation and gay rights and with the backdrop of the Vietnam war raging in the background the time seemed right for a new youth movement to emerge – perhaps one a little less heavy on the peace and love...

Artist, journalist and activist Caroline Coon, who documented the punk scene in the 1970s, describes the feeling of the time in an interview for this book:

'In 1975, the British Labour movement, who many young people expected to champion the underdog, was tearing itself apart and the left, who hated the hedonism of the hippie movement, was presenting itself as puritan, authoritarian and, as Scargillism proved, undemocratic. There was the Cold War freeze, IRA terrorism was escalating and unemployment had reached one million. The atmosphere on the streets was one of palpable stagnation mixed with suppressed fury at the sheer awfulness of life. Furthermore, 1960s white rock music heroes had become inaccessible millionaires, while rock music played in rundown pubs was hackneyed and "old". The best music and fun was to be had in underground black shebeens, or gay discos. What was white heterosexual youth, a generation younger than me, going to say and do about all this? I began purposefully looking out for their reaction. I began asking questions: how was the new generation, who thought that hippie Peace and Love had failed, going to pick up the baton of rebellion and change? How was the new generation going to confront Establishment power? Were the new teenagers on the block going to be as angry as I predicted?'

By 1975, the Sex Discrimination Act was passed in England, Wales and Scotland, to protect women from discrimination on the grounds of gender.[8] However, for many this legislation was simply a symptom of wider social change, which saw women actively reinvent their roles in the work place, the home and wider society. Inevitably, this was reflected in the youth culture of the time where young women (inspired by a potent combination of sheer boredom, liberalism and creativity) took advantage of the greater formal freedoms offered and actively fought social and cultural boundaries and restrictions.

In her 2010 documentary film *She's a Punk Rocker*, Zillah Minx, singer with UK punk band Rubella Ballet, explored what attracted women to the scene. Minx interviewed a diverse group of women punks that included vocalists, musicians, artists and journalists. It becomes clear that what is understood to be 'punk' was realised within an uncoordinated, spontaneous moment in which men and women, with a shared sense of isolation and rebellious desire, came together without a prescribed agenda or particular aesthetic style. Despite the many texts and cultural commentators which proclaim otherwise, few punks, least of all punk women, would recognise themselves in the standard descriptions laid out by the academics, journalists and historians.[9] The women in Minx's film talk openly about actively creating their own scene, with a sense of proud ownership. They were not blind followers, but rather instigators, as Minx remarks:

> 'Punk was the first youth movement where women were equals. Prior to punk, women were seen as the girlfriends of skins, mods, hippies and teddy boys, but a female punk was a punk.'[10]

Equality at the word 'go'?

Many of the women involved in the early scene agree that punk was something of an egalitarian movement. Penelope Houston, singer of one of the first San Francisco punk bands, The Avengers, echoes this notion, as she explains how gender seemed almost irrelevant:

> 'The scene was so small that just being a punk was enough … the idea that there were boy punks and girl punks or male punks and female punks or something was not really something anybody thought about.'[11]

Rock photographer, Erica Echenberg, who has photographed X-Ray Spex and The Slits, amongst others, agrees. She describes how, prior to punk, women were marginalised by the masculinity of popular rock culture:

> 'As girls, we were being accepted for the first time. All the huge dinosaur bands like The Who, Queen and so on, wouldn't give you a look in. They just saw us as sex objects. Now you could get involved, front a band or take photographs. It was up to you.'[12]

Why being pretty didn't matter

The lack of idealism attached to punk (as opposed to, say, the hippy culture that bewitched many of the preceding generation) was attractive to many women because they were free to define their own agenda, or even dispose of an agenda altogether. Deliberately making themselves 'ugly' with extreme make-up and anti-fashion clothing become a norm for female punks, as they rejected the social conventions that dictated what young women should wear, how they should act and what they should aspire to be. In her series of articles on 1970s punk, for online magazine *The F-Word*, zine-writer and author Cazz Blasé describes how the mainstream media of the time was utterly focused on guiding women firmly towards their traditional role in society:

'Quick study of mainstream women's magazine *Honey* and teenage girls' magazine *Jackie* suggests a strange world in which women were seen to exist purely to be married off at the earliest opportunity. One particularly nauseating 1972 ad in *Honey* read: "When the time comes to tell the world you love him, take the third finger of your left hand to H. Samuel and they'll show you how to say it beautifully."'[13]

So the reaction, of course, when women and girls began to openly reject this path was one of intrigue, horror and shock.[14] *What's this? Girls who don't want to be just 'the guitarist's girlfriend'?! Girls who perhaps don't necessarily aspire to be the picture-perfect Jackie magazine cover model version of femininity?!* This unconventional presentation of what it meant to be feminine had a two-fold effect. Firstly, it ensured that punk women were simply impossible to ignore, be it from the words they were saying (or screaming), the sounds they were making together, to the clothes they were wearing (or not wearing). And secondly, acting as a beacon, a mouthpiece if you will, announcing to the world with a mighty yell that, actually, there is another way: *Little girls no longer have to be seen and not heard…*

Aesthetics and sexuality

Whilst it is easy to dismiss punk followers as young kids simply latching on to another uniform (albeit a rather unconventional one), by dressing in a way that upset and angered the establishment, women punks specifically were refusing to be defined by the traditional boundaries that helped to shape them via their gender.[15]

Social conventions of the time insisted that *ladies* should dress modestly and that their demure appearance should reflect their sedate nature, as well as being pleasing to the eye (the ultimate aim in this fantasy being, of course, to ensnare a suitable husband). With punk anti-fashion adhering to its own internally created codes and conventions, women explored their own tastes, often stretching the limits of public decency with exposed flesh, extreme make-up, bondage gear, ripped clothing and customised accessories. 'Fashion was political,'[16] Zillah Minx recalls, describing how even before the term 'punk' was bestowed upon the innovators of the movement, clothing was used to not only as a public sign of allegiance to the fledging scene, but as an anti-consumerist statement. The hive of creativity that stemmed from the desire to wear something no one else had worn was liberating for the people involved, terminating the reliance between creator, seller and consumer, as people crafted and customised their own clothes and accessories. Minx describes how the atmosphere of the time was one of burgeoning creativity and co-operation, as youngsters ignored the traditional institutions of authority: 'We were like: "We're just going out and doing it… We don't care what you think!"'

However, the function and significance of the aesthetics behind punk is something that commentators and participants alike cannot agree on. Whilst the stereotypical British punk look might be limited to spikes, chains, leather and mohawks, many believe that the anti-fashion element of the culture served a

You Create, We Destroy: Punk Women

very significant purpose, in particular for women. By rejecting the niceties of commercial fashion, as dictated through shop windows and the media, male and female punks alike were making a visible public statement of their rejection of society and its expectations. Soo Catwoman (Lucas) was a well-known figure in the scene, credited with partially creating the punk look. Her spiked hair and extreme make-up has become an iconic punk image and such was her reputation that her 'character' was portrayed in the Julian Temple mockumentary *The Great Rock n Roll Swindle*. She describes the significance of her strong look:

> 'The catwoman look wasn't a fashion statement: it came from inside. When I was young I'd always been this little girl in a frilly dress, but I never felt like a little girl, so it was kind of, "Don't tell me I've got to wear a flowery dress: I don't want to be pigeonholed."[17]

Whether desired or not, punk women inevitably attracted a lot of attention. Pamela Rooke was a shop assistant, model and performer who became best known under her stage name, Jordan. Despite not being a musician, she is another iconic female who has since become synonymous with the very concept of the female punk. Jordan both innovated and embraced the aesthetics of the movement, describing how she viewed herself as 'a work of art'. Well known for outlandish outfits and behaviour to match, Jordan in many ways set a precedent for others. However, she admits that her outward appearance could be as isolating as it was liberating:

> 'I was always looked on as a bit weird. When I was fifteen I had my hair dyed red and pink, which caused a lot of problems at school. But I wasn't someone who looked in magazines for ideas, it was just me... When I went up to London the first time to visit Vivienne's shop I was wearing gold stilettos, a see-through net skirt and

I had my hair in a big white bouffant. When you look like that you're very lucky if can find somewhere where you fit in and feel comfortable. I ended up working in Sex [Malcolm McLaren and Vivienne Westwood's iconic clothing boutique] for years. It was my time.'[18]

All-girl punk music: style and substance

The subversive styling of punk, meant that the usual rules were not only disregarded, but actively distorted, including those that dictated the definition and presentation of gender and sexuality. Author and academic, Lauraine Leblanc, talks in *Pretty In Punk (1999)* of how for the first time in rock's history, even without taking into consideration the contribution of women to the genre, punk music took the lyrical focus away from the tedious, clichéd subjects of girlfriends and sex, despite remaining a male-dominated scene, 'allowing punk music to avoid gender stereotyping in large measure'.[19] Women in bands, therefore, deliberately placed themselves in a position of influence and by choosing to opt out of many of the usual conventions regarding beauty, womanliness and artistic merit, they quickly became figureheads for the burgeoning scene.

X-Ray Spex and Poly Styrene

One woman drawn in by the first adrenaline rush of the early punk scene was Marianne Joan Elliott-Said, who became better known as Poly Styrene, vocalist for X-Ray Spex. Born in 1957, to a young legal secretary from Hastings and a Somali stow-away, Styrene became one of the most recognisable and admired women in punk. Intelligent, articulate and '[not] particularly good with authority', she was a hard worker, 'fiercely independent' and absolutely determined to make a career out of music.[20]

You Create, We Destroy: Punk Women

The developing punk scene was appealing to Styrene because it enabled her to achieve the adventure, fame and financial independence of her dreams, without compromising on her radical outlook. By striving to create a platform for her work, she became one of the most celebrated and successful women of the era, whilst refusing to be anything other than herself, or being self-restrictive simply because of her gender. Placing an advert in *Melody Maker* and the *NME*, looking for 'Young punx who want to stick it together', Styrene recruited a trio of enthusiastic musicians who could provide the perfect backing for her screaming: Jak Airport, Lora Logic and Paul Dean.

Critically, X-Ray Spex were well received and widely considered one of the best, most competent punk bands of the era. Saxophone player, Logic (born Susan Whitby) had grown bored of piano, violin and guitar lessons before, at thirteen, finding the instrument that would go on to make such a huge contribution to the band's distinctively punchy, pop-tinged sound. Taking an instrument previously best known for its smoothness, Logic used it to simultaneously counter and complement Styrene's abrasive vocals.

> 'Rather than shaping her instrument's tone into lite jazz's smooth lines, she squealed and skronked with it, breaking melodies apart with destructive glee… you can't get more punk than turning unexpected instrumentation into something seemingly unmusical, then turning *that* into music.'[21]

As well as gelling musically, the pair found themselves drawn to each other in a broader sense – perhaps finding certain camaraderie through their various adventures as young girls making it big in a male-dominated scene.

> 'We just seemed to click, like we'd known each other before. I thought [Poly] was wonderful, bubbly, creative,

and completely alternative. We were both wearing the
same sort of granny clothes, too.'[22]

For many, punk became synonymous with the levelling of
the playing field that was rock 'n' roll, as strong women took
to the stage with radical lyrics, non-conformist attire and their
own interpretation of beauty.

Styrene herself openly rejected the notion that conventional
beauty should be desirable, or a particular help, or hindrance
to success. As a biracial teenager with dental braces and an
arresting, unconventional prettiness, it's easy to see why she
could garner so much attention simply from *being*, let alone
climbing on stage to front a punk rock band. Her oft-quoted
comment about rejecting the 'sex-symbol' status that usually
goes hand-in-hand with being female and fronting a band ('I
would shave me 'ead tomorrow if I became a sex symbol'[23])
cleverly summarises these women's bold outlook.

Fashion: losing the point

To some, however, the dress-to-shock mantra that became
synonymous with the punk movement meant that any political
message was undermined, especially when scavenged by major
fashion labels and repackaged for sale in the sanitised haven
of the high street. It became a safer version of punk, with a
hefty price tag. Additionally, the blatant sexualisation of some
women who adopted what eventually became punk fashion,
caused concern for many and not just the establishment's moral
commentators. Arguably, as soon as punk had a recognisable
'look' attached to it, it failed to be punk – thereby pushing
others into more and more extreme forms of self-expression.

Many embraced the joyfulness of creativity, relishing in
the freedom to distort the standards of acceptable beauty
that had enslaved so many women. Shaving heads and caking
on make-up was a way of openly refusing to conform to the

rigid standards that instructed women on precisely what was beautiful, acceptable and normal, as well as being a fun way of irritating straight-laced parents.

Caroline Coon believes that the dress adopted by many punk women was certainly a genuine tool of resistance, as she says:

> 'Following fashion and creating your own style can be both political and a pleasure. Youth is a time for the spectacle of style and part of the thrill and fun of it is to provoke adult denunciation of youth fashion as "unsuitable"'.[24]

Performance and reception

Compared with the roar of modern hardcore punk bands, the sound of '77 era punk might sound somewhat kittenish, but at the time it was so utterly beyond anything that had come before that it might as well have been called 'A Soundtrack to the Apocalypse'. In the same way Elvis, two decades earlier, had people fainting in front of their televisions at the sight of his overworked pelvis, the snarling hellballs who spat and sneered and screeched their way into the public consciousness appeared to many to be little more than untamed, untrained kids battering away at instruments whilst yelling obscenities. So where could girls and women fit into this testosterone-charged chaos? The simple answer is: they didn't 'fit' into anything, they just got on with what they wanted to do. For the first time in popular culture men and women, to a certain extent, as fellow punks, co-created a scene cooperatively.

Of course, with the rose-tinted glasses of retrospect wedged firmly on our noses, it would be easy to fall in love with a storybook version of punk, entirely free of prejudice, but that would undermine the struggle that many women experienced when joining bands. Perhaps exacerbated by the stereotype that punk was an entirely amateurish art, it is clear that for women and girls there was the dual challenge of acceptance.

Even the most successful girl bands of the era were dogged by the cries, particularly by male journalists, that they were musically inept or simply a gimmick. Individual women, such as Gaye Black ('Gaye Advert') of The Adverts and Blondie's Debbie Harry, were often singled out for discussion almost exclusively in terms of their appearance, with the assumption that they were only in the band because of their sex appeal. Both women have openly criticised the media's response to them as performers, with Black remarking that:

> 'The media would concentrate on irrelevant things like clothes or be extra critical of my playing, in the same way that some men are prejudiced against women drivers.'[25]

With both the mainstream and alternative press, women and girls were judged mercilessly and, as with many women, the harshest judgements focused on appearance. Nigel Wingrove, founder of *Stains* fanzine typifies the attitude of some:

> 'There were very few sexy women in punk. For me, Blondie, Siouxsie and Gaye Advert were the only ones that were OK.'[26]

As with any minority within a scene, it is easy for critical eyes to over-scrutinise those who stand out, holding them up as being representative of the whole of that group whilst merrily ignoring any contradictory evidence. Whilst many women may have been put off by such hostilities, others found it inadvertently inspired them to aim higher. Shanne Bradley, founder of The Nipple Erectors, describes her experiences:

> 'There weren't that many female musicians around. It was tough. I felt I had to be able to play harder and faster than a bloke to be accepted, taken seriously. It ain't funny when ya have a couple of skinheads gobbing [at you]

for target practice in an empty hall in Farnham…and the long-haired sound man smirking. One bloke even cut off the guitar strings to stop me from playing. That was when I was first learning.'[27]

The women who picked up instruments were by and large not content to be novelty acts simply giving a tokenistic nod to the righteous women's libbers, but were competent musicians in their own right. Helen McCookerybook says:

'There is a myth that women musicians never learned to play: all of us did, and some like Gaye Black [The Adverts], Gina Birch [The Raincoats] and Viv Albertine [The Slits] became brilliant. Out of my original punk band, I was the only female and I'm the only one still playing thirty years later.'[28]

Diversity and style

Lyrically, as well as stylistically, the music produced by the women of the era demonstrated not only their creativity and talent, but their diversity. It is impossible to pin down a specific 'girl punk band' sound, because the genre itself seems to refer more to a mindset than anything else. Of the first wave of all-girl punk bands it is probably The Slits that remain the most well-known (although the line-up shifts meant the band was not always exclusively female). By the time they recorded their first album *Cut* in 1979, The Slits' wide-ranging sound referenced reggae and dub and the band later embraced increasingly experimental, avant-garde stylings, illustrating perfectly the array of sounds used by bands categorised simply as 'punk'. Forming in 1976 and playing their first gig in 1977 as support for the Clash, The Slits were fronted by the fourteen-year-old Ariane Forster (Ari Up), with Tessa Pollitt of the Castrators and Flowers of Romance's Viv Albertine. Today, they are widely regarded as one of the most ground-breaking punk bands of the era, but as Ari recalled in an interview with Maria Raha in 2005, the reception The Slits received initially was less than welcoming:

> 'We were totally put in exile, we were totally sabotaged, we were totally hated, most of our reviews were of outrage, and just, "Ew! These girls look disgusting and they can't play music, they can't do anything!"'[29]

It is worth reiterating that until fairly recently, for the most part, male journalists have tended to exclude the contributions of all-girl bands. It is therefore perhaps only with retrospect that, as Caroline Coon says: '...feminist writers and scholars have begun to insert women back into the punk canon,'[30] which allows hugely important bands such as The Slits to gain the recognition that they deserve.

Using their art as a weapon, rather than simply presenting themselves as entertainment, women in the first wave of punk were (knowingly or not) challenging the very essence of what it meant to be a girl and woman, through their lyrics, lifestyle, aesthetics and performance. Many lost friends and family, as Simone Stenfors (previously mentioned dancer, model and punk) describes:

> 'I'm the black sheep of the family. My mother now says she really admires me, but my sister disowned me years ago. My dad was very Victorian: he always wanted me to be a certain way and I always wanted to be different.'[31]

In a society which demanded women be demure, sexless and utterly passive, every step away from that was a progressive step towards liberation. Certainly, every aspect of the punk performance, including vocal style, sartorial choices and lyrics, jarred with the era's social definition of a 'lady'. The vocal delivery of performers such as Ari Up and Poly Styrene, with their high pitched screams implying a person teetering precariously on the edge with the distinct possibility of completely losing control, to the deep growls that traditionally present as a masculine trait, were not only impossible to ignore, but were overtly confrontational.

Music journalist, Nitsuh Abebe described how Styrene's vocal delivery demanded attention.

> 'She'd been trained for opera, but with X-Ray Spex she used those pipes to thrill and needle you, singing in a flat, keening yelp. It's bold and commanding, and many female vocalists have come back to it when they're looking for a way of singing that's fierce, but fiercely feminine – that sounds like it's bursting free from expectations.'

Being a girl punk vocalist meant there was no room for coyly delivered whispers, or harmonic vocal acrobatics. This was hard sounding music, to suit the often hard to hear messages that the performers wanted to deliver.

Lyrics: upfront and in your face

Playing around with the aesthetics of the movement was not the only way to show resistance. Women and girls, empowered by the radical nature of the genre, used their lyrics to explore themes that had previously been glossed over, or ignored altogether. Lyrically, all-girl punk bands straddled an enormous range of topics and the provocative nature of the words crafted by the performers was hard to ignore. Poly Styrene explains:

> 'I was writing protest songs in the playground. Our dinner lady used to make me eat meat and I didn't want to so I wrote a song about it.'[32]

Whilst some performers wrote personal lyrics (such as The Slits' *Ping Pong Affair*), others were plainly political in nature (*Offending Article,* Poison Girls' caustic critique of sexism and *Oh Bondage, Up Yours!*, Poly Styrene's smart, sarcastic take on consumerism), dealing with issues encompassing everything from animal rights to feminism, to the global effects of consumerism and war. Women and girls who used music as a way of expressing political viewpoints was not radically new, particularly after the hippy era but there was a certain raw power and volatility to their lyrics that had previously been absent.

Even when claiming to have no interest in a feminist philosophy, women in punk bands in particular presented a refreshingly alternative view of girl/womanhood than that which was broadly represented at the time – a view where women were stronger, more independent, bolder, brasher and just simply atypical. Crass, were a prime example.

Crass and Poison Girls

Formed in 1977, Crass were an English punk band that used lyrics and performance poetry to express explicitly political, specifically anarchistic, viewpoints. Although not an all-girl band, Crass became well known for promoting the messages of feminism through their lyrics. Gee Vaucher (visual artist), Eve Libertine (vocals) and Joy De Vivre (vocals) were the feminine components of Crass and it was their 1981 album *Penis Envy* that saw the group tackle head on many of the pertinent issues that affect women. Controversial, poetic, honest and direct, Crass' lyrics cover topics that many other bands would shy away from. Sexual violence, beauty standards, environmental concerns and gender roles were recurring themes, with tracks like 'Beta Motel', appearing to tell the tale of the brutal rape of a woman, disabled by her 'red high-heels', whilst 'Poison is a Pretty Little Pill' cleverly utilises overtly aggressive, war-like vocabulary in a description of the various beauty products and services available to the modern woman.[33] By broaching taboo subjects in such a direct, unapologetic manner punk bands were expressing the thoughts, feelings and experiences of many women, which had perhaps been lost in other music genres and youth subcultures.

There was a certain sense of proud rebellion expressed in the lyrics of the women punks. Brighton-based punks Poison Girls were fronted by Vi Subversa, whose writing displays a definite anarcho-feminist slant. In 'Real Woman' Subversa ironically defines the stereotypical facets of womanhood as she claims:

> 'I'm not a real woman
> I won't cook your food
> And I only want sex
> When I'm in the mood.'[34]

The nursery rhyme-like refrain is deceptively challenging, as she demonstrates a self-possession and decisiveness notably absent in the average female recording artist of the time. At forty-four years old, Subversa was already a mother of two when Poison Girls began and through her involvement in the scene she defied numerous stereotypes about the notions of age, femininity, motherhood and even the punk genre itself. Overall, perhaps weary of the apparent failure of the hippy movement, this was a more demanding form of protest from a group of women who saw their involvement as a tool for encouraging (or demanding) social change, rather than simply delivering a bleak commentary.

Certainly, sexuality was something that was played with, manipulated and distorted by punk bands, for fun as well as for political means. Some performers, notably Siouxsie Sioux (Siouxsie and the Banshees) and the Plasmatics' Wendy O Williams, used their body as their art, utterly annihilating what was previously deemed suitable for their gender. Both women traded in a hyper-sexualised version of themselves, but rather than using it to deliberately attract, it was a means to repel, with their provocative dress becoming a powerful statement against sexual repression, rather than an invitation for fawning admirers (although this was an inevitable by-product).[35] Predictably, there was a certain backlash against women who chose to flaunt their sexuality, with some arguing it was irresponsible, a bad example to girls who wanted to start bands, a publicity stunt, or simply fashion going too far

Regardless of political intent, or lack of, visibly identifying as a punk came with its own risks. The dressing up and posturing might have been part of the act, but the offence caused (and the often violent consequences) were frighteningly real, as Helen McCookerybook says:

> 'Most of us feel like survivors … It seemed as though everyone was against us, so it didn't matter what we did. If something went wrong, no matter how violent or frightening, there was no question of any support or help from the police. It was a frightening time, to bear the brunt of so much public hatred … I got sexually assaulted and so did many other women I knew because of what I wore. I suppose it annoyed our parents, but in terms of proper resistance, it was useless.'[36]

It could be suggested that the disgust and violence shown to these individuals was a perpetrator's way of expressing their fear of boundary-free, independent, strong-minded women. Assaults and violence (including sexual violence) were commonplace, as society struggled to accept the sartorial choices made by many punk women. London-based dancer, model and punk, Simone Stenfors, was victimised because of her punk identity during the early 1970s:

> 'In the beginning the punk look was whatever you could find in the wardrobe. I remember being at Hampstead

tube station one night and I was wearing a little dog collar with fake diamonds, a T-shirt with all the zips in it and a 1950s' skirt with a drape jacket and very high-heeled spiked shoes with studs in. I'd just got off the tube and I heard this, "Oi slag," from behind me and this Teddy boy and this Teddy girl got off and the next thing I know they grabbed hold of me by my head and smashed it against the wall and ripped a great big thing out of this drape coat... It was quite dangerous, really, going out, you either got beaten up or had your picture taken.'[37]

For Wendy O Williams, who generally appeared on stage in a state of undress, using her body in her performance was more than simple attention seeking. She may have been objectified, but she was doing it on her own terms.

'You know this is something that really makes me sick. All my idols in rock 'n' roll have all been male. And me going out and being an overtly sexy female and doing what I feel and what every male performer has done for years, like straight eroticism ... Our record company, the only pictures they are interested in are with my tits ... I'm proud of my body, I work out ... but there's more much more to The Plasmatics than my body ... My body is just part of my whole attitude ... It's that censorship thing, that male thing that chauvinistic attitude. They have all these roles women are supposed to play. Women are supposed to be barefoot pregnant and in the kitchen. Women onstage are supposed to be almost asexual, a prude. It's bullshit and it really infuriates me. In the front of our shows there's always lots of girls ... Girls like having a female out there doing all this stuff ... it's about time they had someone to relate to who's not afraid to be a woman stepping out and doing my thing and not being inhibited.'[38]

In contrast, some bands including Rubella Ballet and X-Ray Spex rejected the notion of a punk uniform, preferring instead to experiment with bright day-glo colours and home-made outfits that injected an element of cheerful abandon into their performances – a sharp contrast to the black leather bondage gear get up that has become the stereotypical legacy of the female punk.

One of the greatest successes of early punk is that there were no limits, or strictly defined dress code. Women had choice and whether they presented themselves as sexualised, desexualised, or anti-sexualised, that choice was theirs to make.[39] However, no matter how forward-thinking the performers might have been, that didn't guarantee that the irony of their statements was always respected or understood, with many women being labelled as whores, sluts and perverts by people on the outside of the subculture.[40]

The Iconoclasts, an all-girl group from Liverpool described their reception:

> 'Round here girls are automatically classed as slags if they're punks. We get a lot of abuse, just because you wear a short skirt at some time or other ... you're going onstage and your audience are going to be mainly male and they're all going to be shouting things at you, taking advantage of the fact you're girls.'[41]

The sexualisation of the punk woman is something that still resonates in today's 'alternative' scene, with the boom of 'alt-models' and soft-core pornography, such as the male-owned Suicide Girls. Trading on the 'punk' image of the models, whilst claiming to 'give women control over how their sexuality is depicted',[42] Suicide Girls-style pornography is portrayed as either the next logical step for the acceptance and liberation of the punk woman, or cynical, irony-free exploitation of the legacy left behind by those original punk trailblazers.

Feminism and 'the girl punk'

Much has been made about whether women punk bands defined themselves as feminist, or if gender politics was a specific agenda for female punks as a whole. By the 1970s, there was a significant backlash against the feminist movement, despite several new laws that encouraged equality for men and women alike. Women punks were able to participate as 'more equal' partners invested in a subculture than at any previous time, but the implication that feminism required a structural revolution of sorts intimidated people. Feminism became an ugly word, with its supporters demonised.[43] Bands and performers including The Slits, Siouxsie Sioux and The Raincoats have all denied setting out with a feminist agenda, but few could argue that the overall message, whether intentional or not, was of female empowerment. As The Raincoats guitarist/vocalist Ana da Silva explains:

> 'When we started we didn't say, "Let's form a feminist band," but by merely starting a band and defying stereotypes, we became one. I'd rather have us considered on musical terms, as well, however.'[44]

Liberation and defiance: punk's legacy and the girl band

Punk, they tell me, is dead, or so say the T-shirts at least... In February 2008, Cazz Blasé and fellow writers Sara Shepherd and David Wilkinson conducted a street poll on behalf of *The F-Word*. They were motivated by the desire to explore the public perceptions of punk.

Though they interviewed only a small sample of people, the results are interesting. The poll suggested that the public perception of punk is still very much a male-focused one, with just two interviewees mentioning bands that contained a woman when questioned about punk in general. When asked specifically, a third of the sample could not name a single woman in punk, with 60% of respondents having never heard of The Slits. Blasé describes the experiences as suggesting 'that there's still a lot of work to be done when it comes to documenting, and highlighting the female punk experience'. But does this really matter? Surely punk has always been about shunning the mainstream and hiding in the dark corners waiting to be discovered by those who will truly learn to love it?

And what of the legacy that female punks have left behind? The early days of punk felt like a genuine revolution, like anyone was welcome to help shape this exciting movement, simply by being their own, unique, expressive and creative selves.[45] Modern punk may no longer bear any resemblance (in terms of aesthetics or sound) to the bands and individuals who developed the subculture, but what is clear is that the forward-thinking women and girls who picked up instruments, wrote lyrics, took photographs, crafted fanzines, used their bodies as art and 'performed the wonderful spectacle of punk on the streets'[46] were performing an utterly essential role and therefore shaping their own legacy in a completely new way. By using a vast range of skills, women punks created something utterly captivating and entirely necessary that has empowered (and continues to empower) generations of women over the last thirty-five years. Their screams, their aesthetics, their brattish posturing and irrepressible vigour translated into genuine progress for girlhood and womankind as they bravely refused and redefined the labels that society would thrust upon them.

The way punk continued to grow and be continually reinvented, enrapturing a new audience with the passing of each decade, demonstrates that the genre is as relevant and as powerful as ever. As the glare of publicity turned from punk in the early 1980s, the movement simply did what all underground movements do – go back underground. Some women (actress and SEX Boutique model, Jordan) deliberately moved away from their punk past, whilst others reinvented themselves as bone fide pop stars (Blondie's Debbie Harry).[47] Some, like Ari Up and Poly Styrene, continued making music until their untimely deaths, letting their sound naturally evolve beyond the constraints of traditional punk, whilst retaining that essential, undefinable punk spirit. Others, such as The Raincoats, are still very much alive and kicking to this day.[48]

Of course, the business of punk nostalgia and punk retrospectives have since given bursts of publicity to the most popular bands of the era, ensuring they may be gone, but not forgotten.[49] Advancements in technology mean those previously impossible-to-get-hold-of early demos, or 7 inch singles can now be easily found and shared, protecting the legacy of those early punk artists. Moreover, the public tributes made in the pages of broadsheet newspapers to both Ari Up and Poly Styrene following their deaths, are testament to how the press seems to have re-evaluated punk and its cultural significance, with the *Guardian* commenting on the latter:

> 'It did not take long for the punk rock movement of the 1970s to lose its creative impetus and lapse into tedious repetition, but Poly Styrene, who has died of cancer aged 53, remained one of the era's true original talents. She became a flamboyant feminist punk icon through her work with her band X-Ray Spex, and continued to carve a boldly idiosyncratic path in both her subsequent solo recordings and her lifestyle.'[50]

Similarly, Ari Up's significant contribution to punk and to the music scene was in 2011 hailed in the broadsheet's obituary:

> '…The Slits have been enormously influential, not least thanks to Ari's stage presence and fierce vocal style. She helped to reinvent the role of women in music.'[51]

Women Make Noise

From the ashes of the first wave of punk, came post-punk, hardcore, pop punk and riot grrrl, all of which had their moments in the spotlight and by referencing the key elements of the punk sound and performance, whilst embracing DIY punk ethics, it was possible to see the influence of those early punk women. Each sub-genre saw notable girls and women working together to produce powerful, captivating music, but nothing penetrated the consciousness of mainstream society as the original punk scene had. However, there have been and continue to be a steady stream of all-girl bands, too numerous to mention – though a few contemporary examples with a notable punk influence (including Bikini Kill, Red Aunts and Petty Bone, to mention just a few) have continued to push boundaries and challenge the expectations that society still puts on women today, through their lyrics, sounds and aesthetics.

Formed in China in 1998, all-girl band Hang on the Box use their band as a platform to address their dissatisfaction and anger on a range of topics, as the punk women of the 1970s did before them. Although their sound has evolved significantly over the years, referencing an array of genres including new wave and electronica, the band formed and identified as punk from the start. Their website biography tells of their inception and early live performances as a cheerfully shambolic affair:

> 'With their non-existent skills and only their punk attitude, they received a storm of booing, laughter, and violent words, but this is when they decided to become the best punk band only possible by girls.'[52]

Gender inequality and relationship issues are often subjects of Hang on the Box's songs, with titles including 'Asshole', 'I'm Not Your Baby' and 'No Sexy'. Singer/guitarist Wang Yue explained to the webzine www.womanrock.com why these topics were frequently referred to in her lyrics:

You Create, We Destroy: Punk Women

'There're many things I'm not satisfied with in life, also about the relationship between the female and male. Because I'm not pleased with it, then I take my lyrics to reflect that rage.'[53]

Hang on the Box might be a world away from the British street punk experiences of say, Ari Up, or Vi Subversa, but it remains clear that their shared experiences and opinions as women have led them towards creating music together as a cathartic platform. Other bands have faced censorship, and worse, in similar endeavours. For example, Secret Trial Five from Vancouver, fronted by 'Pakistani-Canadian drag king' Sena Hussain, use their songs as vehicles for political protest, with titles such as 'Hey Hey Guantanamo Bay' and 'Middle Eastern Zombies'. Russian punk collective Pussy Riot combine a fast, ferocious punk sound with vocals that swing from anguished screams to melodic harmonies. Consisting of between three and ten members (all women) and writing songs and conducting interviews as a collective, the group exudes a spirit that transcends narrow musical boundaries, presenting themselves 'as on the border between punk rock and contemporary art.'[54] Performing impromptu concerts/protests blurring the lines between activism and art in a way reminiscent of Crass, Pussy Riot have adopted the traditional anti-authority punk ethos, inspired by concepts of self-organisation and self-governance. They have been persecuted for their efforts, most notably in 2012 when the band were imprisoned following a protest against the Russian Orthodox Church's close ties with the state. They say:

'Our motivation is ethical; we see that entire strata of population find themselves under unjustified discriminatory pressure. For instance, conservativeness dictates a definite role for a woman, which is guaranteed by social mechanisms of encouragement and punishment.

This role doesn't allow her to fulfill herself in another, alternative way that doesn't correspond to the ideals of classic femininity.'[55]

Would such artists, who have since found the courage and conviction to come together, united by their passion and anger, to create music and form bands, have done so without the pioneering women who came before them?

Now what? Protecting a hard-won freedom

After being involved in what I would loosely term 'the punk scene' for almost fifteen years, I have to say that I have never known a genre of music able to generate such intense debate. People take punk very seriously and feel extremely protective over their scene, with a keen sense of involvement and, yes, to some extent, ownership. (See websites like Maximum Rock 'n' Roll, Bridge 9 and Punktastic for the continuing debate).

To me, at its best punk sees like-minded individuals working co-operatively to form a resistance against a world that tries to dictate who you should be, what you should do and how you should look. At its worst, there is nothing to separate it from any other teen culture out there, aside from the current on-trend jeans. For a scene that set out to be progressive, it can still be remarkably backwards in terms of gender inclusivity, with all-girl punk bands sidelined as novelty acts and I have witnessed first-hand, detailed discussions on internet message boards and in person about whether or not particular performers are 'fit enough' to front a band. I have known politically 'right-on' individuals who pride themselves on their punk attitude, to blanche at the idea of sharing a stage with an all-girl band.[56]

It is not clear whether this is a particular problem in the current punk scene, or simply a reflection of society as a whole. What we can establish is that despite still being told they are not wanted, still being told they are not 'doing it properly', still being made to feel that they 'don't look right', there are still hundreds of girls and women picking up instruments and microphones and creating punk music. Simply by refusing to shut up and go away they are openly resisting the oppressive powers that are unnerved by outspoken women and long may they continue to do so. We, as punk women, look to the past for inspiration and as a source of strength, rather than nostalgic indulgence, and in doing so take comfort in the fact that it is the hardest battles that bring about change.

But perhaps change is creeping up on us. Take the global literary phenomena that is the leading character in Stieg Larsson's ridiculously popular crime novels of his 'Millennium Series'. The so-called 'girl with the dragon tattoo' has earned him sales in their millions and she has all the classic punk traits. Not just the haircut, the piercings, the tatoos; I'm referring to the attitude, the independence, the absolute refusal to conform to a standard feminine package that she just doesn't fit. Perhaps the figure of a punk woman is becoming a recognisable, even acceptable, heroine after all.

I'll leave the final word to Caroline Coon, the woman who reportedly first labelled this genre 'punk rock':

'Because women's achievements have been excluded from historical records and genre canons it has always been difficult for successive generations to appreciate the contributions women have made to politics, science, economics and the arts. Luckily, male feminists have helped to counter the female sexists who collaborate with patriarchy to restrict women to the domestic sphere! Young women have to live in their own time impelling themselves into their future, therefore looking back to the past, appreciating the past, seems counter intuitive. But, the past is there when women need it. The past is there to give women the confidence that with hard work and commitment people can improve their conditions and opportunities. All freedoms women have today exist because of past struggles. A lot more needs to be done and we must be determined that the freedoms we now enjoy must never be taken away.'[57]

Contributor biography

Jane Bradley is a freelance writer and secondary school English teacher from the north east of England. In addition to writing for an educational blog, she runs a copywriting business and has her own blog 'Life After the Storm', dealing with domestic abuse, escape, survival and recovery. Jane initially became interested in punk through her older siblings, but describes discovering riot grrrl as 'life changing', triggering her enthusiasm for fanzines, feminism and female musicians. After moving to West Yorkshire to study print journalism and watch hardcore bands, Jane was inspired to start the Armley of Darkness DIY collective, putting on gigs around Leeds. She provided the vocals for the Magic Finger, Team Rocket, the Radical Possibilities of Pleasure and Late Night Dog Fight and played records at feminist disco, Pussy Whipped. She now lives with her family by the North Yorkshire seaside.

Jane would like to thank: 'Paul Wheatley; Sarah Wheatley; Julia Downes; Alistair Billam and Rob Chapman (at the University of Huddersfield); Caroline Coon; Zillah Minx; Helen McCookerybook and Arlo, Henry, Elsie and Luke Bradley.'

7. Post-Punk: Raw, Female Sound

Rhian E. Jones

The sound, the bands

Post-punk, roughly defined, refers to the wave of musical experimentation which took place in the wake of punk from the late 1970s to the mid 1980s. It was influenced musically by European electronics and the rhythms of reggae, funk, disco, jazz, dub and world music, and informed conceptually by the art-school background and grounding in political and cultural theory of many of its members. Radical in form and content, post-punk was distinguished by musical, vocal and lyrical experimentation and by a frequently self-conscious and self-critical approach to the idea of being in a band and making music. Over the past decade, the relative neglect of post-punk by music historians has been replaced by a rush of books and documentaries on the genre – Scott Crary's *Kill Your Idols* in 2004 and Simon Reynolds' *Rip It Up and Start Again* in 2005 were followed by books on the New York scene by Paula Court, Marc Masters, Thurston Moore and Byron Coley[1] – as well as a clutch of anthologies, album reissues, and a revival of post-punk sounds and techniques by bands like Franz Ferdinand, Interpol, Liars, Erase Errata and LCD Soundsystem. Significantly, much of this rediscovery and renewal has focused on the contribution of women and girls.

Women Make Noise

For example, ESG, a band of four sisters from South Bronx, were an important if somewhat incongruous part of the New York post-punk scene in the late 70s and early 80s. In subsequent years, samples of their exuberant, percussion-heavy sound were used so often that ESG are sometimes held to be the most heavily sampled group in history. Although this use was frequently unattributed and unpaid, its prevalence and the band's resurfacing in the early 90s led eventually to the release in 2000 of the compilation *A South Bronx Story* and some acknowledgement of the abiding influence of ESG's sound. A good year for post-punk revivalists, 2006 saw the reissuing of ESG's first full-length recording *Come Away With ESG*, as well as a new album from a reformed version of pioneering UK girl band The Slits; European performances by their New York contemporaries the Bush Tetras; and a retrospective monograph from Manchester artist, muse and post-punk musician Linder Sterling (alongside her part in the 2006 Tate Triennial). Celebrated post-punk band The Raincoats saw the reissue of their first and second albums and, in 2009, the screening at the British Film Institute of their self-produced documentary *Fairytales: A Work in Progress*. In 2010, cult New York band Ut reformed for a brief US tour. In 2011, the death of The Slits' singer Ari Up was marked by tributes to her band's impact on both punk and women in music, building on the thirty-year anniversary of their debut album *Cut* and Zoe Street Howe's biography of the group two years earlier.[2] As these retrospectives, revivals and personal histories demonstrate, an intrinsic part of post-punk's value and interest was the number of women it involved and the possibilities it presented for making music in an all-girl band.

Some of the all-girl bands and women discussed in this chapter are already justly celebrated, for example: The Slits, whose infusion of punk with reggae and dub, and whose confrontational presence onstage and off, provided inspiration to many subsequent women (see the previous chapter for more

Post-punk: Raw, Female Sound

on their involvement in the 70s punk scene); New York scene doyenne, musician, writer, artist and actress Lydia Lunch; and The Raincoats, based around the partnership of Gina Birch and Ana da Silva, whose gently revolutionary music pioneered an arresting and persuasive kind of female-centred rock. There are others whose influence has been profound, including ESG and their pioneering polyrhythms, and Ut, a London-based New York trio who fused rock, free jazz and the Velvet Underground. Other post-punk bands with all-girl line-ups or prominent female members are perhaps less well-known but no less notable, including the UK's Delta 5, The Au Pairs, The Mo-dettes and Linder Sterling's band Ludus; New York No Wave bands the Bush Tetras, Mars, the Bloods, DNA, Daily Life, and Y Pants; and the wave of European girl bands which included Switzerland's Kleenex/LiLiPUT and Chin Chin, Germany's Malaria!, and Holland's the Nixe. This chapter will look at how these musicians extended the gains of the punk revolution, becoming wellsprings of musical originality, subversion, and political and sexual self-expression, and how their ability to do so was facilitated by their opportunity to create and perform in all-girl environments or as part of all-girl outfits.

Although I was born well after post-punk began to blossom, some of my formative musical moments were those of the early 1990s, especially grunge and riot grrrl, and the referencing by figures like Kurt Cobain of post-punk bands like The Raincoats inspired me to find out more about them. Discovering these often forgotten or marginalised groups was fascinating, as was uncovering the motivating spirit of the post-punk era: the extension of punk's democratisation and demystification of music; the application of political and cultural theory to music-making and performance; the attempt to create self-sustaining communities and networks of alternative culture independent of an inhospitable mainstream; and of course the still-astonishing number and variety of women involved as artists, critics, fans and influential figures. In an era of worsening socio-political conditions and increasingly class-constricted access to arts and entertainment, the ideals and practices of post-punk seem increasingly relevant and vital. Researching and writing this chapter was a chance not only to further analyse these ideas, and to relate them to the history of the girl band, but also to pay tribute to many interesting and inspirational women, especially The Slits' bassist Tessa Pollitt and Ut's Nina Canal, Jacqui Ham and Sally McFall, whose interviews have made a valuable contribution to this chapter. (Unless otherwise noted, all quotes from these artists are from interviews for this book.)

Origins and outlook: the social, cultural and political context

Despite its subsequent influence on a wide variety of musical movements, the origins of post-punk and the US No Wave scene lie in a specific congruence of socio-political circumstances. Lydia Lunch defined No Wave as an angry reaction to 'political corruption, rampant poverty', Vietnam and 'the failure of the Summer of Love'.[3] The post-punk scene evolved during a period marked by recurrent social unrest, economic crisis, and the displacement of a post-1960s left-liberal political consensus, criticised as compromised and stagnant, by the divisive monetarist conservative ascendancy exemplified by the elections of Thatcher and Reagan.

In the UK, US and northern Europe, the resultant rise in mass unemployment, widening social divisions, industrial strife, nuclear escalation and return of neo-fascist street politics occasioned by these dislocations found expression in the feelings of instability, paranoia and dread which informed much of the period's culture. This was happening not only in music but also in visual art and film, including the experimental work of figures in the transgressive cinema movement like Vivienne Dick, whose short films were staged around the New York post-punk scene and revolved around female protagonists. Socio-political stagnation and crisis generated explicitly radical musical movements like the anti-fascist Rock Against Racism, alongside the work done by grassroots organisations to counter police racism and other sources of antagonism. The era also witnessed widespread industrial and social unrest, campaigns for nuclear disarmament, the rise of gay pride and the birth of hip-hop. When interviewed for this chapter, Ut remembered the post-punk period as one of international cultural change and the Slits' Tessa Pollitt recalled: 'revolutionary times… violent, uncompromising times'. The feminist film-maker and music writer Mary Harron's experience of New York at the time of No Wave was of a city in decay, 'infested and crumbling, but wonderful', in which the individual could feel as though they 'were about to disintegrate, go the way of the city'.[5] Much post-punk seemed similarly intertwined with contemporary social and political turbulence, anxiety and gloom – though the music was often anything but.

While the movements known as oi! and hardcore responded to worsening social and political conditions by drawing on punk's more directly confrontational and less cerebral aspects, many post-punk bands, finding their dissident politics out of step with an increasingly right-wing broader culture, attempted to construct an independent and experimentalist cultural alternative. Punk had developed alongside an infrastructure of independent labels, distributors, record stores, and locally organised and promoted gigs, with small magazines and fanzines functioning as an alternative media. These attempts at an alternative collaborative culture were facilitated by an abundance of collective living spaces; young people were able to live cheaply by squatting bomb-damaged and abandoned family homes in west London and the run-down deserted tenements and railroad apartments in New York's Lower East Side. Musician Thurston Moore defined late-70s Manhattan as 'a place that young artists could come to, knowing they could find a place to live and a job that wouldn't kill them.'[6] These areas duly began to house communities of artists and students, supplying living, rehearsal and performance space, in which lack of financial pressure allowed inhabitants to concentrate on creative projects. Affordable rent was frequently supplemented by other ways of living cheaply, whether sharing space and resources, blagging free entry to clubs and gigs, or shoplifting food and clothes.

Female freedom in the aftermath of punk

For women in particular, the impact of punk had gone some way towards altering their perceptions of possible opportunities open to them, offering an alternative to their expected roles as workers, wives and consumers. In London's Ladbroke Grove, these conditions yielded The Slits and The Raincoats. Slits' founder Paloma 'Palmolive' Romero had moved to London from Spain as a seventeen-year-old in 1972, leaving behind a restrictive political and domestic background. After a short-lived stint as drummer in The Flowers of Romance, alongside The Sex Pistols' Sid Vicious and future Slits' guitarist Viv Albertine, she was determined to form her own band, recruiting the fourteen-year-old Ari Up as vocalist after spotting her at a Patti Smith gig. Rehearsing in a succession of squats while they underwent several line-up changes, The Slits eventually settled into their early incarnation in which Ari and Palmolive were joined by the latter's former bandmate Viv Albertine on guitar and Tessa Pollitt on bass, both art students. After writing several of their early songs and appearing on their 1977 Peel Sessions, Palmolive and The Slits parted ways. She later joined fellow London girl group The Raincoats, who had themselves been galvanised into action by her former band.

The Raincoats' Gina Birch remembered seeing The Slits play while a student at Hornsey School of Art as 'extraordinary, and so... doable somehow... I didn't know if I could do it,

[but] suddenly the possibility was there'.[7] Inspired, Birch 'just ran into a guitar shop and, not knowing what I was doing, I just bought the cheapest bass they had' – an adventure she found 'gut-wrenchingly embarrassing... [it was] at the time, so humiliating to go into a shop and admit you didn't know what you were doing, being female.'

The space provided within punk for the untrained to make music enabled post-punk women to overcome a lack of precedent in forming bands and taking non-vocal roles. The majority lacked a trained musical background and learnt their instruments as they went along, unhindered by their consequent lack of technical expertise. The emotions involved in overcoming these social taboos, and the painstaking process and embarrassing nature of 'learning to play in public', both reflected and intensified the efforts of many female musicians to convey similar emotions through their lyrics and music.

The all-girl post-punk outfit: an organic creation

What the music writer Greil Marcus described as the 'disorderly naturalism' of female post-punk music[8] can be seen in the organic and spontaneous way in which all-girl bands were formed, a process rooted in encouragement of participation and performance coupled with demystification of how to do so. Bands like The Slits and The Raincoats were thrown together through their involvement in punk-generated cultural networks based around music, art and politics, in an atmosphere described by celebrated feminist film-maker Mary Harron as one of 'spontaneous amateurism'.[9] Musician and graphic artist Linder Sterling recalled of the scene in late-70s Manchester:

> 'Everybody around me was making music, it seemed like a very obvious thing to do, and it seemed so easy for everyone else, so I got musicians together and it's not that hard after all'.[10]

Women and girls' participation in post-punk was an acceleration of the opportunities which punk set in motion. The Raincoats' Gina Birch recalled that it was

> 'a great time to be a woman ... It was the most genderless time that one could imagine ... You could do what you wanted, so it didn't make any difference if you were male or female'.[12]

In particular, the punk-inspired increase in female instrumentalists, and the consequent potential for all-girl line-ups, marked a distinct change from previous female modes of musical expression. June Miles-Kingston, drummer for the multinational post-punk girl band The Mo-dettes, formed in 1979, noted the relative advantages of being in an all-girl band when facing hostility from both audiences and the rock press. She claimed that both they and The Slits:

> 'came across as ... sort of strong, you don't mess with us ... Whereas one woman in a predominantly male band probably looked as though they were out on a limb a bit.'[13]

Tessa Pollitt locates the blues period as the nearest equivalent in terms of opportunities for women, adding that the relative paucity of female musicians before punk:

> 'made it a great challenge for us to be accepted and respected ... [There were] so many limitations on female musicians that had to be broken'.

The Slits were instrumental in this, but female involvement was also encouraged by the generally experimental and inclusive nature of post-punk musicianship. Ut's Nina Canal claims that the No Wave scene 'was at once anarchic and inclusive: everyone was equal for the blink of an eye, so the field of possibilities just went wide open'.[14] According to Lydia Lunch, 'everyone was the most unlikely person to be in a band' during No Wave.[15] Musician Christine Hahn, who in 1977 New York formed the short-lived Daily Life with fellow post-punk musician and photographer Barbara Ess, was inspired both by Lunch and by the inclusion of women in No Wave bands Mars and DNA: 'I loved the idea of women having an equal voice and power in bands with men... it hadn't really been done up to then'.[16]

What made post-punk all-girl bands so good

The impact of The Slits on perceptions of the girl band is highlighted by their concern with defining themselves against their US peers The Runaways, who were perhaps the highest profile all-girl rock band of the time. Ari Up maintained that The Slits were 'the first girl band that weren't put together as a gimmick or by a man'.[17] Tessa Pollitt viewed The Runaways as 'a manufactured group who played like men', whereas The Slits' own music was 'very new, raw and female'. Similarly, Lydia Lunch's defiant and confrontational stage presence differed markedly from that of existing female performers like Blondie's Debbie Harry, and from what contemporary music writer Annene Kaye called 'the cloying, hackneyed mannerisms traditionally adopted by "chick musicians"'.[18] The untried and experimental nature of post-punk allowed women in particular to junk traditional techniques and received wisdom on women in rock.

Post-punk is often considered to be an unwritten history of the 1980s, its sound and aesthetic deviating sharply from the standard conception of the decade as dominated by glossy and manufactured synth-pop, with the implicit corollary that most post-punk bands did not achieve the same kind of fame and fortune as their mainstream counterparts. While to some extent the nature of post-punk itself mediated against chart success and major label attention, it was also simply not a primary concern of many within the movement. (Lydia Lunch, interviewed for the 2002 documentary *DIY or Die: How to Survive as an Independent Artist,* quipped: 'I would be humiliated if I found out that anything I did actually became a commercial success'.[19]) Although a handful of groups became sufficiently successful to tour internationally, the performance and delivery of much post-punk music was bound up with small and localised gigs, independent record shops and labels – ZE and 99 Records in New York, Rough Trade, Factory, Mute and 4AD in the UK – and self-published and distributed fanzines. Through such networks, and specific outlets like John Peel's radio programmes or the New York club scene, bands achieved prominence within their respective scenes but attained less in the way of commercial success.

The Slits were the last prominent group of the first wave of punk bands to secure a record contract with a major label. They signed to Island Records in 1979, a decision which followed multiple offers from labels keen on exploiting the novelty value of an all-girl band.[20] Such strategies were resisted by the bands themselves, or, where they were not, often gave rise to discomfort and interband tension, as with Decca Records' request that The Mo-dettes alter their sound to that of traditional saccharine girl-pop for the 1981 single 'Tonight'.

Similar debates surrounded the *NME*'s 'Women in Rock' issue in March 1980, in which journalist Deanne Pearson credited punk for the sudden influx of girl bands and noted their distance from their 'sweet-girl vocalist' predecessors.[21] The feature brought together post-punk bands including The Raincoats and The Au Pairs with new romantic vocalist Barbara Gogan, all-girl metal band Girlschool and a grudging participation by The Mo-dettes, who criticised the whole enterprise as reinforcing an artificial gender-based division between musicians.[22] These discussions themselves suggest the growing interest in and awareness of all-girl bands, but also signify some of the nuances and difficulties inherent in how they were seen and presented.

While all-girl groups tended to tour and perform in support slots for other bands, with exceptions like The Slits' 1979 promotional tour for *Cut,* this could perhaps be seen as a function of post-punk bands' collaborative and cooperative tendencies, rather than demonstrating that girl groups were taken less seriously or regarded as more of a commercial risk. The 1980 Beat the Blues Festival, held in London, was headlined by The Slits, along with the Pop Group, The Raincoats, Essential Logic, The Au Pairs, John Cooper Clarke and Linton Kwesi Johnson. That said, women in bands still frequently faced audiences – and journalists – hostile to or dismissive of the idea of female musicians or more interested in their value as eye-candy, as the intentions and principles behind their performance and presentation were not automatically apparent or uncritically received.[23]

Style and content: breaking with tradition

In New York, No Wave musicians made a virtue of actively rejecting established musical technique, aiming to sever all links with previous rock traditions and reduce the music to its basest elements. This 'Year Zero' approach made inexpert playing a conceptual centre to their music rather than a function of inexperience. Ut's Jacqui comments that, while:

> 'a few people were coming [to No Wave] from a trained perspective', those involved were influenced less by their background and more by 'how much they were, or chose to be, indoctrinated by their past'.[24]

Lydia Lunch, eschewing knowledge of chords and 'all those progressions that have been used to death in rock', played guitar using knives and beer bottles.[25] Mars' Connie Burg 'knew barre chords and all the other chordings, but I more or less left it all behind'.[26] She, Lunch, and Pat Place of No Wave bands the Bush Tetras and, previously, James Chance's the Contortions, all used slide guitar as a way for musical novices to create arresting sounds.

Whereas this aspect of post-punk was, in the above cases, based on considered artistic principles, it could also result from a simple spontaneous engagement with music. This was the case with ESG, a band mentioned briefly at the start of this chapter, composed of sisters Renee, Valerie, Deborah and Marie Scroggins and their neighbour Tito Libran. Officially formed in 1978, the sisters had been making music informally well before then, basing their sound on a mutual love for James Brown, Motown, and the disco and Latino rhythms of their South Bronx neighbourhood.

ESG were spotted at a New York talent contest by Ed Bahlman, whose 99 Records shop and label fostered numerous No Wave bands. As ESG's manager he booked them into New York clubs where their spare and unpolished sound dovetailed neatly with the No Wave scene. Subsequent support slots for acts including Public Image Ltd., Gang of Four and A Certain Ratio led them to cross paths with Factory Records' Tony Wilson and producer Martin Hannet, which in 1981 resulted in the three-song single You're No Good. Subsequently widely sampled and still highly influential, ESG's blend of polyrhythmic hip-hop and girl-group lyrical sensibility was produced with a complete lack of high concept, allowing the band's music to chime with the No Wave movement despite their lack of punk background or self-conscious artiness.

From such impulsive or artistic experiments, arresting musical novelty arose. The tiny and close-knit punk scene in Switzerland gave birth to Zurich's LiLiPUT (initially Kleenex), who formed in 1978 and lasted five years with various line-up changes. Vocalist Astrid Spirig, who joined in 1979, claims that the band's initial practices produced:

> '...four hours of noise and absolutely no music. We
> recorded it all. Then suddenly we discovered that, hey
> wow, right there at that point, hour and a half into it,
> something wonderful was coming together. So we
> rewound the tape, listened to that part again and took it
> from there ... We were always searching for new sounds'.[27]

Ut developed a similar method of 'spontaneously
composing', explaining that, 'the main thing was for us to
serve the music and take everything further'. The Slits, too,
were 'constantly developing and looking for new ideas, both
musically and visually.'[28]

The sound itself: 'new, raw, and female'

The departure from established norms of making and
performing music, although common to bands across the post-
punk spectrum, has been identified as a particular characteristic
of all-girl groups. Mavis Bayton's study of 70s and 80s groups
informed by feminist thought found that their creation and
performance ethos stressed cooperation and mutual support
rather than inter-band hierarchies and the breaking down of
barriers between audience and band.[29] Post-punk musician and
writer Vivien Goldman dubbed The Raincoats' debut the first
'woman's rock album' she had heard, its self-effacing musical
communalism marking 'a conscious change from the top-dog/
underdog pattern set up by the patriarchal structure'.[30] Post-
punk was full of such subtly subversive manoeuvres as female
musicians attempted to realise a self-consciously radical sound
dealing with emotions – embarrassment, awkwardness, anxiety
– infrequently expressed in mainstream rock. The consequent
search by female music-makers for suitable modes of musical
expression led them to interpolate dub, reggae, jazz, disco and
world music, contributing to the experimental, dissonant and
eclectic nature of post-punk musicianship.

The Slits' distinctively experimental sound – a slippery, loose and spacious dub-punk hybrid – stemmed partly from an absence of established rock 'n' roll references of the kind motivating their male contemporaries. Whereas fellow bands like the Clash retained older influences like rockabilly and mod, according to their founder, Palmolive, The Slits 'had never really followed rock 'n' roll' and therefore drew on more eclectic musical impulses.[31] Palmolive's own musical background included flamenco and African drumming. But there was also a deliberate rejection of masculine precedent: Viv Albertine recalls of The Slits' early attempts at music-making that, rather than simply copying their predominantly male forerunners, 'We kept saying to ourselves, "How do we feel?" If a woman is making music, do we just do habitual copying of what men do?'[32] She argues that, 'Women do play… in a very different way from men, if they have the confidence to … it's coming from the heart, totally honest.'[33] For The Slits, this female consciousness expressed itself in a rejection of artificially 'girly' vocals in favour of naturalistic ragged harmonies, and in tempos and rhythms that were loose and elastic rather than strict and steady, a style of composing that Ari Up described as 'not as mathematical as the boys' stuff' and more 'like an ocean wave, in and out'.[34]

The influence of reggae and dub on post-punk was an obvious function of the environment in which it was produced: the Ladbroke Grove scene was immersed in reggae, dub and lovers' rock through its clubs and house parties, and a defining factor of Rock Against Racism gigs and tours was their bringing together of punk and reggae performers. Academic and former punk musician Helen Reddington suggests that this reggae influence may have resulted from the masculinist and exclusionary nature of contemporary rock and punk, with which female musicians felt less affinity[35]; however Tessa Pollitt, noting that The Slits were themselves 'a multinational band' with Spanish and German members, recalls that reggae was 'more interesting than a lot of punk music [and] had a militancy we could relate to'. Viv Albertine considered reggae 'the most important thing happening from about '77 onwards'.[36] She also theorised The Slits' attachment to dub as a conscious rejection of 'the ugliness of the punk sounds', considering dub 'a more beautiful version' of punk minimalism: 'ethereal, sensitive' rather than 'aggressive, metallic'. The Slits adopted the Jamaican tradition of playing version into their music, as well as following early jazz traditions which favoured incorporating melodies from other compositions.[37]

The Raincoats applied non-traditional instrumentation and music from folk cultures which emphasised participation over expertise, including Inuit singing, gamelan percussion and Celtic violin. Loose-knit textures and frequent switches in tempo lend their songs a feeling of fragility and unsteadiness, with understated, almost incidental percussion used as decoration rather than driving force, while Birch and Da Silva's vocals veer from a hesitant, mantra-like intonation, through fretful brooding, to a compulsive, confessional patter.

Jazz and funk influences became increasingly visible as post-punk progressed: the Los Angeles band 45 Grave's metal-punk compositions were written in jazz chords, the end results defying categorisation, while NYC's The Bloods drew from traditional funk as well as from emerging hip-hop culture, Motown, free jazz, and anthemic rock 'n' roll. In an example of post-punk's consistently questioning and playful ethic, Barbara Ess' band Y Pants recast the sounds of dub and reggae through the use of toy piano, drums and ukulele, subverting their predictability as stylistic touchstones and, according to Vivien Goldman, expressing 'the spirit of the times, which was fun'.[38] Playfulness, alongside more serious boundary-pushing, was evident in The Slits' cover of Marvin Gaye's 'Heard It Through the Grapevine', and The Raincoats' cover of the Kinks' 'Lola', in which the bands produced versions which blurred musical boundaries as well as questioning those of gender, race and sexuality.

Rock solid rehearsals, fluid performance

Despite the movement's emphasis on amateur and often anti-musical efforts, many female musicians treated rehearsing and discipline with a quasi-military fervour, rather than glorying in inexpert messiness. Ari Up described The Slits as 'extremely disciplined. A lot of work, 24/7 – we were thinking, living, breathing music',[39] while Tessa Pollitt recalls that they 'practiced diligently, like soldiers… the early gigs were often chaotic, but we were very disciplined at the same time'. Gina Birch states that The Raincoats 'rehearsed solidly', and Lydia Lunch that 'we rehearsed ad nauseum and were pretty fucking tight...I was the fucking dictator'.[40] For Lunch, however, ultimately the extent of her musical ability 'wasn't the point. I developed my own style, which suited the primal urgency I needed to evacuate from my system'.[41] The accordingly urgent, short and frantic sets by Lunch's first band Teenage Jesus and the Jerks (not an all-girl band but women centred) were a notable break with rock tradition, and Lunch's performances were, according to contemporary music writer Roy Trakin, 'very influential in freeing people from the idea of technique as being somehow prerequisite to talent'.[42] Tessa Pollitt believes the lack of structure, coherence, and technical prowess in The Slits' notoriously shambolic live performances could be a positive asset, claiming that:

> 'If we started a song wrong, say with the wrong tempo, Ari would stop us and we would start again … the audience could relate to our human error, and the humour was a big part of The Slits'.

The egalitarian nature of post-punk also found expression in collaborative songwriting. The Slits 'all worked on each other's guitar, bass, everything... fucking painful, but we were very strict with each other...everyone would have things to say about each other's parts', working on the principle that 'if everyone worked on the music, it belonged to everyone'.[43] This communitarian approach extended to swapping instrumental roles, as The Raincoats did for much of their second album *Odyshape,* while The Slits have songs on which both Tessa Pollitt and Viv Albertine take over Ari's vocalist role. The technique became a notable part of Ut's live performances, where the band claim it functioned to 'subvert the hierarchical thing' but also to heighten the perspective of each musician by allowing them to play from multiple perspectives in a way that enriched the song.[44] Swapping roles also enabled band members to occupy a broader musical identity and avoid pigeonholing. Ut describe their changing instrumental roles as part of a more general democratising strategy by which each band member got to be 'the controller and the dustbin collector' by turn.[45]

Playful music, revolutionary themes

Post-punk's ideological concern with the politicisation of the personal, and with identifying and promoting authenticity in the face of popular cultural stereotypes, lent itself to exploration from a feminine and feminist angle. This concern with authenticity was expressed in the songs themselves, which were produced, structured and presented in a way which set them apart from the slick and manufactured products of more mainstream artists. It was expressed also in lyrics which demystified and deconstructed conventional femininity, love, sex and romance, and which analysed social and cultural pressures on women or the tensions of personal relationships in implicitly political ways. The Raincoats' violinist Vicky Aspinall identified:

> 'areas which are supposed to be traditional female areas, to do with emotion, the house and the domestic sphere … we haven't avoided it altogether, but just tried to write about it in a way that's true to ourselves'.[46]

Post-punk songs duly explored mundane and unromantic areas of female experience, notably consumerism, self-consciousness, and body image, problematising and politicising them.

The Raincoats in particular mapped a landscape previously foreign to mainstream rock – a female-centred one of self-consciousness, self-doubt, embarrassment and anxiety, its borders defined by the pressure to conform aesthetically and cosmetically, as well as by family, society and biology. In The Raincoats' lyrics, punk's preoccupation with mundane daily routine – bus rides, tower blocks, shopping, boredom – is rendered with drab watercolour realism rather than the gritty outlaw glamour with which The Clash tended to sculpt their cityscapes. (The same quotidian impulse, as their name suggests, motivated Barbara Ess' and Christine Hahn's 1977-78 band Daily Life.) With songs like 'In Love', The Raincoats attempted an unsweetened representation – embarrassing, unsettling, haunting – of the romantic experience for women.

Elsewhere, Delta 5's 'Mind Your Own Business' and 'You', and The Mo-dettes' 'Two Can Play', performed relationships as struggles for autonomy and control, while The Au Pairs' 'Come Again' satirised the self-conscious absurdity of those who considered themselves sexually enlightened 'new men'. ESG's arch and energetic 'Erase You' celebrated female agency and independence. The Slits gleefully burlesqued the banality of conventional heteronormative relationships in 'Love und Romance', described the thrill of anti-consumerism in the self-mythologising 'Shoplifting', and addressed retail therapy as addiction in 'Spend, Spend, Spend'. In 'Typical Girls', mainstream femininity is identified as a profit-driven invention, 'another marketing ploy', and its attendant anxieties and insecurities about 'fat, spots, and natural smells' are scathingly rejected. The stinging lyrics of the Bush Tetras' 'Too Many Creeps' conflate love, romance and consumerism, ultimately dismissing the whole package as the fruitless and frustrating result of 'shopping around' only to find 'nothing that's worth the cost'.[47]

Political engagement/musical confrontation

In the heightened social and political tensions of the post-punk era, gigs could become critical moments of consciousness-raising or confrontation, and women in post-punk bands developed a political sensibility which could take ideological and outspoken form. In the early 1980s, Birmingham band The Au Pairs, led by politically vocal feminist Lesley Woods, criticised the British presence in Northern Ireland in songs like 'Armagh' and opposed Thatcherism and US imperialism. While their candid politics were the subject of growing press obsession, The Au Pairs' bassist Jane Munro recalls that 'most of the bands we were gigging with or who were influential at that time also had political and/or feminist lyrics'.[48] Despite ambivalence towards conventionally organised politics and demonstrations, many post-punk bands participated in the tours and festivals organised as part of Rock Against Racism's opposition to the rise of neo-fascist groups. Leeds' Delta 5 were notably aligned with the movement, while The Slits, in common with many of their peers, developed 'a natural affinity' with London's young Caribbean community in their opposition to police antagonism. LiLiPUT also considered themselves 'very political... [although] we didn't throw stones and smash windows. We stood there and played songs'.[49]

The F word

The question of explicit allegiance to feminism was a more divisive one for post-punk women. Often it was a function of broader political consciousness – New York's The Bloods, the only openly queer female band of their day, contributed to the 1983 anarcho-feminist science-fiction film *Born in Flames*, as did The Bush Tetras' Pat Place. LiLiPUT's Astrid Spirig's advocacy of women's rights was bound up with her interest in 'political and union organising, drugs and fighting the system'.[50] Linder

Sterling was unequivocally militant in her feminism.

The Au Pairs and Ut wrote lyrics which directly referenced the personal and systemic oppression of women, even though, for the latter group, 'we came together because we shared a radical sensibility … we didn't see ourselves as being female musicians.'[51] The Slits were similarly ambivalent, stating in an early interview: 'We are feminists in a way … we just want to show them what we're doing, what girls can do', but later eschewing the label.[52] Palmolive 'never liked the feminist movement, like the political side of it', while Tessa Pollitt says retrospectively that the band 'were not consciously being political, just trying to change the things we were not happy about and question the injustices of the world … it wasn't just about female matters'. Karin, guitarist with the early-80s Swiss pop-punk band Chin Chin, was 'never particularly interested in the endless male-female discussion anyway. We are all musicians, I don't like to be defined by my gender'.[53] The Mo-dettes were explicitly critical of partisan feminist politics, their bassist Jane Crockford declaring that female musicians should earn respect rather than feeling automatically entitled to it by virtue of their gender, while vocalist Ramona Carlier distinguished between her situation as a female musician and the feminist principles of equal rights and access to abortion, to which she did subscribe.[54] The band's lyrics reflect this ambiguity: songs like 'White Mice' champion sexual autonomy, while 'Foolish Girl' wryly catalogues the misadventures of a girl who renounces feminism only to end up in an unhappy conventional marriage.

It can, of course, be argued that simply by their chosen appearance and behaviour, post-punk women were making a political statement, one which was often widely perceived as threatening or provocative. The Slits' associate and one-time manager Don Letts described the UK at the time of punk's first flowering as 'the dark ages' in terms of gender relations and women's freedom to dress and behave in ways that differed from contemporary conventions.[55] Both Palmolive and Ana da Silva had moved to England to escape restrictive political regimes in Spain and Portugal respectively. Palmolive's background was one:

> 'where you had to do things a certain way … [The Slits] just basically wanted to be whatever we wanted to be, do the things we wanted to do when we wanted to.'[56]

During punk and post-punk, these basic tenets of liberation and emancipation came into conflict with die-hard social restrictions on female behaviour.

Research by Helen Reddington has established the high degree of objectification, harassment and assault to which female musicians were often subject, both within the music scene and industry itself and as part of their daily lives. Gina Birch and Linder Sterling echoed the sentiments of many women that:

> 'In those days, you were kind of running the gauntlet every time you stepped outside the front door … a lot of men really took it as a provocative stance [as though] you were personally offending them by dressing in a way that was … anti the conventions of femininity.'[57]

The Slits, in particular, as the first prominent all-girl punk band, found their appearance, attitude and behaviour attracting press and public hostility to rival anything thrown at their male contemporaries. Tessa Pollitt recalls that 'It just seemed to others that we were asking for it. The vibe towards us was "know your place woman!"' Even when the group became more established, hostility persisted: Viv Albertine says of one period in the early 1980s that 'every step there'd be staring, comments, swearing, physical stuff' which forced her to 'toughen up' to a point where she found herself unrecognisable.[58] Lydia Lunch too found herself adopting a permanent 'boxer's stance' in order to deal with the daily aggression she encountered.[59]

As Ari Up acknowledged, they 'were automatically women's rights by being who we were'.[60] Mars' Connie Burg declared her generation of women 'totally uninterested in taking the roles that were typically assigned' to them.[61] Awareness of issues like the omnipresent threat of assault, and the struggle to confidently occupy public space, informed songs like The Raincoats' 'Off-Duty Trip', The Slits' 'Ping Pong Affair' and The Bush Tetras' 'Too Many Creeps'.

Typical girls: engaging with femininity and sexuality

While women in post-punk could not entirely avoid traditional sexism, objectification and sexualisation, they were largely able to resist attempts by male management to reductively present them as sex objects. Here the Slits again proved pivotal, in their pioneering of an active and confrontational sexuality which took place on their own terms rather than within male-defined conventions and to which other women were able to respond. Most notably they appeared clad in loincloths and mud on the cover of their debut album *Cut*. Dismissed by some as a cynically sexualised ploy, and derided by others because of the group's deviation from a conventionally desirable body shape, the band's stated aim for the cover was to 'show that women could be sexy without dressing in a prescribed way. Sexy, in a natural way, and naked, without being pornographic'.[62] Tessa Pollitt claimed that the band were:

> 'celebrating the freedoms we were creating ... and being dressed in nothing but mud and loin cloths for the front album cover of *Cut* was one of the most liberating things I have done'.

Post-punk: Raw, Female Sound

Vivien Goldman embraced the cover as a defiant reclamation of the female body, and Pauline Black, who went on to form 2-Tone band the Selecter, saw the cover as:

> 'so joyous, innocent and natural that it just seemed like a celebration of womanhood rather than any cheap titillation.'[63]

However, this reading was by no means universal. Sexuality itself was something about which The Slits, in keeping with their consistent refusal of seriousness, described themselves as 'very tongue in cheek'.[64] Ari Up's notable youth during the band's early fame enabled her in particular to draw on and subvert the image of the bratty, untamed wild child and the hypersexual nymphet. According to her bandmates, she had:

> 'that Lolita type of sexuality, which she also quickly became aware of and became a parody of ... Can you imagine a young woman, with all the pressures on women to be pretty and acceptable ... [feeling able] to just hoick down her knickers and piss onstage? She didn't care what she looked like, what she smelt like...'[65]

This refusal of shame in bodily functions, nudity or sexual agency was present not just in stage performances but also in songs like 'Slime', 'Vindictive' and 'Ping Pong Affair', as well as in interviews where Ari spoke frankly about her good and bad sexual experiences. The Slits' aesthetic and behaviour onstage and off was repeatedly referenced in terms of wildness and ferocity – even an analysis as recent as Simon Reynolds in 2005 refers to them as 'a feral girl gang' – which reinforced their performance of an exoticised, 'untamed' sexuality not subject to social convention.[66] The Slits' contemporary Siouxsie Sioux remarked that the band 'weren't glamorous, they were very earthy'.[67]

Elsewhere in post-punk, Linder Sterling was notably concerned with confrontational critiques of femininity, taking to the stage at Manchester's Hacienda in 1982 in a dress made of discarded raw meat sewn onto layers of black netting, a provocative use of signifiers that predated Lady Gaga by almost three decades. Lydia Lunch's mode of engaging with femininity saw her subvert the glamorous sex-kitten trope itself, taking on conventionally masculine attributes of sexual aggression and predation in songs like 'Lady Scarface', as well as referencing the torch-song's tradition of female catharsis in her cover of 'Gloomy Sunday'. She described her subversive cabaret album *Queen of Siam* as her decision to let 'the sick little girl out to play'.[68]

The Raincoats, meanwhile, effectively pioneered a 'third way', deconstructing and demystifying female sexuality both through their songs and through the refusenik strategies of anti-glamour with which they performed them. Their aesthetic has been described as 'plain', 'dowdy' and 'dreary', but in fact it contained a greater degree of agency and strategy than is usually acknowledged. The Raincoats' deliberately mismatched outfits, featuring clothes and accessories in clashing styles and colours, represented a disruption and refusal of any cohesive female aesthetic, a conscious de-emphasising of feminine adherence to fashion and style, and consequently a de-emphasising of gender and sexuality. They certainly didn't appear to be dressing in expectation or anticipation of an appreciative male gaze. As Gina Birch argues:

> 'We weren't trying to be Plain Janes ... it was a protest!
> And it was quite deliberate ... it did threaten ... the boys in
> black leather, who wanted girls in a tutu'.[69]

Ana da Silva wrote retrospectively that being female should involve:

'...reacting against what a woman is told she should   be like ... Try and avoid ... playing the games constantly proposed to you'.[70]

The Raincoats' demeanour and dress was a strategic rejection of these 'games' in favour of writing their own rulebook.

Legacies and inspiration

Where did post-punk women go? Many groups in the post-punk vanguard were short-lived, while others increasingly developed away from its aesthetics, as they had originally left punk behind in favour of greater innovation and experimentation. The mid-80s saw the increasingly distinct offshoot of new wave achieve some chart success, along with nascent developments like alt-rock, indie and hip-hop, but much of the infrastructure supporting independent music seemed lacklustre and directionless, despite attempts by labels like Rough Trade to challenge their mainstream counterparts by adopting corporate strategies of management and promotion.[71] Meanwhile, 'we women were obliterated. We did it ourselves,' says Gina Birch. 'We didn't expect to always be in bands … When the scene started dissipating, we let it flow away'.[72] Helen Reddington notes similarly that despite the initial influx of women into bands, they failed to 'secure the conditions for their own continuance' and by the mid-1980s were either absent or back in their established vocalist roles.[73] For Ut, the movement 'just ran its course'.[74] Following the scene's dissipation, many female musicians sought to continue their artistic self-expression in related fields, turning to photography, visual art, writing, television production, academia or law, or remaining within music but outside the confines of the industry. Lydia Lunch, for one, viewed her music as one of several artistic mediums available as tools 'to get across the emotional impact' of what she produced.[75]

The musical legacy of post-punk, including that of its many female members, remained deeply embedded in underground and alternative music, breaking the surface at various junctures before the early-2000s revival in British and US alternative rock which saw the rehabilitation of many post-punk groups. ESG in particular had seen their standing rise throughout the 1990s, with their work sampled by acts including the Beastie Boys, TLC, the Wu-Tang Clan and Tricky, as well as indie bands like Unrest and Liars – although the lack of royalties received antagonized the band, who addressed the issue with pointed panache in the 1993 single 'Sample Credits Don't Pay Our Bills'. After third album *Moving* in 1984, The Raincoats scattered to solo projects, reconvening in the early 1990s as the grunge movement took them to its heart. In 1993, longstanding Raincoats' fan Kurt Cobain spearheaded efforts to reissue the band's out-of-print albums and invited them to support Nirvana on tour. The evolution of post-punk into twee, riot grrrl, grunge and electro also displays the musical and sartorial hallmarks of its female participants. The Raincoats' 'messy hair thing, and looking like you've slept in your jumper' had an obvious influence on the grunge aesthetic.[76] A musical and political influence, too, can be seen in the subsequent eruption of riot grrrl, as well as electro acts like Chicks on Speed, Peaches and Le Tigre.

The Bloods' retrospective biography namechecks several bands whom they consider to be 'keeping the fierce flame burning', including The Gossip, The Yeah Yeah Yeahs and Erase Errata.[77] Viv Albertine has praised contemporary female musicians including Meg White, Talk Normal and Grass Widow. The latter, a San Francisco trio, echo The Slits in their collaborative stage performance and their blend of distorted post-punk riffs with ragged vocal harmonies. Swedish pop-punks Leichtenstein are overtly influenced by the sound and aesthetic of The Mo-dettes. The experimental and deconstructionist approach of post-punk is continued in

Post-punk: Raw, Female Sound

the music of several other all-girl bands, from the Tokyo-based instrumental trio Nisennenmondai to the Manchester collective Womb, whose sound revolves around free improvisation, incorporates world music and utilises homemade instruments and found objects. The use of sound and genre pastiches by Austin's Deep Time continues post-punk's self-conscious self-critiquing. The spontaneous and collaborationist songwriting of Afrirampo, featuring improvised vocals and tribal percussion, also displays the influence of post-punk, as does the guitar playing informed by African fingerstyle patterns, group vocals and wordless singing of London afro-punk trio Trash Kit, and the innovative and experimental music of Azita Youssefi's first musical project, The Scissor Girls, which was accompanied by onstage attire, including matching uniforms, goggles, tutus and heavy eye make-up, which mocked and subverted received ideas of feminine aesthetics. The current proliferation of angular melodies, odd tunings and departure from conventional band configurations are all features made possible by post-punk experimentalism.

Post-punk, even in retrospect, lacks the spectacular and cinematic narrative arc which made punk infamous. Its disorderly, category-resistant, subversive and ironic nature has seen it marginalised in both popular and academic accounts of its era, but its significance and value are readily apparent. Initially inspired by punk, post-punk women were able to take their music in radical new directions, employing innovation and deconstruction in band configuration, lyrical content, musicianship and performance. The Slits, says Tessa Pollitt:

> 'were never a punk band in the "follower" sense of the word. We always carved out our own path, strove for something fresh and new'.[78]

Post-punk's acceleration of and extension of the female self-expression which punk had initiated laid solid foundations

213

for many subsequent musical movements. It especially encouraged the female potential within them, making post-punk a pivotal movent for women in music which continues to influence and inspire.

Contributor biography

Rhian E. Jones grew up in South Wales before studying at Goldsmiths College and Oxford University. She now lives and works in London where she writes on music, history, politics and popular culture. Her writing has appeared in *Wears the Trousers* magazine, McSweeneys Internet Tendency, *New Left Project*, *Red Pepper*, the *New Welsh Review* and the *Morning Star*. Her first book will be published by zer0 Books in 2013. Her blog is Velvet Coalmine. See http://velvetcoalmine.wordpresscom

8. Subversive Pleasure: Feminism in DIY Hardcore

Bryony Beynon

'As women artists, we were branches of the same tree called INVISIBLE.' *Yoko Ono*

'The whole angry young boys thing was very romanticised. Angry young girls were a threat.' *Sharon Cheslow, guitarist from Chalk Circle.*

From a curious vantage point in the centre of the unlikely venn diagram where feminism, punk and cultural theory meet (and usually eye each other suspiciously) I can't help but notice a gaping hole in those library shelves. Thirty years on, hardcore punk – the wayward child of New York's art-damaged noise and California's sprawling suburban decay – remains almost entirely overlooked in the coverage of punk. When granted a mention, hardcore is at best an unsavoury footnote, a foolish sonic experiment in extremity destined to annihilate itself. At worst, it is painted as a complete dead end, a cultural desert of violence and machismo, a youthful misdemeanor; the worst excesses of punk's death drive. More pertinently, hardcore in the history books maintains an unpleasant reputation as a scene off-limits to women, queers and people of colour, almost by design. Meanwhile, the smattering of books dealing exclusively with women in punk tend to focus either on the more gender-fluid exuberance of '77-era punk, where Siouxsie and Poly's pioneering screams echo, or on rewriting the flash of activity around riot grrrl in the early 90s to act as a convenient 'ground zero' for punk rock feminism. So the stories of women in hardcore and DIY punk outside of these overexposed punk postcards remain, for the most part, unrecognised, their work uncredited, experiences marginalised, names forgotten. While Henry Rollins and Rollins Mackaye are the closest thing punks have to the proverbial household names, how many know Cheslow, Pickering or Droogas?[1]

English punk rock may have emerged 'as the result of unmaterialised promises of economic rewards'[2] but America's hardcore (and its subsequent global offshoots) had no such financial fantasies. Distilling the noise of its predecessors down to a lethal shot of rage and speed (arguably as far back as 1978 with LA's Middle Class and their seminal *Out of Vogue* EP), hardcore lacked that soaring pop sensibility that once had major labels flocking to first wave punk. Participants were instead pushed to create new models of self-reliance for their music, to find a way to spread it through independent channels that did not rely on external endorsement. This meant fusing the ingenuity of 'do-it-yourself' innovators like the Buzzcocks (whose *Spiral Scratch* single was one of the very first self-released punk records in January 1977) with the stringent separatism of UK 'anarcho-punk' groups like Crass. This transformed bedrooms into record label HQs, and gig-goers into tour bookers, photographers and self-published zine writers, not to mention the thousands of teenagers getting acquainted with guitars and drumsticks, revelling in their amateurism as an outlet for the sharply felt, universal alienation of youth.

Crucially, this was *not* a spread from the US to the rest, but a groundswell amongst disaffected young people across nearly every urban centre in the world. There were punk bands in Turkey, Brazil and Japan at the same time as The Sex Pistols were being manufactured! (Yes, just as the role of so many women has been minimised or written out, so cultural imperialism has also insidiously had its way with the historical narrative of punk and hardcore, but that is another chapter for another book!)

So why explore women's contributions to the hardcore scene? From my perspective, as that punk in the library, I'm left wondering why the bands, songs and stories of the women from hardcore history that I know off-by-heart have been left out, why all those that have challenged and inspired me to intercept and unpick the complacency of 'dude-rock', to write and create from my own lived experience, why they should be denied their dues? In truth, I was fifteen years too young for riot grrrl, and anyway always much more a fan of the abrasive, corporeal buzz and howl of hardcore from the get-go in my mid-teens. Alienated by boys, obsessed with noise, I collected records diligently while resigning all hope of ever hearing a voice like mine break through the static at any point.

A girl gang underground

Discovering the secret underworld of thousands of all-girl or at least women-centred bands – existing parallel to the dominant timeline of the more popular and inevitably all-male bands I knew about – was to break once and for all with the doubts that hound every girl who's a minority in their own subculture. This experience quickly brought about a shift from being a consumer to a producer, a process that the men engaged with DIY culture find much less challenging, for reasons the women I have interviewed will tell you next. All this would never have happened for me without the encouragement of these stories and meeting those who had done the same; they forced their way in and showed me that I could, should and had to do it too. Ten years into organising gigs, booking tours, writing about punk and running a record label, while singing and playing in a bunch of bands, I am still endlessly thankful and in love with these secret histories and the new ones forming even now, so call this a love letter (still realist and still critical, I hope) or just my tiny attempt at payback. As well as shedding light on these punk women of hardcore past and their often overlooked bands, I wanted to restore some diversity to this narrative, and contribute to a richer, more representative version of hardcore history, for those who seek it out, whether curious or already obsessed, by highlighting the achievements of my peers still active in DIY feminist punk rock organising today.

'Riot grrrl sounded like folk music compared to, like, the Cro-mags!'[3]

Many of the women involved in hardcore's first wave expressed frustration and alienation at increased violence and macho behaviour, and some chose to disassociate or move to other forms of outsider music in protest. As Jennifer Miro of The Nuns (San Francisco, USA, 1979-81) explained:

> 'There were a lot of women in the beginning. It was women doing things. Then it became this whole macho anti-woman thing. Women didn't even go to see punk bands because they were so afraid of getting killed. I didn't even go because it was so macho and so violent that it was repulsive.'[4]

However, other reactions to these frustrations, initiated by those who stuck around, helped to form a blueprint for DIY punk rock feminism. Indeed, the persistence of many in claiming an active role for themselves in spite of unwelcoming attitudes was even more significant as they swam against this rising tide of violence and machismo. Racism, sexism and

Subversive Pleasure: Feminism in DIY Hardcore

homophobia existed in hardcore as much as it did in 'the straight world' but the idea that punk women abandoned their affiliation *en masse* (and picked up keyboards or something) is misleading. For example, Sharon Cheslow, guitarist of all-girl post-punk innovators Chalk Circle (Washington DC, USA, 1981-83) created discussion and response to these conflicts in her zine *If This Goes On*, where she began writing about sexism in the punk scene as early as 1982.

Six years later, Cheslow and others from the female DC cohort (including Cynthia Connolly, Amy Pickering and Lydia Ely) were still organising, still critically analysing the social structures of their community. In June 1988, *Maximum Rocknroll* would publish a collection of interviews these women had conducted with notables from the 'harDCore' scene on the subject of gender. A key aspect of their discussion was the fact that, despite ostensibly hoping to create an 'alternative society,' the roles taken up by women were overwhelmingly 'backstage', whether they be 'working for Dischord, promoting, or booking at clubs'.[5]

This illustrates how that boring old patriarchal paradigm that women merely support whilst men take the spotlight had insidiously replicated itself within hardcore punk as an accepted social norm. Kim Nolan, active in the 90s straight edge hardcore scene, recalls how 'the roles that I was being assigned made me feel like half a participant […] because the aggression in the music was masculine.'[6] Interestingly, she also felt like a space that other punk women had carved out for their own empowerment was not for her either, because 'while I supported it […] riot grrrl sounded like folk music compared to like, the Cromags'!'[7]

I relate to this a whole lot. Nolan perfectly illustrates the contradictions that women (and indeed those of any gender who don't fit certain stereotypes of masculinity that get replayed and magnified) participating in male-dominated musicultures work hard to disprove and deny, crushing gender essentialism and proving that of course it is totally possible to be a radical feminist and love this supposedly 'macho' music, raising a critical eyebrow to the oldest lies about 'music for boys' and 'music for girls.'

No barriers

DIY punk specifically developed and continues to have a plethora of sometimes overwhelming nuances relating to both ritual and style (from dancing to dress) as requirements for authentic participation, there are things that strongly and sometimes physically enforce this suppression. I would argue for three extra dimensions to that alienation from 'within', as it were; three community-and-consensus-enforced barriers to equal participation for women. These are: alienation relating to lack of musical aptitude and alienation as a result of female physicality – through both the body and the voice.

The first, the idea of a somehow inherent lack of skill or inability of women to 'play', is common to the wider 'women in rock' paradigm and has already been discussed at length elsewhere in this volume; an experience common to both first wave punk musicians and 'women in rock' generally. However, the fact that this persists in hardcore, where lack of musical expertise, simplicity and amateurism is generally considered a badge of pride, seems to speak volumes for the latent tendencies of rock conservatism often inherent across punk, sadly furthering the facile aphorism that, as once proclaimed by Julie Burchill, 'a woman behind a guitar looks as unnatural as a dog on a bicycle'.[8] Of course, a key strategy to subvert this was to consciously choose to play with other women. As vocalist Amy Pickering (Fire Party, DC, USA, 1986-90) insisted, 'Fire Party formed around music, not around sex,' but goes on to say: 'We were on the same musical level, so it made more sense for us to get together.'[9] While the theoretical rejection of 'skilled musicianship' is considered a natural tenet of punk regardless of style, in practice a genre with a thirty year history has become its own worst enemy when it comes to limited focus and obsessive boundary drawing. The focus on 'playing right' still plagues punk and creates a conservative undercurrent holding back the discovery of new musical frontiers, and nowhere is this stronger than when women take to the stage and play.

The second two modes of alienation are corporeal: specifically of the body and the voice. They relate to those highly codified physical ways of expressing enthusiasm for a live performance that have developed and been passed down over time, to show 'authentic' appreciation. This might involve 'slamdancing' or 'moshing' (for anyone not familiar with these terms, at many gigs, not just hardcore, audiences in front of the stage form a group that slam into each other and/or jump up and down en masse), sometimes grabbing the microphone from the singer (who may offer it) to sing along in the process. It is important to note that, as these scenes have evolved organically all over the world, cultural difference and incidental factors can affect experience and acceptable behaviour. While all would scoff at the suggestion of there being 'rules' *per se*, any observer or indeed participant can spot the reactions dished out for those who deliberately or otherwise go against these norms. Calvin Johnson from K Records observed of hardcore as far back as 1981, how 'when a girl is dancing, she gets special abuse.'[10]

The different sonic and stylistic subsections of hardcore have historically placed a varying amount of significance on those physical forms of participation, but it is telling that, in those hardcore communities where people moshing as an almost essential badge of authentic 'fandom', less women tend to be actively involved. This is not to say that all conform to the same standards in any way but, in my experience, a vocal female contingent inevitably produces a scene less tolerant of sexism and more open to women. For instance, Vic DiCara of 108 described the period of 1986-89 as 'when hardcore hit its nadir, at least in terms of female involvement,'[11] and it was that period's dominant style (known as 'Youth Crew') prominent in cities like Boston and New York, where both the above focus on dancing 'hard' as a badge of authenticity, as well as straight edge (a kind of quasi-ascetic philosophy where adherents avoid drugs, alcohol and smoking) were rampantly popular. As a teenager, Glynis Hull-Rochelle worked at legendary warehouse venue the Anthrax in Connecticut and attended many of these gigs. She recalls how witnessing bands still considered seminal for hardcore, for example her friends' band Youth of Today, left her with a clear sense that:

> 'Had I ever said one hundredth about women's rights or feminism as those boys said about straight edge, I would have been burnt at the stake as a castrating dyke witch bitch.'[12]

Sub/cultural academic Angela McRobbie has said that 'the dance floor is the most public setting for music as sexual expression'[13] and where hardcore is concerned, this space in front of the band is also somewhere to express physical aggression: sex and violence. This performative strutting echoes the roots of moshing as something that 'separate the kids from the posers [by] swinging your arms to hit everyone within your reach.'[14] No-one would deny that, on the whole, the evolution of these changing styles of movement have always been dictated by a male-majority crowd, and thus the tension between authentic participation and being a woman comes into simple, sharp focus. Of course, girls can and do stage dive and crowd surf too, but there are plenty for whom the certainty of landing breasts-first on a crowd of pumped-up young men has its downsides, to say the least, plus, 'getting touched by a bunch of sweaty male strangers has all-too-familiar, nightmarish connotations' for many women.[15]

So what does all this add up to? In practice, how many of the young men attending hardcore gigs, engaging in moshing, are really likely to stop to ponder how their right to this physical abandon might feel threatening or 'triggering', perhaps, to those in the audience who may have experienced assault? Furthermore, is it unrealistic and over-sanitising to expect this kind of consciousness? Punk feminists would argue that this kind of consideration would certainly encourage more women to move from the peripheries to the stage. Moreover, when women are visible on stage, the sense of being party to an unregulated wrestling match beneath or in front of it understandably diminishes, not least because a crowd often takes cues of physical movement from the band.

More recently, online media has provided a space for debate and discussion about the building and breaking of this sub/cultural consensus, allowing arguments to reach many more than a heated exchange at a gig might do. In her submission to a collaborative blog on this subject called *I Live Sweat*[16] Jennifer Twigg (bassist of The Ambulars, Chicago, IL) recalled:

> 'I remember standing in the back of a large room once and still getting punched hard in the face by a beefy dude. Afterward, I was talking with my ex-partner, just beginning to realise how much I was not into these displays of performative machismo, and he kept saying "this is just how it is, how it's always been. It's not going to change."'

It seems these activities are staunchly defended precisely because they're so wrought with codes and meanings inscrutable to the eyes of perceived 'outsiders', and are thus more resistant to being co-opted by the mainstream. However, by their very existence, they help to reinforce what Twigg calls the 'antiquated notion that men will be men and need to blow off steam.' That this same notion is so commonly used outside of punk as justification for other forms of gender-based violence is clearly troubling.

Defiance at all costs

Strategies for resistance seem to take on different dimensions depending on the era. In the early 90s US hardcore scene, for example, one group of women created a cult of personality around themselves. They made a deliberate spectacle of being a minority, uncommon, of their identity as 'hardcore girls', stagediving, moshing and singing along with their favourite bands as enthusiastically as possible. This was at a time and in a scene where women's participation was at its lowest, and thanks to the kind of dancing fashionable at the time, often downright dangerous. They called themselves XChicks up FrontX, and as participant and zine writer Vique Martin recalls, they were known for 'taking up the stage front and banding together to sing along, to have fun [and] protect each other from getting kicked in the head.'[17]

Instigator Daisy Rooks explains how she and her sister Margaret initially invented this mythical group in reaction to their own sense of being in a minority, creating a fantasy of a 'huge movement of straight-edge women'[18] and began referring to it at every available opportunity, as though they could will it into existence. Obvious parallels to riot grrrl's inception aside, this speaks to the enduring appeal of secrecy in girl culture and the quasi-mythology of girl gangs as a strategy for solidarity, creating allies in an unwelcoming world (think Joyce Carol Oates' *Foxfire: Confessions of a girl gang*, but with more XL band T-shirts). More than offering each other physical protection in a violent environment, Nolan recalls that XChicks up FrontX 'tried as a group to become more visible than one woman alone.'[19]

Through their visibility they reinforced the idea that men did not have a monopoly on the physical and mental release offered by hardcore. Daisy recalls:

> 'At one point there were thirty or forty women that were affiliated with it, that would run around and scream at people.'

The problem with this strategy is that not all women have the capability or the desire to match or exceed the physical response they might see happening around them at a gig, and that in doing so they could end up reinforcing this as the most authentic way to participate. Then there are the general dangers of factionalism in any youth culture setting, in raising questions about who gets to decide who is in or out. Still, these resistance strategies do have to be seen in context to avoid homogenising 'women in hardcore punk' as some kind of singular group with singular concerns, which, as the wide range of opinions we have heard so far shows, they never have been.

If moshing is at once an anarchic expression of consensual violence and a kind of elaborate skin-touching ritual, it is unsurprising that the power dynamics of hardcore are at their most obvious in this area. Steps have been taken in a new conversation around how we might reinvigorate these kinds of physically confrontational aspects of hardcore with a sense of inclusion. As Jenn Twigg explains:

> 'There are ways to get stoked and go buck wild without being violent and creating an oppressive space; I've seen them at a million other shows.'

Discussions in both zines and online spaces make the effort to bring female experiences of overtly violent dancing and its effects to the forefront. The responses are usually revelatory and contested precisely because these experiences are usually silenced or marginalised. Most people, men and women, involved in these discussions see moshing as part of the hardcore tradition, and few would advocate for making it socially unacceptable. Some do now admit that it is problematic in that it physically reinforces the power dynamics between the moshing and the 'moshed,' whilst allowing that, when mutual respect is prioritised, women who do choose to dance can do so with significantly less fear of injury, humiliation or molestation.

Finally, there is alienation via means of the voice. This aspect may seem more related to women singers, but in fact it has wider repercussions for audience members. This is again specific to hardcore punk women and girls at gigs, some of whom shared anonymously that they did not sing along into the microphone when offered it because of fear that, amplified, their voice would sound 'wrong'. The dominant hardcore paradigm of vocal delivery is a throaty, hoarse, low-register and certainly 'male' shout. Such is the level of that dominance that it is not uncommon for women who have stepped up to the mic and raised their voice to have their endeavours dismissed under the apparently irreproachable guise of personal taste – 'I'm not sexist, I just don't like the sound of female vocalists' is a common rebuttal, and not only from men. Why?

Stephie Cristol, vocalist of all-girl hardcore punk band Hysterics (Olympia, WA, USA, 2010-present) suggests dryly that 'the voice of "the other" could sound threatening to the sacred dude-circle.' She goes on to explain how:

> 'for several years as a teenager I "didn't like female voices" either, and I only figured out later that that reaction was totally a by-product of my own internalised sexism, or resentment toward being born into a gender that didn't match that of my musical heroes at the time.'[20]

Thus, the vicious circle of women's outsiderdom, even in this supposed haven for outsiders is completed. Let's remember though, that the bands that form to break these cycles of subordination, either by voicing the lived experience of the members, or through the simple act of playing together, also easily prove the potential of punk at its most vital and subversive, as a tool for decimating the status quo.

Punk's matrilineage

> 'It would be possible to write the whole history of punk music without ever mentioning a male band, and I think a lot of them would find that very surprising.'
> *Caroline Coon, quoted in The Lost Women of Rock Music: Female Musicians of the Punk Era (2007).*

> 'We think back through our mothers if we are women.'
> *Virginia Woolf (1929)*

So who creates and provides access to the accepted history of hardcore punk, and why oh why do they keep 'forgetting' all the girls?! McRobbie[21] has suggested that 'women's sexual attractiveness is their most interesting quality, both for participants in subcultures, and the writers who do work on them' and the best-known oral history of hardcore in the early 80s US rigorously confirms this. Steven Blush's *American Hardcore* (2001) is a resounding example, falling victim to both his orthodox insistence that hardcore was an exclusively American phenomenon, that it 'died' in 1986 (conveniently at the precise point the author's interest waned) and more dangerously, to a bitter misogyny that laments how 'few gorgeous women participated in hardcore, many were nasty, ugly trolls.' If even the insider historians take this view, what hope, you might wonder, is there for the representation of women's punk experience not predicated on their looks or sexual availability?

Many pioneering all-girl hardcore bands delivered a howl of protest and aggression specific to their own experiences in a male-dominated, sometimes startlingly conservative music culture, only to be roundly forgotten in the grand narrative of spikes, rage and boys, boys, boys. Why is this? Jessica Skolnik, a veteran Chicago promoter, musician and feminist/labour activism organiser gave me her opinion:

> 'Women tend to be marginalised in punk because it's challenging to a lot of people to think of women as people who embrace aggressive energy, even though, you know, there are plenty of us who have been involved in punk since the very beginnings.'[22]

No more heroines

For many of the musicians and organisers I spoke to, actively championing these less-revered all-girl bands from the past is a key strategy in combating the dangerous yet enduring essentialism over women's cultural tastes. Everyone I interviewed for this chapter identified at least one woman or girl-identifying band or musician that acted as their personal catalyst and primary influence in both picking up instruments, and in the shaping of their political lives as activists and organisers. For Wick Bambix (of all-girl-hardcore band Bambix, who have existed in various incarnations in Holland since 1984) it was a band of her peers, seminal all-girl hardcore band Nog Watt (1984-1985, Amsterdam, Holland). Wick recalls accidentally discovering them on a compilation LP and thinking 'they were the first *real* all-female punk band from Holland and they were exactly what I wanted to do.'[23] Things like expensive instruments or lessons were jettisoned in favour of new female heroes and, in Bambix's case, metal washing powder containers for drums(!) and a bass plugged into a record player for an amp.

Representation is another battleground. Bands' names like Beyond Pink (Malmo, Sweden, 2004-present) play on the history of stereotyping and marginalisation that has been so key to feminist struggles against patriarchal media forms. The previously mentioned Hysterics (Olympia, WA, USA, 2010 – present) subvert the quintessential Black Flag logo of the four black bars re-imagined as four bloody tampons. This playful visual metaphor is not hard to decipher, but is also a direct challenge intended to 'mess with the macho hardcore paradigm.'[24] That this logo draws polarising reactions of awkwardness or discomfort (from the men I showed it to) speaks volumes about the marginalisation of the female experience in terms of shaping the everyday reality of hardcore punk.

Many felt frustrated at finding their gender to be the main focus of discussion and reviews when their band was highlighted, annoyed that interviews ostensibly about the band would instantly turn to the question of their being women. Recently, Beyond Pink published a disclaimer on their MySpace website profile advising promoters:

> 'Please don't book us on the basis that we're an all-girl band. We want to believe that we are able to get shows because people like our music, not just because it looks cool to write something about girls on your poster.'

There were others for whom, through using an acceptance strategy of being 'one of the boys', felt they were never stigmatised for being female. Tara Johnson, the bassist (and only female member) of 1990s metallic hardcore band Disembodied recalls:

> 'I didn't feel like hardcore was a boy's club because I just didn't give a fuck. I didn't ever feel like I needed to be a spokesperson for girls in hardcore.'[25]

Johnson does conclude, though, that her outward behaviour of not being a 'girly girl' allowed men to accept her more easily. This sort of strategy of acceptance through gender minimising/outright invisibility was mentioned frequently by women I spoke to. Mish Bondage of The Braphsmears (Portland, OR, USA, 1980-82) and later Sado Nation told me she remembers deliberately:

> 'not dressing provocatively, I really wanted to force the audience to accept me on my ability and not look at me as the band's 'hood ornament.'[26]

This fear of being judged on looks rather than ability is nothing new. Amy Pickering spoke out about just wanting Fire Party to be accepted as a band, rather than a band of women. Her personal lyrics never dealt directly with feminist issues, but she recognised, as many others after her would, the radical potency in playing music with other women in a culture that said 'No'.

> 'It's not that we don't want to make a statement, just the fact that we do this is a statement on its own.'[27]

The climate of continued political upheaval in the 1990s saw many hardcore bands begin to foreground myriad issues relating to social justice struggles and activism. One of their rallying cries was 'the personal is political.' (A phrase tellingly inherited from Second Wave feminists, also forerunners of the DIY method self-publishing and creating spaces for radical discussion; a neat history lesson for the next person who tells you there is no precedent for the link between feminism and punk!) In many cases, the agenda and lyrical concerns of all-girl hardcore bands has developed side-by-side with the development of Third Wave feminism, often characterised by sex-positivism, trans-inclusivity, and an acute awareness of the intersectionality of class, race and gender in both feminist and social justice debates and also in hardcore which is still, in America and Europe, overwhelmingly white and often middle class.

Subversive Pleasure: Feminism in DIY Hardcore

Overt violence towards all-girl bands was a common denominator for many of my older interviewees. Wick of Bambix recalls having lit cigarettes thrown at her hair on the stage, not to mention overt threats of rape. Mish Bondage counters that she found the crowd in early 80s Portland punk a more dangerous place than the stage.

I interviewed Adrienne Droogas, the singer of Spitboy (Oakland, CA, USA, 1990-95) a band whose confrontational, inventive hardcore always split opinion. The band, all sharing vocal duties, often spoke earnestly, both during songs and in between, about issues such as rape and sexual assault. They would often stop mid-set to confront sexist behaviour in the crowd, responding to catcalls by inviting the person on stage to repeat his heckle into the microphone. Droogas (2011) recalls:

> 'There was one show [...] while we were playing, this guy kept running to the front and lifting up his shirt and screaming "show me your tits"[...] I saw him do it twice, and on the third time I threw down the microphone, literally jumped off the stage (which was a few feet high) and landed right next to him. He saw me coming and was turning to run away and I grabbed his arm, swung him around, and started talking to him. I held his arm and was right in his face and explained to him why his actions were awful. What he was perpetuating by treating women this way. How he had just made me feel.'[28]

Such direct confrontations challenge the idea that the band are a spectacle to be watched, not engaged with, and on top of this, in the all-girl band's case, objects to be looked at. Still, Droogas maintains her responses while playing were:

> 'never a conscious, thought out process. We would simply respond from the heart and let it all unfold as it was meant to unfold.'

She also pushes the idea of audience accountability in terms of constitutional power and being conscious of privilege in her response, whilst furthering the punk tradition of breaking down the barrier between band and crowd.

'Those women put up with a lot of shit so now we don't have to'

Twenty years on, sexist attitudes in contemporary punk and hardcore persist in new and ever more insidious capacities. The more nuanced or subtle the manifestation of sexism is, the more prone to intellectualised derailing any resistance to it may be. So certain attitudes are more defendable than a spontaneous shout of 'show me your tits' might be. Sadly this is not to say that I have not experienced very similar heckles myself or been groped whilst on stage within the last two years. This means that strategies for resistance and confrontation have also had to develop. Many of the women involved in hardcore today that I spoke to credit outspoken bands like Spitboy, as well as Bikini Kill and the riot grrrl innovators, with creating a space for them. Stephie Cristol of Hysterics explained:

> 'Those women put up with a lot of shit so now we don't have to...at least not to the same degree. Their impact is still really felt […] so if you're new in town and you're not down with women, trans, or queer people being in bands, it's like, "get with it." I think we encounter significantly less sexism here than we do in other cities, but when it does pop up in Olympia punk, it tends to be more subtle.'[29]

Is this the punk matrilineage in action? It certainly feels like it. As radical feminist punk and hardcore women and their allies across the world continue to highlight these histories and create their own, so the possibilities for bringing this sense of agency and opportunity to bear on parallel, more systemic injustices outside of punk rock come into focus.

'But after the gig…'

It's been suggested that 'participation in punk rock subcultures and feminist activism have been two separate pathways for young women's liberation and empowerment'[30] but increasingly women involved in these kinds of projects tread both paths simultaneously. Collective organising and self-determined cultural work based around the principles of mutual aid and cooperation have proved an effective antidote to the multiple alienations mentioned before. Collectives-based radical punk feminism imbued with a social justice agenda have made a large impact on the DIY music communities across the worldWhile some of these groups have been influenced primarily by their involvement in or reaction to the legacy of riot grrrl (see chapter 10 on girls' rock camps) there are many other thriving collectives and projects that have come out of the experiences and struggles of women engaged with hardcore and punk. The following is a selection of diverse examples with different focuses, that illustrate how initial resistance to marginalisation within a music scene can bear incredible fruit, not only creating frameworks for support and encouragement for women in hardcore and punk, but initiating action and change on a wider scale. Upholding the commonalitics and exploiting the intersections and cross-fertilisations of the punk, hardcore, activist and anarchist cultures are crucial in this respect.

Punk feminist projects

Philly's Pissed

Jessica Skolnik has pointed out that: 'sexual harassment is still rampant in both activist and punk scenes, and the places where they intersect.'[31] *Philly's Pissed* and *Philly Stands Up* are two punk-led projects that evolved directly from an incident of sexual assault within Philadelphia's hardcore punk community. They began as a mixed-gender collective made up of radical punk women and their allies, providing substantial support and works towards restorative justice for all people affected by an assault. See www.phillyspissed.net and phillystandsup.com

C.L.I.T. Fest (Combating Latent Inequality Together)

C.L.I.T Fest began in Minneapolis in 2004, as 'two nights of music and a day of workshops dedicated to the active participation of women, as well as combating sexism, rape and abuse within the punk movement.'[33] The use of the term 'movement' is telling as to the integration of the 'more than music' principle in regards to punk. The concept has now spread as eight *C.L.I.T Fests* have taken place yearly in cities across the US, including Richmond, LA, Chicago, Portland and most recently Washington DC. (For more information and details of events in your area search 'clitfest'.)

Emancypunx

Emancypunx is an autonomous, all-volunteer 'anarcha-feminist' group of women from the ages of sixteen to twenty-eight years based in Warsaw, active since the mid 1990s. Formed in reaction to a rising tide of sexism and homophobia in Poland, with the aim of:

> 'promoting feminism and reproductive rights [in a time when] feminist literature was hard to access, the same goes for any art or music done by women. In order to promote females within a still male-dominated hardcore scene the record label was initiated.'

Subversive Pleasure: Feminism in DIY Hardcore

As well as the record label and tour booking, Emancypunx organise several annual festivals across Eastern Europe and run a zine library and archive. As an established radical female presence in the European punk scene, they have considerable influence and reach (see www.emancypunx.com).

Maximum RocknRoll

Maximum Rocknroll (MRR*)* has been publishing a monthly newsprint zine focusing on DIY punk and hardcore from around the world from its base in San Francisco since 1978. Whilst the magazine's coordinators and columnists have historically taken a hard stance against latent racist, fascist and capitalistic traits found within the sprawling interconnected punk scenes around the US and then the world, for the duration of the 80s there was sometimes little attention paid to issues of sexism and homophobia amongst punks in MRR's pages. This has gradually changed, and in 2010 the live-in coordinator roles were simultaneously filled by radical feminist punk women. What is the significance of this, if any? Layla lays it out:

> 'Myself and [fellow coordinator] Mariam both have a feminist agenda in terms of both this work and our existences, so we do what we can to make more space for women in the magazine.'[35]

Taking on column-writing tenure for the magazine a few years ago meant, in a strange way, taking my own rambling place in punk history, at least in the eyes of those who may, in years to come, happen across some browned old copies of the magazine. The current coordinators efforts, and those of the women and men before them, have resulted in the foregrounding of feminist issues within MRR's editorial focus, together with a more stringent analysis of punk records and zines from this viewpoint.

Looking forward

I've tried to shine the spotlight on just a few of the punk women who've formed bands, written zines, put on gigs and started trouble, and included examples of those who've used this proactive spirit gone on to create social change both within and beyond their own musical communities. The role of women in DIY punk and hardcore has always been crucial, but our stories tend to get sidelined in all subcultural grand narratives, punk rock and beyond. Like so many that have gone before it, here is an underground culture that prides itself on the 'idea' of autonomy, but in practice slips back into reproducing the social inequalities of the 'straight world' time and time again. That punk is, for better or worse, and with some mutation, still here, is testament to the enduring power and attractiveness of rebellion, so the feminist punk must be the rebel squared. In a world where true inclusivity and tolerance seem more and more radical qualities by the day, the tide is starting to turn globally within a punk underground that's better networked than it ever has been before, to a positive groundswell of productive rage. Only time will tell what this energy might create, but the history books have nothing on us.

Contributor biography

Bryony Beynon is a writer and community organiser originally from South Wales, and has been involved in DIY punk for ten years. She plays or has played in Back Stabbath, The Sceptres, Good Throb, Tortura and Croup, while running Dire Records. She is a columnist for *Maximum Rocknroll*, publishes *Modern Hate Vibe* zine and crops up trumpeting for radical feminism in *The Guardian* and on the BBC as co-director of Hollaback London. Bryony is a graduate of Sussex University and the Culture Industry MA programme at Goldsmiths, writing and researching on knowledge hierarchies in volunteer-led radical cultural practice and international secret punk histories, as well as gentrification, psychogeography and creative economy. As a promoter she has taken gigs out of the pubs and into abandoned buildings, railway arches and the roof of the Hayward gallery with the Big Takeover project, and is currently working on setting up a permanent autonomous DIY space for London.

Bryony would like to thank: 'Adrienne Droogas, Jenn Twigg, Stephie Cristol, Mish Bondage, Wick Bambix and Jessica Skolnik for their contributions, and to Charlotte Percival, Layla Gibbon and Angela McRobbie for continued support and inspiration.'

9. Queercore: Fearless Women

Val Rauzier

'We're tired of your abuse. Try and stop us. It's no use.'
Tribe 8, 'Rise Above' a Black Flag cover[1]

Queercore, or 'homocore' as it was first called, was a loose
community of isolated, like-minded individuals who developed
a culture of fanzines, films, art and music. Initiated in Canada
and North America during the mid-1980s, queercore spread
throughout the US and Europe during the 1990s and 2000s.
It was inspired by feminist, postmodern and queer theories
that rejected binary understandings of sexual identity as
homosexual/heterosexual and gender identity as man/woman.
These theories were put into punk practice to confront
heterosexist society.

   Central to queercore were all-girl bands, Team Dresch,
Sister George, Tribe 8 and Fifth Column, whose music
confronted lesbian invisibility, misogyny, homophobia and
sexual violence and who created vital spaces and communities
for different ways of doing and being queer. In this chapter,
I focus on these women. Firstly, because as a dyke in my late
teens in the beginning of the 90s, I owe these bands a lot.
They were the role models I had lacked; the comforting loud
voices that could tear down the walls of my own isolation,
humiliation and fear. They helped me challenge the feeling

Queercore: Fearless Women

that I was 'wrong', 'sick' or deviant' – my homophobic self-hatred – and offered possibilities for queer strength, love and desire. As a dyke and a die-hard punk fan, I had difficulty finding music in which I could find myself, let go of my frustration and rage and fulfil my needs. Queercore made me feel like I could fit into the world.

Of course, I found an affinity in punk, in its freedom, speed and anger, but I was not blind to the (not always latent) sexism and homophobia that had crept into the scene. I found myself reinventing boys' songs about girls, listening to gender bending tracks (The Raincoats' cover version of 'Lola' is still one of my favourite songs) or seeking out tracks of 'lesbian music' singer songwriters like Cris Williamson, Meg Christian and Ani DiFranco. Of course, on the post-punk side, I got my kicks from The Au Pairs' Lesley Woods, the German all-girl band Malaria!, The Raincoats, Crass, The Slits and Delta 5. Later, Bikini Kill's 'Rebel Girl' (particularly the version where 'slut' is replaced by 'dyke') and Excuse 17's 'Wedding Song' among other riot grrrl music allowed me to gasp for air... until I found all-girl, all-dyke, politically engaged bands who sang about sex, love, violence and homophobia. They were loud, direct and fun. They were at war against homophobia, lezbophobia, racism, ageism and used music and performances to address power, patriarchal strategies and divisions.

As a queer teenager I was not alone in my alienation and attraction to fragments of queer culture in punk. Joanna Brown, co-organiser of the Homocore night in Chicago, described her situation:

> 'When I was fifteen, I lived in a small town in Louisiana, and the record store carried *New York Rocker*. I knew I was queer, but it was horrible because I was the only one. The magazine had a spread on famous couples in punk, and there was Adele Bertei of The Contortions and her girlfriend, Lesley Woods, of The Au Pairs. I was

> so impressed that there was a lesbian couple; I realised,
> maybe it was OK to be queer if you were into punk.[2]

The discovery of queercore not only helped me be proud of who I am but it also inspired me to become a radical queer cultural producer. In 1997, I started working on radio shows about women in music (Babes In Boyland in Montpellier, France, OvaryAction on Oslo's feminist independent radio station RadiOrakel in Norway and rAdiOrAgaZZa on L'eko des Garrigues, in France), writing fanzines (Ovary *Action*, *The Laugh of the Strip(p)ed Hyena*, *Barbie Kills Ken*) and organised live music events. All these projects challenged the traditional representation of women, queers, lesbians and dykes.

The role of all-girl bands and women within queercore is not particularly well documented. Most accounts of the queercore scene (e.g. Ciminelli & Knox's *Homocore*) tend to focus on predominantly white men and marginalise trans-individuals, lesbians and queer women. In this chapter, I celebrate lesbian and queer bands and artists who have drawn on discourses of girlhood, femininity, womanhood, lesbianism and queerness within radical music-making, lyrics and performances affiliated with queercore. I will first explore the social, cultural and political context and role of LGBT social movements since the 1980s in order to trace the musical manifestations of the independent DIY queer culture that these women played a pivotal role within.

Homophobia to homonormativity: The struggle for LGBT rights

Picture the scene: you are in the mid-1980s, Reagan and Thatcher are shaking hands mobilising repressive and conservative acts across the UK and USA. Smiling to the television camera – always smiling. Bloody conflicts and weapons of mass social destruction (cuts, privatisation...) provoke public outrage in strikes, blackouts and protests. Violent aggressions rage on international and home fronts. In this climate of social division, the privilege enjoyed by the traditional white middle-class heterosexual family is defended by discourses of fear, panic and exclusion of difference. In particular HIV/AIDS, is used as a vehicle to justify fear of diverse sexualities, genders and foreign 'others'. The slow response and silence about the new epidemic and cultural stigma translated into the deaths of thousands in pain and shame. Although HIV/AIDS was first reported in the medical and popular press in 1981, it was only in October of 1987 that Reagan spoke publicly about the epidemic. By the end of 1987, 59,572 AIDS cases had been reported and 27,909 of those women and men had died.

Understandings of same-sex desire as pathological and perverse re-entered the mainstream, supported by powerful institutions of religion, medicine and the law. In England and Wales, private homosexual acts between men over the age of twenty-one had been decriminalised with the passing of the Sexual Offences Act in 1967 (this was eventually passed in 1980 in Scotland and 1984 in Northern Ireland). However, conservative attitudes to queer, lesbian and gay practices persisted in society and culture. On 24th May 1988, Clause 28, initially introduced by Conservative MP Jill Knight, was passed into law. This controversial clause prohibited local authorities (public-funded services including schools, health, social services, Universities, libraries and museums) from 'intentionally promoting homosexuality or publishing material with the intention of promoting homosexuality'. Same-sex relationships were dismissed as 'a pretended family relationship'. Homosexuality was represented as a threat to the health, morality and future of the nation. Crises around sexuality, including HIV/AIDS, Section 28 and the age of consent, mobilised LGBT (lesbian, gay, bisexual and transgender) social movements in the UK and US such as ACT UP, Gay Liberation Front, Stonewall and Outrage! who felt that achievements in the recognition of gay, lesbian and bisexual practices and identities during the 1960s and 1970s were under attack. As writer Des Harmon explained:

> 'The 1980s were perhaps the most frightening years in which to be gay in the United States since the Stonewall Riots. As represented by lawmakers and major news media, AIDS read like a neat morality tale: the excesses of the 1960s sexual revolution, including increased tolerance of gays and lesbians, had been "repaid" in the form of a dreadful plague that threatened to destroy the transgressors.'[3]

However, high profile protest actions (which included four women interrupting the BBC's six o'clock news live on air in 1988[4]) actually increased the visibility of gay, lesbians and bisexual identities within cultural arenas. It also sparked a new determination in LGBT social movements to rehabilitate LGBT identities and practices as normal, healthy and positive in society. It is now hard to imagine, but queer youth in the late 1980s and 1990s had no legal protection against homophobic discrimination, recognition of their relationships or right to parent children. In the UK, key organisations like Stonewall, Outrage! and the Gay Liberation Front campaigned for gay, lesbian, bisexual and trans rights resulting in the right for gays and lesbians to serve openly in the military (2000), equal age of consent (2002), Clause 28 was overturned (2003), the right to change gender (2004), recognition of same-sex relationships and civil partnerships (2004), the right to adopt children (2006), anti-discrimination laws in all areas including employment, provision of goods and services and hate crime (2007) and the right for lesbians to access IVF (2008) to be secured. Even today, proposals to lift the ban on same-sex marriage is controversial for politicians, religious groups and campaign groups in the UK and US.

Queercore: Fearless Women

Despite the steady stream of successes for LGBT groups, to some, this strategy of normalisation does not go far enough in its acceptance of diverse sexual practices and life. Simply put, legal rights and recognition are rewarded to some relationships, identities and practices but not to others. For instance, monogamous relationships, a binary model of gender identity, nuclear family structure, employment, property ownership and consumption are all legally protected. But where did that leave those who practiced non-monogamy, gender queer identities, poor and/or anti-capitalist lifestyles who did not want to (or could not) conform or assimilate into the norms of straight society? Furthermore, with activists confronting laws that punished sex between men, did this push lesbian visibility further to the margins of culture and society?

Increased LGBT recognition provided lucrative new markets for commercial minds to cash in on: gay bars and clubs, magazines, fashion, music and civil partnerships. A queer agenda to counter this 'homonormativity', and exploitation of the 'pink pound' or 'dorothy dollar' grew alongside and within LGBT social movements. Inspired by the punk rock ethos – and a need for more independent queer culture to express the complexity of queer life and counter the dominant capitalist, patriarchal, homophobic and homonormative discourse – the seeds of Queercore were planted.

In the beginning there was Rhythm 'n' Ink: the origins of queercore

The literature came before the music. It started out as a loose collective, trading fanzines and letters, and evolved to include dozens of bands.[5]

In a similar fashion to riot grrrl, the term queercore was coined in fanzines created during the 1980s. *JDs* (Juvenile Delinquents), edited by GB Jones, underground film-maker, artist and musician (member of Fifth Column), and Bruce

LaBruce, also an underground film-maker, were based in Toronto, Canada. This fanzine inspired the California-based fanzine *Homocore* created by Tom Jennings and Deke Motif Nihilson.[6] In *JDs*, Jones and LaBruce, represented a community of diverse like-minded fanzines, film-makers and bands who shared the same oppositional ideas, values and experiences of gay and lesbian mainstream culture. As GB Jones described:

> 'all the JDs gang had been thrown out of every gay bar in Toronto... It was obvious we weren't a consumer of the "right" clothes, shoes, hairstyles, music and politics that the rigid gay and lesbian "community" insisted on: we didn't subscribe to the racism and misogyny and their ridiculous segregation of the sexes, either, plus we were poor.'[7]

Annual gay pride marches were also a target for acts of queer rebellion and resistance to the established institutions of power. Silas Howard, from Tribe 8, testifies:

> 'One of the big moments was a gay pride parade in 1989. We saw a float obviously crashing the parade – a tow truck pulling a cop car – and on the front was a big banner that read, "No Apologies, No Regrets." It was surrounded by punks and queens. There was this big high-heeled show on the cop car, and a bunch of punks pulled out baseball bats and started beating the shit out of the car.'[8]

However, this feeling of alienation did not only exist in the gay community: some felt that the punk and hardcore punk movement had evolved into a straight white male world that reproduced openly sexist as well as homophobic attitudes. The scene was growing very far from its original queerness and gender playfulness. For example, Derek Jarman's 1977 film *Jubilee* documented iconoclastic polymorphous punk sexualities such as the Electric Chairs' Wayne County (now known as Jayne County), an integral queer male-to-female punk performer. By the mid-1980s, though, the gender-bending mood inherited from the 1970s was slowly eroded by rigid gender definitions, divisions and hierarchy. Bruce LaBruce explained:

> 'The early punk scene was much more adventurous and sexually experimental. Like the early gay scene, it was a refuge for all sorts of people who engaged in non-conformist behaviour. By the mid-80s, however, with the advent of hardcore, a certain sexual conservatism crept into the scene. The macho posturing of the speed metal heads and the skinheads and the other mosh-pit habitués resulted in the regression to a kind of high school mentality, with the jocks on centre stage and the girls and fairies on the peripheries like wallflowers.'[9]

Queercore emerged from the margins and seized power back from punk:

> it 'bristled against what it saw as the bourgeois trappings of a mainstream gay lifestyle and the macho, hetero hardcore scene that punk – a movement founded by women, people of colour, and gays – had become'.[10]

Hetero-mono-culture: Queercore and DIY tactics

Queercore, as punk had before it, emerged as a movement of resistance, an antagonistic reaction to the dominant media industry. It was based on direct action and DIY approach to cultural production and distribution that challenged the passive consumption of mainstream culture. As GB Jones explained:

> 'The culture in this society is designed for spectators and consumers, not participants. It's one immense mono-

culture, where everyone shops at the same stores that are in every mall, eats the same food at the same fast food outlets, listens to the same hit songs as everyone else, sees the same blockbuster movies, and watches the same television shows ... But really there are a lot of people who can't stand to live like that, and there are more of them every day. They don't want to watch a television show about someone else's life, they want to live their own life. They aren't willing to settle for what this culture offers, and they do whatever it takes to make their own culture [...] It's a lot harder to try and create your own culture, to make a little place for yourself and your friends in the world. Let's face it, it's not for everyone. But once you notice how little mainstream culture has to offer you, once you want more, there's no going back. People will use whatever they can, by whatever means necessary, to make a culture they can live in[11]

Queercore was therefore inspired by punk and gay and lesbian social movement, whilst simultaneously reacting against them – or what they had become. Queercore sought to question narratives of sexual identities as stable, natural and healthy and focused instead on the construction of disruptive practices of diverse genders and sexualities based on subversive notions of freedom, pleasure and fun.

Riot Grrrl and Queercore hold hands: queering grrrls

'We need a girl culture.'[12] *Tammy Rae Carland*

Queercore also evolved in parallel with riot grrrl culture (see chapter 10) as Jody Bleyle commented:

Queercore: Fearless Women

> 'In the early 90s the queercore and riot grrrl scenes were so intertwined [...] that was a very strong part of where queercore came from'.[13]

In 1992, the year riot grrrl broke through to the mainstream, Fifth Column released 'All Women are Bitches', Outpunk released 'There's a Dyke in the Pit' 7 inch EP, and God is My Co-Pilot released the 'I Am Not This Body' LP. Riot grrrl provided space for girl-centred culture and enabled the exploration of diverse sexualities and relationships between girls and women. However whereas riot grrrl garnered significant international media attention in the early 1990s queercore did not attract as much attention. This has meant that many popular accounts have ignored crucial links between riot grrrl, lesbian feminism and queercore.[14] Although it can be argued that riot grrrl was a white heterosexual subculture, which may have explained its popular appeal, Catcall record label owner, Liz Naylor felt that exposure to girl-positive sentiments in her own youth would have eased her experiences:

> 'Women aren't particularly taught to respect each other in society, this is what's so amazing that there are these ostensibly heterosexual bands Bikini Kill and Huggy Bear saying "yeah love other women" though there is a certain amount of fear that 'oh well they're all dykes' that is actually a big fear people have. I think it's a very brave thing for them to say and it's a message that I wish had been around when I was younger because it would have stopped me going through pain.'[15]

Whether grrrls bands were openly queer or not, queer women and girls were drawn to riot grrrl's queer positive anti-sexist and anti-homophobic discourses and practices. However, the desire for a visibly queer band grew as Tribe 8's Leslie Mah explained:

'It would have been a whole lot of a difference to me had there been an out band at the time when I was sixteen. Or even for a band to say that they were queer positive. It would have just been like '"wow, it's acknowledged, I exist".[16]

Kaia Wilson, of Team Dresch, described how she developed her experience of an all-girl band into a desire to form an all-queer girl band:

'I originally sought out other women musicians to play music with, because I knew intuitively that I wanted to play with other women. And that graduated to, "OK, I want to play with other dykes."'[17]

Therefore queercore answered a need to extend beyond the heteronorms of riot grrrl, the lesbian invisibility of mainstream culture and rigid models of lesbianism in dominant lesbian and gay social movements and culture to focus on diverse queer sexualities on the terms of women and girls:

'While several of the female performers who participated in the riot grrrl scene were in fact gay, and the riot grrrls zines often dealt with the topic of homosexuality, the focus of the movement was not lesbianism, and participants were understandably angry when their music was dismissed as "dyke rock". Perhaps because of this, several of the homocore scene's key players branched off to form bands that were made up chiefly of lesbians.'[18]

Jody Beyle, bass/guitar player in the all dyke band Team Dresch argued that:

'Lesbians have always been integral to the queercore movement. Queercore is girl-rooted. The bands that started the scene – they were all lesbians. There were almost no guys".[19]

Punk lesbians connected rapidly through queercore, Donna Dresch remembers how she immediately wrote to GB Jones after reading her fanzine. She was soon after featured in Jones' underground film *The Yo-Yo Gang*, the Fifth Column song 'Donna'.[20] Girls communicated, exchanged and bridged their isolation. Queercore provided queer girls and lesbians with a space, a scene, a community where they could feel empowered and find a voice and be loud, without apologies ... or compromise:

> 'We are not politically correct... We are dykes, we are queer as hell. If you can't deal with that then we suggest you don't read any further.'[21]

Lynnee Breedlove of Tribe 8 also refers to this communal framework:

> '...queercore was important at the time that I was touring with Tribe 8 because we were often between metropolises in these queer cultural wastelands. So to know that other bands like Team Dresch and Pansy Division and Sister George and Harum Scarum were out there too and were gonna be at the show was a huge support.'[22]

There's a dyke in the pit: performing queer girl music

> 'I just want a public place
> where girls can meet each other's stare.
> Sometimes that's what it takes to know you're alive.
> To feel yourself burning just for some girl's stare.'

'Remember Who You Are,' Team Dresch[23]

Women Make Noise

Leslie Mah, whether she played in her radical punk band Anti-Scrunti Faction or in the San Francisco-based infamous queercore band Tribe 8, has long embraced her own strength, (stage) presence and personal space, and she knows the empowering qualities of such a move:

> 'I am acknowledged as a personality that takes up space ... When we play I want the dykes to take all the space in this club, in this hall.'[24]

Her statement goes beyond space, though. It also implies the personal experience of all the actors involved. Indeed, what she also refers to here is the value, power and pleasure of the interaction between the audience and the performers.

Expectation, experience and excitement are essential parts of live acts. Sex and pleasure (and their regulation) in music has been theorised using Derrida's exploration of a 'theory of sound as erotically penetrative'.[25] For example, scholar Hillary Chute develops her theory of political power of pleasure to focus on how individuals access their bodily senses and escape the authoritarian regulation of the body by the mind.[26] One can therefore understand the liberating effect of music as a 'public and reciprocal transmission of pleasure', and understand its value as a queer and feminist mode of political expression that explicitly challenges not only the mainstream figurations of sexuality but also hierarchical structures of knowledge dissemination and practices of cultural consumption[27]. Empowered subjects can resist – and exist beyond – the consumerism (and objectification) of the capitalist logic and regulation of human relations. The traditional boundary between the performer and the audience is blurred, all the actors, as physical, sensual, affective and sexual subjects, make sense of sound and situations. Individuals are thus exposed to the radical possibilities of communion in transgression. These feminist performance practices, often referenced by Kathleen Hanna in Le Tigre's performance, were at the core of Tribe 8's own 'true dyke punk rock'-ness.[28] Lynnee Breedlove described pleasure and power in the combination of theory and practice, genre, gender politics and fun in Tribe 8:

> 'As musicians we all followed dude bands or het[erosexual] bands, like Leslie [Mah] liked Sonic Youth and the Clash. Silas [Howard] liked thrash and metal. I liked Black Flag. So to take these styles and twist them into queercore was fun, but to be part of an army of bands creating a whole new genre was more akin to the camaraderie that those bands experienced in their movements. Having studied 2nd wave feminism in the 70s and 80s, I got a crash course and 3rd wave feminism from the first babe I dated in sobriety. There were feminism and queer theory books everywhere in her apartment, and I compared the two side by side, as 1990 was the year I got sober and the year of the cusp of the 2nd and 3rd wave. There were play parties and butches and femmes and punks and sober anarchists and zines and tats and homemade piercings of body parts I never dreamed of pokin' a hole through. Dykes were outta control.'[29]

This radical challenge and shift of power challenged the dominant and sustained Gayle Rubin's (and Foucault's) idea that sex IS political[30]. The all-girl queercore band who pushed dyke politics to the fore was, in my opinion, Tribe 8. Not only were they loud and fun, lyrics precise and straight [sic] to the point, but their performances were radically confrontational. As writer Maria Raha sums it up:

> 'Where lesbian desire has historically been packaged under the folk music umbrella in the form of love songs or softer protest anthems, or in the angrier punk folk of

Phranc and Ani DiFranco, Tribe 8 gives audiences the
liberating and unapologetic spectacle of true dyke punk.'[31]

Behind Tribe 8's goofy performances, the artists harboured
radical political motivations. For example, on their album
Role Models for America, the song 'Prion Blues' is followed by a
presentation of the lesbian collective Out of Control, involved
in the support of women political prisoners and of California
Coalition for Women Prisoners. The band often performed
topless, playing with S&M aesthetics and acts. They were sexual,
sexy and ... offered an experience of deep, in-your-(puritan)-
face punk practice. Lynnee Breedlove, the lead singer, would
wear a strap-on, inviting a boy from the crowd to come on
stage to be handcuffed, kneel down and fellate her dildo. As
Breedlove stated: 'the blow job thing is all about being on
your knees and you're in a submissive position.... it's good for
everyone to be tied up and penetrated', especially if 'you feel
like you constantly need to be in control'[32]. The live music
performances of Tribe 8 put a 'mirror' effect into action 'that
forces audiences to face their own homophobia, sexism, racism,
sexual repression, and, worst of all humourlessness.'[33] Not only
was the band mobilising serious challenges to dominant gender
stereotypes and sexualities, they were crucial to the validation
of lesbian identities and dyke-centred queer punk community
in San Francisco. As Lynnee Breedlove says:

'San Francisco was full of out dykes with Mohawks,
going nuts and moshing at punk shows. And there was
occasionally a chick drummer like Killer in Typhoon,
who later played in Third Sex. She's like a big old butch
and you're like: "yeah, she' a dyke!" But no one was
up there singing about "I'm going to **** my chickie
babe." You know, people were starving for it, and they
were really happy (with Tribe 8) as a result of this big
hole. I felt connected to my community ... I was creating

something I believed in and they were hearing it and going "yeah! Thank you. You're talking about shit that we need to hear on stage, because this is the stuff we hear every day." Nobody ever sings about that shit, and when people don't hear their lives are accepted in pop culture or in the media or anything, that's when they feel invisible and that's when they start blowing their brains out and vandalising other people's property.'[34]

To fully understand the power and impact of queercore, it's important to examine some of the topics that were openly dealt with by the dykes. Queercore talked about their personal (and collective) experience in their own terms. I will now focus on the main themes in the lyrics of girl bands involved in queercore.

Tuff lovin': love/hate songs for dykes

One crucial concern is the creation of alternative queer and lesbian identities. For instance, in 'Remember Who you are' Team Dresch urged lesbians to proudly break free from the lack of confidence, worries and hesitation in order to 'Send out signals telling who you are. Transmit messages about who you are'.[35] Throughout the song, the instruments and Kaia Wilson's vocals become louder, more self-assured and urgent. The confessional first-person, who tells the listener about her worries and fears, transforms into an imperative form of self-empowerment, support and encouragement of the listener. These themes of queer identification and visibility are closely connected in queercore music. Playing with roles, stereotypes, rumours within the community itself constructed Tribe 8 as honest and authentic queer dykes. For example, in the song 'Butch on the Street', Tribe 8 mock the femme sexual practices of lesbians with a defensive butch public persona: 'butch in the street, femme in the sheets'.[36] Queer and lesbian sex was a central theme in queercore, criticising dominant misperception of sex between women and representing queer sexual practices and desires. For instance, Ellyot Dragon, of Sister George opens the song 'Virus Envy' screaming the loud, powerful line: 'so you think that dykes don't fuck'[37] before her guitar joins in the bass and drum in a furious riff. Tribe 8's use and references to S&M are numerous both in their lyrics and their performance. Queercore girls and women also used music to explore the everyday dilemmas in trans and gender-queer life. For instance encounters of comments and misrecognition in women's toilets from other women. Tribe 8's 'Wrong Bathroom', or the German band West Dyke in 'Dyke', reveal daily struggles with a rigid idea of gender.

Violence against women and lesbians is condemned. For example, Fifth Column's song 'All Women are Bitches' describes the hatred of women using reflective tactics similar to punk and riot grrrl. The song opens with a dialogue:

'Which are more dangerous, men or guns? Both are dangerous, but only a man can kill you, or at least try'.[38] Fifth Column sample gun shots and laughter and imitate the voices of the different characters (a man talking to his son and perpetrating misogyny) to culminate in an explosive assertion that 'All Women are Bitches'.

Confronting misogyny and homophobia (or 'lezbophobia' as Tribe 8 called it on their *By the Time We get to Colorado* EP) is a central topic in queercore. Gay bashing was a very common occurrence that often went unreported and unpunished by authorities. For instance, Joanna Brown, co-organizer of Homocore Chicago, described her experience: 'I came out when I was sixteen, I got beaten up the next day.'[39] Donna Dresch and Jody Bleyle of Team Dresch also reported being seriously assaulted after playing live.[40] Rape revenge and survival of sexual abuse are also prominent themes in queercore lyrics. Tribe 8 call for revenge by castration in the song lyrics of 'Frat Pig': 'You did it in the name of fraternity. You say you just won a game of hockey. You were dealing with some leftover energy.

Frat pig. It's called gang rape. Let's play. Gang castrate.'[41] During the band's performances, Breedlove would then carry out a dildo castration. In 'All I can Do', they deal with the revenge fantasies of a lover that stem from disassociation commonly experienced by women survivors of childhood sexual abuse:

> 'Your eyes are wide.
> You've gone away
> Just like you used to when he would touch you
> Floating above us there you can watch us
> Under me lies someone I don't know
> Someone I've seen a few times before
> What do you feel when I back you up
> Against the wall in the kitchen
> My legs pressed between yours
> Do you feel him push you, do you see the
> Pictures of him as he stands with his feet wide apart
> His hands on your shoulder, his belt in his hand....
> I'm not that prick wielding his dick like
> Some kind of weapon
> I'm not the sick bastard that did this to you
> I'm not him it's only me I hate him, I love you
> I'll kill him/I want you
> I want you
> I want you to live
> We'll make him pay now.'[42]

Acknowledgment of physical and sexual violence against women and lesbians led to the development of initiatives like Home Safe and Free to Fight.[43] Self-defence workshops were organised to help girls and women to protect themselves against perpetrators.

What these songs have in common is that the artists speak out and resist prejudice, violence and oppression. In doing so, they unveil the insidious techniques the patriarchy uses to maintain its power and hierarchy. Of course, queercore did not stop there. These all-girl queer bands played a crucial part creating a legacy and space for future generations of women, girls and queers to use music to mock straight and lesbian and gay society and construct alternative queer sexualities and genders.

Post-Queercore: the future of queer girl bands

For many, experience with queercore impacted on their future projects preferring to instigate a pro-girl and queer not-for-profit economy. As Lynnee Breedlove, reflected, 'being in Tribe 8 taught me to create organisations like Lickety Split an all-girl courier chick bike messenger company that lasted 10 years in the 1990's, and Homobiles a non-profit queer car service 20 years later, which is sliding scale, no one turned away for lack of funds and has drivers of all sexualities, genders, ages and races.'[44] A retrospective of GB Jones' underground films and artworks was held at the Lexander in Los Angeles in December 2010. Although Team Dresch split up in the late 1990s they reunited in 2004 to play Homo-a-go-go and have since played other reunion events in 2009 and 2010. Online projects like QZAP (the Queer Zine Archive Project) dedicated to preserving the living history of queer culture provide an accessible resource of queercore ephemera.[45]

At the turn of the 21st century queer music culture picked up momentum in what has become known as the queer music explosion. Radical queer-orientated cultural festivals (Homo-a-go-go, Queeruption, Up Your Ears, Dirty Bird); record labels (Mr Lady Records, Chainsaw records, Emancypunx, Retard Disco, Queer Control); and collectives (Homocrime, Queer Mutiny) have continued to create spaces for queers and allies to meet, exchange and create cultures. Queer punk bands and performers have proliferated: Limp Wrist, The Third Sex, Excuse 17, The Butchies, Dominatrix, Lorena and the Bobbits, Sarah Dougher, BoySkout, Team Gina, The Hidden Cameras,

Queercore: Fearless Women

Bonfire Madigan, Tami Hart, Sleater-Kinney, Lesbians on Ecstasy, Gravy Train!!!!, Le Tigre, The Moves, Men, Rhythm King and Her Friends, CWA, Peaches, Scream Club, Erase Errata, The Need, Ste McCabe, Homousexual, Vice Cooler, Homosexual Death Drive, The Haggard, STLS, Katastrophe and The Gossip. These contemporary bands build on queercore all-girl bands to challenge dominant gender and sexual categories using music, sound and performance to construct alternative genders and sexualities not visible in mainstream society. Contemporary queer performers and bands, like Le Tigre and Peaches, have used electronic sounds and choreographed dances to create pro-queer space and culture. Lesbians on Ecstasy have used electronic music technology to produce a sophisticated homage to 'women's music' legacies.[46] Rhythm King and Her Friends have integrated 'drag kinging' into their performances. Radical spoken word queer collectives like Sister Spit and performers Dr Madelyn Hatter, Alix Olsen and Corey e. Houlihan have found audiences amongst punk and literary fields.

This chapter has focused on the role of all-girl bands, lesbians and queer women in what has become known as queercore in the 1980s and 1990s. These bands, Tribe 8, Team Dresch, Sister George and Fifth Column, used music to disrupt and challenge dominant heterosexual ideals, sexism and misogyny, lesbian invisibility and homonormativity (a politics that sustains rather than contests dominant heterosexual ideals, 'promising the possibility of a demobilised gay culture' – see L.Duggan, 2003). Queer women and girls reconfigured punk, DIY culture, gay and lesbian public spaces to carve out radical cultural lives in a hostile world that could adequately express the complexity of queer lives and practices. The all-girl bands of queercore left a lasting legacy and cultural memory that continues to this day. The presence and popularity of queer performers like Beth Ditto of The Gossip is both a testament to the legacy of queercore and an indication of what a queer future can offer.

Contributor biography

Val Rauzier is a strong believer in DIY cultures and their power to change the world and save lives (and the other way around). In her struggle against the hatred perpetrated by patriarchal and capitalist powers, she has been involved in zine-making (co-editor of Barbie Kills Ken, OvAryAction and the Laugh of the Stri(p)ped Hyena) and DJing (as ovARyAction SoundSystem, DJ Garcons ManquEes and rAdiOrAgaZZa). She also has hosted shows dedicated to women in music on independent radio stations (Babes in Boyland on radio Clapas, France, OvAryAction on RadiOrakel, Norway and RadiOgAgaZZa on l'eko des garrigues, France) for the past fifteen years. She currently lives and works in Oslo and is a PhD candidate in English and Cultural Studies at the University of Montpellier. Her thesis focuses on Diamanda Galàs and Kathy Acker.

Val would like to thank: 'Her Noise archive for fixing everything, including the vcr for the archive still in the analog format. Anne Gidde for driving so I could write and for asking the right questions ... and then patiently read the rough draft ... on her holiday. Chrystel Dg for support, encouragement and knowing when/how to kick my lazy ass. To Lynnee Breedlove and artists and queer activists for answering my questions and being ready to go through hours of discussion.

And of course, last but not least: to the bands then, there, here and now for writing the songs and for the passion of performance, to the zinesters and the power of the pen, of the words, of the lines: a massive thanks!'

10. Riot Grrrl, Ladyfest and Rock Camps for Girls

Sarah Dougher and Elizabeth K. Keenan

All-girl bands, all-girl activism

This chapter discusses three unique and interconnected strategies that girls and women have created to link music-making with feminist activism. The networks of women and girls involved with riot grrrl in the early 1990s and the thriving, sustained efforts of organising present within Ladyfests and rock camps demonstrate a continuous engagement with musical activism in feminism. Each network has encountered challenges to effective organising, including issues of inclusion and the ideological conflicts inherent in feminist political activism.

Riot grrrl describes a politicised movement of young feminists in the early 1990s that organised around many different cultural formations – including music, art, writing, self-publishing, consciousness-raising and direct action. Created in opposition to sexism within the punk scenes of Washington D.C. and Olympia, Washington, as well as wider rollbacks in reproductive rights and in response to increasing visibility of sexual violence, Riot grrrl was less a specific style of music than it was a socio-political identity that found

259

expression in part through music. The idea of the 'all-girl' band was important to riot grrrl because its participants used all-girl (or girl-only) space to create areas of safety and resistance within their punk scenes. Some of the bands associated with riot grrrl include Bikini Kill, Heavens to Betsy, Huggy Bear, Bratmobile, Skinned Teen and Emily's Sassy Lime, to mention only a very few. It is important to note that although the creation of all-girl space was an important strategy within riot grrrl, the bands sometimes included men, and often counted men as their supporters. Within riot grrrl, forming an all-girl band was an act of solidarity, mutual support and resistance against larger cultural narratives that suggested girls/women could not play music, fight back against violence, or be powerful (critically acclaimed and/or popular) within their chosen cultural forms. Most riot-grrrl bands were short-lived, but left a legacy of music, writing, film and art that would reverberate through underground music culture in the United States, Europe and beyond.

Approximately ten years after the heyday of riot grrrl, Ladyfest and the Rock 'n' Roll Camp for Girls emerged in the Pacific Northwest, and quickly (using the internet) spread throughout the United States and Europe, providing models of organising and community-building that drew on some elements of riot grrrl ideology. It would be a mistake to assume a direct evolution between these phenomena, even though some individuals involved with Riot Grrrl found roles within Ladyfest and Rock Camp structures. Each has a distinct set of assumptions and was created in opposition to specific events and wider cultural trends. The Ladyfest model undertook grassroots community organising to create showcases for local and national women artists and musicians within a festival-style atmosphere, usually lasting one to three days and donating proceeds to a local woman-centred or social-justice based non-profit. Similar in style to the riot grrrl 'conventions' that occurred in the early 90s, Ladyfests create a place for like-minded people to get together, listen to live music, attend art shows and attend workshops based on feminist political and social issues. Unlike riot grrrl conventions, however, they were open to the general public and operated within a context of a more developed indie-rock music industry that emerged throughout the 1990s. Rock Camps for Girls were created to serve young women and girls (generally aged eight to seventeen) in a formal environment, providing music and self-empowerment education, as well as mentorship for day camps taking place over a week during the summer. Rock Camps and Ladyfests emerged in reaction to the dearth of girl/woman-centred musical opportunities within a larger underground, indie DIY culture, as well as to the perception of still pervasive sexism within the mainstream music industry.

As authors of this chapter, we have a variety of relationships to the material that we are discussing, for more information see the contributor biogs at the end of this chapter.

Riot grrrl: politicising the girl band space

'A movement formed by a handful of girls who felt empowered, who were angry, hilarious and extreme through and for each other. Built on the floors of strangers' living rooms, tops of Xerox machines, snail mail, word of mouth and mix tapes, riot grrrl reinvented punk.' *Beth Ditto of The Gossip*

In the past few years, riot grrrl has received new focus, both within a context of 1990s nostalgia (catalysed by the 20th anniversary of the reissue of Nirvana's album, *Nevermind*) and within a more specific move to historicise the moment as a turning point for the intersection of feminism and music. Riot grrrl is entering institutions, including Fales Library at New York University and the Museum of Modern Art in New York, in ways that legitimise it as feminist history and art. Meanwhile, books such as Sara Marcus's *Girls to the Front* (2010) seek to deconstruct it as a politicised music scene. Within this archiving and remembering of riot grrrl, institutions have often focused on the most prominent musicians, such as Kathleen Hanna and Johanna Fateman,[1] rather than zinemakers[2] and visual artists.[3] While the limited budgets of archives and the need to draw museum attendance no doubt influence this focus on the most famous members of riot grrrl, the materials on display often bring out just how deeply riot grrrl intertwined music, zine-making, feminist theorising and political action, and ultimately how connected these areas of cultural production were to the young women who participated in the movement. Fales Library's collection, for example, began with the Kathleen Hanna papers, which include personal letters and zines, as well as CDs and 8-track recordings.[4] MoMA's 2011 exhibit *Looking at Music 3.0* included listening stations with music, video screens, posters and zines. That this historicising often focuses on the contributions of a few musicians, but incorporates multiple media, suggests a tension between and raises questions about the formulation of the 'girl band' within riot grrrl. Was the 'girl band' the focus of riot grrrl? Was it part of a broader re-framing of 'girl space', in which grrrls could articulate their value, both as people and as political activists? And, finally, in writing histories of riot grrrl in the present day, is it possible to resolve the tension between telling the stories of individuals and the idea of the 'girl gang' or 'girl band' or 'girl space' that formed a central tenet of riot grrrl?

Riot grrrl: origins and the all-girl space

In considering riot grrrl as a holistic movement encompassing the creation of music, zines and visual arts, as well as a commitment to political action, we argue that the idea of the 'all girl' space formed an intrinsic element for the formulation

Riot Grrrl, Ladyfest and Rock Camps for Girls

of riot grrrl as a movement and in riot grrrls' interpretation of the 'girl band' as a space of equality and political action. From its inception, riot grrrl placed an emphasis on reclaiming the idea of 'girlhood' in multiple ways. For example, the 'riot grrrl manifesto' from 1991 lists a series of reasons that 'riot grrrl is...' Among this list, by Kathleen Hanna, a few reasons stand out:

> 'BECAUSE us girls crave records and books and fanzines that speak to US, that WE feel included in and can understand in our own ways
>
> BECAUSE viewing our work as being connected to our girlfriends-politics-real lives is essential if we are gonna figure out how what we are doing impacts, reflects, perpetuates, or DISRUPTS the status quo
>
> BECAUSE we don't want to assimilate to someone else's (Boy) standards of what is or isn't 'good' music or punk rock or 'good' writing AND THUS need to create forums where we can recreate, destroy and define our own visions...
>
> BECAUSE we are angry at a society that tells us Girl = Dumb, Girl = Bad, Girl = Weak.'[5]

In the riot grrrl manifesto, the idea emerges that the term 'girl', could be a source of revolutionary fervor and a source of strength. This radical reframing of a term that Second Wave feminism had largely eschewed would go on to shape Third Wave 'girl power' politics in both good and bad ways.[6]

Instead of cultivating a mere fan-performer relationship, riot grrrl's 'girl bands' actively addressed the need for feminist community within the music scene in order to confront sexist practices. The idea for riot grrrl stemmed from a sense of alienation and inequality within Olympia, Washington's punk music scene. In the article 'love rock, a girl's perspective,' in Tobi Vail's zine, *Jigsaw* 4, from the summer of 1991, Kathleen Hanna wrote:

'At my ideal dance party, no guys would come up and tell the girls that we can't play their guitars cuz we might break 'em or only talk to us if we're wearing tight pants or looking super vulnerable and unchallenging. At my ideal dance party people would talk to each other because they wanna understand and not cuz they wanna win an argument or look really cool. There would be lots of boys who are as concerned as Al is, not about what kind of guitar strings work best to achieve the perfect metal sound, but with things like: How are we all gonna make it more comfortable for girls to be at shows, without being hassled?'[7]

Hanna's piece offered a response to Al Larsen's manifesto, 'Love Rock and Why I Am,' which addressed the anti-corporate, inclusive, DIY ethic which predominated in the Olympia punk scene, an ethic that gave rise to the International Pop Underground festival held in August 1991. Hanna emphasised that the music scene allows girls certain roles – tight pants and vulnerability, with little access to music-making.

The International Pop Underground festival combined Hanna's and Larsen's ideas in an evening called 'Love Rock Revolution Girl Style Now,' an all-girl night that featured many bands already involved in riot grrrl organising, such as Bratmobile and Heavens to Betsy, and side projects from Bikini Kill members Tobi Vail and Kathleen Hanna. Performances throughout the festival reflected the visceral, fiercely amateur aesthetic that had its roots in punk, and that found a revived forcefulness in the passionate and sometimes cacophonous sounds of riot grrrl bands. Headlining an evening of the festival brought visibility to women who shared similar ideologies. But being in a band was not the only way in for women interested in participating in riot grrrl. In fact, in a zine published by Bikini Kill in 1991, Kathleen Hanna writes about reasons 'to be in an all girls band or be a girl in a band':

Riot Grrrl, Ladyfest and Rock Camps for Girls

'- Cuz its fun

- It's a good way to act out behaviours that are wrongly deemed 'inappropriate'

- this is a refutation of censorship and body fascism

- this can deny taboos that keep us enslaved ie. don't talk about sex or rape or be sensitive or corny

- To serve as a role model for other girls

- To show boys other ways of doing things and that we have stuff to say

- To discuss in both literal and artistic ways those issues that're really important to girls

- naming these issues, specifically, validates their importance and other girls' interest in them

- Reminds other girls that they aren't alone

- To make fun of and thus disrupt the powers that be

- It doesn't have to be this intense dramatic self-righteous thing to affect change. It can be fun to talk about scary issues.'

Kathleen Hanna, Bikini Kill A Color and Activity Book 1991

This passage draws the close connections between the activity of playing music and related issues of visibility and voice that were central to riot grrrl rhetoric. Hanna nowhere refers to actually playing music in her 'reasons to be in an all girls band'.

In England, Huggy Bear emerged in 1992 as one of the first bands to embrace and connect with riot grrrl.[8] Like Bikini Kill, this band had a mixed-gender line-up (three women, two men), and their politics resonated with riot grrrl activism and rhetoric. Calling themselves 'boy/girl revolutionaries' they complicated the idea of 'all girl band' even more than did Bikini Kill, which also had a man in the band. Rather than constituting the 'grrrl' band with only biological girls, it was the performance of politics in their music that connected Huggy Bear with their riot grrrl comrades across the Atlantic.

Huggy Bear initially found success in the UK music press, with journalist (and Huggy Bear flatmate) Everett True writing about the band and promoting riot grrrl more generally. However, like riot grrrl in the United States, Huggy Bear soon faced the same dismissal along gender lines, cited as elitist and even contributing to gender inequality in popular music.[9]

Since its inception in the early 1990s, the 'girl band' aspect of riot grrrl has received the most media attention, both in the United States and in the United Kingdom. In a 1992 article in the *New York Times*, Ann Japenga placed Kathleen Hanna and Bikini Kill at the forefront of the riot grrrl movement:

> 'The singer Kathleen Hanna sashayed onto the stage to distribute lyric sheets before a recent Seattle appearance of her band, Bikini Kill. The men in the crowd surged forward, extending their arms to receive the word from this new punk Madonna, with her flailing magenta ponytail and seductive stage manner.
>
> But she slapped the men back. "Girls only," she scolded, putting copies of the lyrics in each upraised female hand. Ms. Hanna's action set the tone for the performance: the band was delivering its wisdom to women, and men had better behave themselves if they wanted to hang around.
>
> Bikini Kill is part of a growing cadre of so-called girl bands that are claiming a place in punk rock. And the rise of groups like Bratmobile, Heavens to Betsy, Mecca Normal and Bikini Kill has inspired a larger movement of feminists in their teens and early 20's who call themselves Riot Grrrls. That's girl with an angry "grrrrowl."'[10]

Japenga's article, among the first mainstream media pieces to cover riot grrrl, offers an initial outsider's view of the movement. Japenga compares Hanna to Madonna, seemingly without irony,[11] and cites her 'seductive stage manner', both of which seem contradictory to the described action of Hanna handing out lyric sheets. In addition to the sensationalistic, star-focused portrayal of riot grrrl, the article provides a few more reasonable tenets that would be repeated throughout media coverage of riot grrrl: 'girls only', 'so-called girl bands', and the idea of a 'larger movement' of young feminists.

As it solidified, however, the mainstream media portrayal of riot grrrl reduced the movement to the bands that offered its most visible representation, often in ways that starkly dismissed their political attributes. In 'Grrrls at War,' a 1993 article in *Rolling Stone*, for example, Kim France conjures the sense of a scene 'catfight' by citing Courtney Love's dismissal of riot grrrl and imagining what other women might feel (without naming them):

> 'Women outside the riot-grrrl camp have complained of a with-us-or-without-us attitude that they find off-putting or sanctimonious. But, no one disagrees that at a time when such strong female musicians as Polly Harvey or Juliana Hatfield vehemently deny that they are feminists, it is important that there are young women who will vehemently assert that they are.'[12]

Despite the hedging tag at the end, the overall impression France gives is a group of women overly occupied with being confrontational, using feminism to demarcate themselves from other women musicians, rather than to build a movement.

The mainstream media portrayal of riot grrrl, however, removed the sense of a larger connection between music and feminist activism that the movement tried to forge: that the music itself was not the only means for creating feminist activism, but part of a larger strategy for fostering 'girl culture'. In her essay 'The Missing Links: Riot grrrl – feminism – lesbian culture' (1997), academic Mary Celeste Kearney has argued that the focus on riot grrrl's punk roots obscures the movement's connections to feminism. Kearney notes that, in the popular media, two main narratives emerged: riot grrrl as girl punks, and riot grrrl as part of a larger 'women in rock' movement. In the *Newsweek* and *Rolling Stone* examples above, both these narratives are present. In contrast, Kearney argues, riot grrrls drew on Second Wave feminism and lesbian separatist ideas, as well as connections with the queercore scene. Kearney writes:

> 'Discursive formulations which position riot grrrl as emerging after and apart from the queercore scene help to reproduce the popular understanding of riot grrrl's members as predominantly straight. Thus, while "girl love" is advocated continuously in riot grrrl music, zines, videos and drawings, its more obvious meaning – lesbianism – has been downplayed, if not outright ignored, in mainstream accounts of this all-girl community.
>
> In an attempt to situate riot grrrls within the larger narrative of homosocial girl cultures, some journalists contextualise the riot grrrl notion of "girl love" as a form of childish play rather than adult sexuality, while others efface the possibility of any homosexual desire or activity amongst riot grrrls by foregrounding the place of boys and heterosexuality in this community.'

Kearney's assessment of riot grrrl's connections to lesbian feminism specifically, and Second Wave feminism more broadly, marks an important departure from the mainstream media portrayal of riot grrrl. While Kearney's presentation of ties between riot grrrl and queercore is absolutely accurate,[13] the idea of homosocial girl culture also simultaneously existed in the music, art, and zines of riot grrrl. Foregrounding idealised relationships between women in much riot grrrl cultural production obfuscated tendentious conflict and the cliquish nature of some riot grrrl organising (see p128 Sara Marcus's *Girls to the Front* as mentioned previously).

Girl bands in punk: exclusions of race, class and sexuality?

Finally, a number of critiques arise from the concept of riot grrrl as a movement of 'girl bands'. As many noted, punk rock at this time and place was a predominantly white, middle class movement. Bikini Kill's 'White Boy' and Heavens to Betsy's 'White Girl' both addressed whiteness and privilege, with the first identifying white, male privilege in the punk scene, and the second calling for self-examination. But, in placing their feminism in punk rock, riot grrrls' message of 'every girl is a riot grrrl' raises questions about exclusions of race, class and sexuality.

Feminist scholars Kristin Schilt (2005), Mary Celeste Kearney (2006) and Mimi Nguyen (2010) have all critiqued the ways that riot grrrl addressed class and race. Both Kearney (2006) and Schilt (2004) argue that, in addition to the boundaries of genre, riot grrrl activities, from playing music to making zines, require both free time and money for instruments or photocopying, making them less accessible to girls below the middle class.

In addition to her critique of the class aspects of zine-making, Schilt specifically addresses (see p48) the ways that zine writers confronted their white privilege, describing them as 'token':

> 'There is frequently an element of power evasion, in which some zine makers recognise the privilege inherent in being white but refrain from discussing what it means.'

Similarly, Nguyen argues (see p5-9 for the following quotes) that riot grrrl zines by white women often repeat problematic tropes of intimacy, confession and absolution:

> 'The white person offers to embrace the person of colour as proof of the former's goodness. The presumption is that intimacy is a pathway to a good relationship is the pathway to justice'.

Nguyen points out, women of colour who responded through their own zines often received negative responses in return:

> 'Critiques of access and intimacy as necessary social goods were often met with accusations of invalidating and more fundamentally, of violating the intimate principle of girl love.'

Most importantly, Nguyen expresses concern that:

> 'Riot grrrl retrospectives will take the form of a story of the loss of a more utopian moment of feminist intimacy, into which race is either a disruption (bad) or an intervention (feeling bad to assure that we are good) and otherwise contained as such.'

However, after the riot grrrl media blackout (in which many riot grrrls refused to speak to the press whom they felt were disorting the riot grrrl message)[14] and after the mainstream media moved on to other 'angry women,'[15] many girls maintained the 'girl culture' of riot grrrl in zines, in bands and through feminist activism. Ongoing activism and cultural production within these groups retained a central focus on women's visibility in music scenes and women's community through music-making. The next part of this chapter examines two subsequent manifestations of this activism, Ladyfest and rock camps for girls. The intervening years between the florescence of riot grrrl and these movements saw the rise of the internet, as well as significant changes in the relationship of underground, punk cultures such as riot grrrl to the mainstream. The deterioration of the mainstream record industry, and the increased globalisation of communication tools gave rise to an environment in which some ideas that found voice in riot grrrl transformed into models that became accessible in diverse geographic and cultural locations.

'Calling all ladies'

At once a festival that looked backward for inspiration and forward in an almost utopian experiment of constructing community, Ladyfest reinserted feminist politics into an indie-rock music scene and raised questions about what that feminism might look like in a post-riot grrrl era. In 1999, as part of its introductory exhibit on riot grrrl, the Experience Music Project conducted oral history interviews in Olympia.[16] Allison Wolfe, lead singer of Bratmobile, participated in the interviews, and, afterward, she talked with some of the women involved in the riot grrrl retrospective, as well as women who had since moved to Olympia, about the need for continuing feminist activism. Soon, Wolfe put out a call for a meeting with the idea of organising a festival – a 'lady' fest – and, eventually, more than fifty women joined the organising committees.[17] The festival set out to organise a gathering, much in the spirit of the original riot grrrl conventions that had taken place through the 1990s, which included not only musical performance, but art shows/performances, films and workshops on subjects such as self-defence, feminist politics, and strategies for creative feminist action.

Inspired by an already-settling nostalgia for the riot grrrl movement and tapping into the popularity of Olympia's Sleater-Kinney, the festival sold out and raised more than $30,000, which was donated to two non-profit organisations. In 2000, Sleater-Kinney was one of the most critically acclaimed rock bands around. In 'Olympia Ladystyle', an article about the festival published August 7th that year in *Time* magazine, writer Benjamin Nugent waxed effusively:

> 'Journalists routinely describe them as the world's greatest rock 'n' roll band, a tag once reserved for the Stones.'

Sleater-Kinney's musical style bridged riot grrrl and the indie rock of the 2000s. Corin Tucker's and Carrie Brownstein's duelling, polyphonic guitars departed from both punk rock predecessors and Corin Tucker's voice developed into one of the most distinctive in rock. The recognition that Sleater-Kinney received no doubt helped create a draw for the festival. However, beyond that band, the first Ladyfest featured some of the most popular 'girl bands' of the 1990s and early 2000s as organisers and performers, including The Gossip, Neko Case, Bangs, Slumber Party, Sarah Dougher, Bratmobile and Tracy + the Plastics. Some of these bands, like The Gossip, were relatively new, but would gain increasing prominence throughout the 2000s. The Gossip's singer, Beth Ditto, added a soulful howl over Nathan Howdeshell's sparse, jagged guitar and Kathy Mendonca's drums. As the decade progressed, The Gossip – especially Beth Ditto – became increasingly outspoken on LGBTQ issues, reframing the concerns of the 'girl band' in a way that more visibly highlighted issues of sexuality. And groups such as Tracy + The Plastics reframed the 'girl band' entirely: each member of the group (Tracy and her two backup singers, Nikki and Cola) was performed by the group's creator, video artist Wynne Greenwood.

If the festival had merely ended, its success would nonetheless be remarkable; however, after tickets sold out, organisers promoted another idea to those unable to attend: start your own Ladyfest. That call has been answered nearly 200 times, in cities in the United States, Canada, Europe, South America, South Africa, Australia and New Zealand.

Riot Grrrl, Ladyfest and Rock Camps for Girls

While the first Ladyfest offered personal, philosophical and political ties to riot grrrl, its successors brought an expansion of politics and musical styles, a tangle of local issues and concerns and numerous debates about what constitutes a 'girl band'. In its expansions, the festival foregrounded concerns about race, sexuality and gender that first emerged in riot grrrl, but now drew on different politics, such as intersectional feminisms, queer politics and trans politics. How could the festival create a sense of relevance in places that had histories of racial division, with genres that appealed to mostly white, middle class listeners? How could white women acknowledge the contributions of women of colour as fellow organisers, musicians and volunteers without rendering them as either token participants or as invisible? How did a commitment to trans inclusion affect the concept of the 'girl band'? Over the next ten years, each Ladyfest addressed these issues.

Ladyfest – the term and its boundaries

The initial debate about the name 'Ladyfest' helps to position the festival in relation to the changing politics of the Third Wave and raises some issues about the ongoing concerns for successive festivals about intersectional identity.[19] When Allison Wolfe introduced the name 'Ladyfest' in an email invitation to the first festival's planning meetings, she thought the name would be ironic, funny and flip. As she explained in an interview for this book (April 10th 2012):

> 'I grew up in the 70s and 80s, and I didn't have the pressures some older women had or have to deal with the classist implications of the word. To me, it was such a funny word. I really just like to reclaim words that are feminine, yet sort of derogatory … I think it's cool and empowering for women to do that.'

After the first meeting, though, some of the women were less certain they wanted to be involved with a festival called 'Ladyfest 2000'. Almost universally, these women brought up concerns of the race and class privilege of being a 'lady'. Although the organisers interviewed for this chapter voiced differing opinions on this point, they generally acknowledged that the word implies a person who is polite, tame, consumer-oriented, sexually passive, white and wealthy.[20] In using this word, 'ladies' attempt to subvert these meanings, but sometimes retain problematic overtones, especially as the first Ladyfest included predominantly white, indie rock and punk artists.[21]

Though the word 'lady' held problematic overtones of race and class, the festival played a role in opening the term 'lady' to queer sexuality.[22] In 2000, 'ladies' were everywhere, from Mr. Lady records, to Kaia Wilson's solo album *Ladyman*, to Sleater-Kinney's 'Ballad of a Ladyman'. In 'Grrrl, You'll Be a Lady Soon', a 2001 'On Language'[23] column in *Bitch* magazine, Rachel Fudge writes that the reclamation of 'lady' opens up a space to redefine gender and sexuality within a punk rock context.[24]

At Ladyfest, punk and indie rock bands often share space with burlesque performers, drag kings, and queer spoken word acts, while workshops highlight issues of gender and sexuality, ranging from 'Trans 202' to 'Coming Out to Your Parents.'[25] Audience members, too, help shape the 'lady' in Ladyfest. At the first festival, for example, attendees queered the name of the festival when they created a personals/'missed connections' bulletin board titled 'Ladyquest'. For organisers of the first Ladyfest, then, the decision to use the term 'lady' helped to reframe the word much more along lines of sexuality than race or class, both in terms of the festival's musicians and audiences.

For subsequent festivals, however, acknowledging the shortcomings of the indie rock scene for fostering an inclusive, feminist space became a greater issue.[26] Many organisers were aware of critiques of Second Wave feminism by feminists of colour,[27] but actively integrating women of colour and keeping to the concept of 'girl bands' became much more difficult. In Philadelphia in 2003, organisers initially hoped their planning committee would reflect the population of the city.[28] But they had posted fliers in typical indie-rock hangouts, like coffee shops and record stores, which had mostly white, middle-class clientele. According to Philadelphia organiser Laura,[29] the group's expectations crashed as they realised the difficulty of fostering an inclusive community:

> 'When we started it, we were like, this will be the only Ladyfest ever that's not all white girls. We're going to Philly it up. There's going to be hip-hop, all this stuff. It's going to be so much fun. And soon, we have sixty members, and they're all pretty much middle-class, white girls. And so, we had a debate about outreach versus tokenisation, and if we should even do outreach on certain things, like to try to get a different demographic, is that fucked up too?'[30]

When white organisers moved beyond music, they were able to connect with women of colour more easily. In Philadelphia, 'It's really not that hard to diversify the spoken-word committee,' Laura said, because that thriving scene crossed lines of race. Music, however, presented a series of challenges, both in terms of race and in terms of gender. In genres like hip-hop, the organisers had trouble finding women MCs and DJs who weren't part of a larger, male-dominated crew.

The issue of gender itself – is a 'girl band' by necessity an *all*-girl band? – arose in nearly every iteration of the festival. At the first Ladyfest, organisers decided only women could be organisers and volunteers, and bands required a majority of women musicians. Subsequent festivals, however, have struggled to define what a 'girl band' and what a 'Lady'fest could be in scenes that were more heavily male-dominated.

Women Make Noise

Ladyfest*East 2001 in New York City featured both female and male volunteers and bands that were all-male save for a frontwoman; the organisers of Ladyfest*East 2002 debated, but decided against, letting male bands perform at the festival if they identified as feminist. Other festivals have addressed the issue of the 'girl band' in ways that address not just composition of the band, but the position that women occupy within it. Ladyfest Olympia 2005 organisers decided that 'girl bands' meant bands with a majority of women, but also promoted a 'drummer showcase' that highlighted women performing one of the most stereotypically masculine roles in a band. Policies for male inclusion give one idea of how Third Wave feminists negotiate the idea of a 'girl space' while not maintaining a completely separatist festival.

While lesbian separatism and gender-segregated feminist consciousness-raising no doubt influenced the grrrls-only space of riot grrrl, changing ideas of the intersection of gender and sexuality have influenced the more fluid policies of Ladyfests. In particular, the growing prominence of transgender participants in queer communities has shaped the idea of who can or should attend, perform in, or organise a women's music festival. While transgender participation at Ladyfest has been much less a controversy than at festivals that practiced and enforced gender separatism,[31] the various permutations of transgender policies at Ladyfest indicate how participants conceive of a 'girl band' in alliance with transgender communities. Many Ladyfest trans policies respond to the controversy arising from the 'womyn-born-womyn' policy of the Michigan Womyn's Music Festival, the United States' largest and longest-running lesbian-separatist music festival, held every year since 1976. In the late 1990s and early 2000s, the MWMF's 'womyn-born-womyn' policy, which excluded transwomen, resulted in protests, most notably Camp Trans, and a boycott of Mr. Lady Records artists who participated in the festival. In response, most Ladyfests developed policies that support trans inclusion but do not boycott artists who perform at the MWMF festival.[32]

As transmen have become a growing population within queer women's communities, the question of who can be a 'Lady' sometimes becomes part of the discussion. Ladyfest Bay Area 2002's mission statement stated:

> 'Ladyfest Bay Area is a non-profit, community-based event organised by volunteers, both women and trans-identified, to showcase, celebrate, and encourage the artistic, organisational, and political achievements of self-identified women'

and goes on to note that it will be a 'safe space' for 'pro-women people of all genders' to attend.[33] Additionally, in its 'Why We Are' section, the festival cited a petition against the MWMF's policy and then specifically invited trans participation:

> 'The exclusion of past, present, and future women from the centres of cultural production has left few points of entry for alternative representations of women. Even within ostensibly "safe" and "woman-only" spaces, some individuals have felt isolated, excluded, or silenced as a result of their race, class status, gender identification, sexual orientation, and/or physical characteristics... Ladyfest Bay Area seeks to capitalise on the incredible diversity of female talent, skill, activism and expression already thriving in our community ... As part of this mission, we actively involve transgendered youth and young women in all areas of the festival, from planning and organising to performing and participating in workshops and events.'[34]

In this policy, Ladyfest Bay Area organisers open the space to transwomen and transmen, a marker of a more flexible notion of gender identity.[35] But, at the same time, the festival organisers indicate that they take seriously the idea of the 'safe space' that the MWMF originally intended – but this 'safe space' now includes trans participants.[36]

Finally, as Ladyfest has become an increasingly international festival, it has also become, paradoxically, an increasingly *local* festival: the first Ladyfest served as a marker of the vitality of women musicians in the Pacific Northwest, but subsequent iterations of the festival have been much more about fostering local scenes, showcasing local women musicians, and connecting with local politics. The balance between fostering a local scene and creating ties to other Ladyfests often raises the question among many festival organisers concerning whether they should splurge on a national act or concentrate on promoting awareness of local musicians. During the course of Elizabeth Keenan's fieldwork with US Ladyfest organisers from 2002-2005, organisers almost always mentioned Sleater-Kinney, The Gossip and Le Tigre as 'Ladyfest' bands, or dream bands that symbolised the national feminist music scene that they wished to tap into and cultivate in their own towns. The reality of festival budgets meant that few festivals could afford these acts.[37]

The local nature of the festival, though, offers opportunities to foster an ongoing sense of a girl-band oriented music scene in many places. The idea that each Ladyfest offers an opportunity for women to learn new organisational skills, book shows and promote bands continues the riot grrrl tradition of DIY in a real, community-oriented sense. That new Ladyfests continue to emerge speaks to the ongoing need for women involved in punk and indie scenes around the world to continue to foreground the 'all girl' band, in an effort to recognise women's contributions to music scenes and to find community with each other. It is important to note that Ladyfest has existed alongside other feminist and queer punk festivals throughout its twelve-year existence. Scholar Marion

Riot Grrrl, Ladyfest and Rock Camps for Girls

Leonard notes that in her conversations with organisers from Ladyfest Manchester (2003), they suggest that they have also been involved with events such as Sheila Autonomista (in Sydney, Australia), Queeruption (held in various cities starting in 1998), and Frock On in Glasgow.[38] The local, grassroots organisation and ongoing interest in putting a punk-influenced feminism into action is evident as Ladyfests continue to be presented around the world. The impetus for a more sustained effort to influence local musical culture on behalf of women and girls has also emerged in the form of rock camps for girls, which share many of the same values and personnel as Ladyfests, with an emphasis on permanent and ongoing educational and community-building systems.

All-girl band, all-girl camp: rock camps for girls

The concept for an all-girl rock 'n' roll camp was developed by a Women's Studies major named Misty McElroy at Portland State University as her senior research project and was first implemented in 2001. The idea of an all-girl camp as a place where girls could have an empowering experience is certainly not new, although notions of 'empowerment' (and, indeed, the cultural definitions of girlhood) have changed significantly since all-girl camps first became a part of American life. Summer camps emerged in the United States in the early 20th century as an antidote to the problems of the industrialised cities of the East Coast; sending girls into nature was thought to improve health and promote self-reliance, while also teaching them social acculturation and good citizenship.[39] Going to camp meant leaving one's day-to-day life and participating in adventure and girls' camps created a safe place for transgression from prevailing gender ideologies. For example, girls could learn to take physical risks, make noise or assert leadership. Although now, as Paris notes, attending camp is 'no longer the challenge to gender conventions that

279

it once was' (see Forman-Brunell, 2001), the Rock 'n' Roll Camp for Girls (RnRC4G) was developed in response to what the founder perceived as prevailing discrimination against girls and women in both the music industry and the culture at large. McElroy developed a camp that not only taught girls how to play music together, but also offered them a range of Third-Wave feminist-inspired activities, such as self-defence and zine-making, which were designed to help them both articulate and address their own oppression both as girls and as girl musicians.

Single-sex activities and learning

This idea of a separate place populated only by girls and women was powerful for the activists who first volunteered at the Portland camp. The single-sex environment removed the competition for and attention from boys, dramatically decreasing the conscious performance of normative gender roles, particularly for teenagers, who make up roughly half the camp's population. The single-sex environment meant that the bands formed at rock camp are necessarily 'all-girl'. The all-girl environment of rock camp is, like the girls' camp at the turn of the 20th century, a fantasy leisure space removed from the outside world that creates a safe environment for what would otherwise be seen as transgressive, non-gender conforming behaviour.

The RnRC4G can be seen as an articulation of girlhood studies, Third Wave feminist activism and its attendant manifestation in punk, aka riot grrrl. 'Girlhood studies', a branch of feminist scholarship emerging in the late 20th century, was awash with ideas regarding the continuing bias against girls in education, despite the gains achieved as a result of feminist activism of the 1960s and 70s. Works such as the American Association of University Women's study, *Shortchanging Girls, Shortchanging America* (1991) and Peggy

Riot Grrrl, Ladyfest and Rock Camps for Girls

Orenstein's 1994 book *Schoolgirls: Young Women, Self-Esteem and the Confidence Gap* describe the ways in which girls' self-esteem begins to diminish once they reach adolescence, and how education and culture at large 'often unwittingly – inhibits, restricts, diminishes and denies girls' experience'.[40] Mary Pipher's influential work, *Reviving Ophelia* was also released in 1994. These works recognised that although the promise of the women's movement had positively impacted women's lives, girls (and particularly adolescent girls) still faced sexism in their private and public lives.

Another issue at the origins of girls' rock camps is consciousness of the roles for women and girls in popular music, and a desire to shift these roles to more active participation, or even a conscious rebellion towards commodification of their gendered selves, a basic feminist media studies approach that was very much part of the riot grrrl critique of mainstream cultural production. In the introduction to their documentary-style book on the Portland camp, the RnRC4G (Rock 'n' Roll Camp For Girls) programme director writes:

> 'In the year 2000, Janis Joplin was the first female artist mentioned on VH1's *100 Greatest Artists of Hard Rock*. Janis broke into the list at number 48, followed by five other female artists. Six women, surrounded by ninety-four male artists.'[41]

This example belies the rock camp's tendency to champion DIY and guitar-based music over its pop counterpart. Mainstream, pop-oriented girl groups like the Spice Girls were generally viewed by camp organisers as a capitalist perversion of the 'girl power' message. With Britney Spears in ascent, and Hannah Montana not even a glimmer in Disney's eye, representation of girls and women playing music (especially musical instruments) had all but disappeared from the mainstream by 2001. RnRC4G acted as a corrective:

in Portland, the walls of the base camp where it's held are covered with murals and posters of women musicians, and most manifestations of the camps include a workshop on 'Women Who Rock', situating musical foremothers as the centre of inquiry and as role models for the young musicians. Most camps also invite local female musicians to come in and perform for the girls. The motto that 'you can't be what you can't see' holds a strong sway at most camps.

You can't be what you can't see: keeping women musicians visible

The creation of the RnRC4G was and remains influenced by riot grrrl ideology and the networks of women who were involved with riot grrrl, who went on to form bands, create zines and artwork and found record labels in women's music scenes in the Pacific Northwest. A June 2011 *New York Times* feature on riot grrrl nostalgia quotes Bikini Kill frontwoman Kathleen Hanna describing rock camps for girls 'the most lasting legacy of riot grrrl' ('A Feminist Riot That Still Inspires' Ryzik, Melena *New York Times,* June 5th, 2011). While correctly identifying that there are in fact cultural and political connections between riot grrrl and rock camps for girls, including women involved with riot grrrl who are involved with rock camps including Hanna herself, these camps emerged in a complex socio-political environment where concern for, and cultivation of, the girl's voice was a central project.[42] Other well-known women musicians involved with rock camps include Corin Tucker and Carrie Brownstein (of Sleater-Kinney), Beth Ditto (of The Gossip) and Sara Bareilles.

In describing the merits of a single-sex environment to their volunteers, the RnRCFG asks, and then answers the important question, 'Why a Rock 'n' Roll Camp for Girls?':

Riot Grrrl, Ladyfest and Rock Camps for Girls

'We want to eradicate all the limiting myths about music and gender that make girls afraid to speak up, sing out and make noise. We want to abolish all the obsolete traditions that restrict many girls' and women's free musical expression and obstruct their access to the world of music. We seek to demonstrate – through lessons, mentorship, positive examples, and the shared experiences of the staff and volunteers – that every genre of music from the heaviest to the most delicate, and every technical job and creative endeavour in the music industry, is available to any girl or woman who wants to explore it … We believe that by teaching these things, we can help girls develop – musically, mentally, and emotionally – toward their own ideas of who and what they want to be.'

RnRC4G Volunteer Handbook v 3.0, 2007, p.4

The ideal outcome for a rock camper is not only to attain some level of skill with their instrument, but also to participate in a community of girls and women and emerge as a self-actualised being. At the RnRC4G, many girls come with little to no experience with the instruments that they encounter at camp. They have small-group instrument instruction that often serves as a rudimentary introduction to noisy, amplified music. They also form bands with others their own age, in an exercise designed to help girls define and ask for what they want in a band and bandmates. Working with adult mentors, the bands collaborate to write an original song and practice it for a cacophonous end-of-camp celebration/rock show in front of friends, family and the general public. Girls may attend workshops about self-defence, image and identity, media literacy and zine-making. These activities foreground the connections that rock camps have with riot grrrl culture. Volunteers and staff who were interviewed in 2010 were usually familiar with riot grrrl, but also recognise the limitations both the politics of this music and the music itself have in connecting with girls at camp. The punk, amateur aesthetic so widely prevalent in riot grrrl music is nearly absent in the mainstream culture that campers have access to before coming to camp, and the confrontational political engagements that constituted riot grrrl demand a level of maturity not all campers have. One volunteer, in an interview for this book, noted:

> 'We recognise that only a small percentage of our campers identify with [riot grrrl] culture or are interested in it, so it doesn't make much sense for us to emphasise those politics, since the goal is to build confidence using music, any music, all music, not just the music we like.'

This sentiment is particularly pertinent for girls who are participating in camps in urban areas where the dominant popular music is mainstream hip-hop. At some camps, like the Willie Mae Rock Camp for Girls in New York, the majority of campers are girls of colour, while the majority of staff and volunteers are white women. The conflict between riot grrrl-style empowerment narratives and the kind of music that girls who come to camp actually like[43] is most often resolved by invoking the camp rule that you can't dismiss other girl/women musicians. Even this rule demonstrates the ideological connections between riot girrl thought and the camps' central mission. Writing twenty years ago, Bikini Kill member and prolific feminist writer Tobi Vail stated in her 1991 zine *Jigsaw*:

> 'This is all about making the transformation from being an object that is acted upon to becoming a subject that is an active participant in the world ... To incite participation in punk rock for girls – one form of girl culture – is to politically mobilise them for the real work of the rest of their lives.' *The Jigsaw Manifesto' Jigsaw 4, Summer 199*

Riot Grrrl, Ladyfest and Rock Camps for Girls

For rock campers, the 'real work of the rest of their lives' is not a foregone conclusion. In the current cultural climate where fewer and fewer women (or men) self-identify as feminists, rock camps tread a fine line between doing explicitly political work and couching their feminist ideology within the more acceptable (to parents/funders) rhetoric of girls' empowerment. In her work on rock camps, Danielle Giffort identifies the idea of 'implicit feminism' to describe:

> '...a strategy practiced by feminist activists within organisations that are operating in an anti- and post-feminist environment in which they conceal feminist identities and ideas while emphasizing the more socially acceptable angles of their efforts.'

Her field work reveals the tensions organisers have between their own personal politics and creative expressions, and the front they need to put up in order to run a summer camp, paid for by parental funds and private and foundation dollars. Within the everyday language of the camp, feminist ideas are not explicitly expressed; within the day-to-day activities of the camp, however, girls are taught resistance to pervading (male-dominated) systems within music, including that they can in fact be cultural producers, not simply consumers.

Rock camps now

In the ten years since the Portland camp was founded, there have been significant changes in both the landscape of popular music, and the mainstream messages about girls and music that girls get from school, their families, the internet and the radio. Disney pop princesses have emerged, generating information and images about girls and music across a wide swathe of media and featuring artists such as Hannah Montana and Lizzie McGuire. Born into a complex media environment of ever-increasing interactivity, they deliver both product and messaging that is attractive to many tween girls, and at times both welcome and problematic to their parents. Disney and other child-oriented channels/entertainment conglomerates have created stars with accompanying vehicle-shows. These TV programmes highlight the value of being an 'ordinary' girl at the same time as being a 'rock star,' fictionalising both ordinariness and fame, putting a new twist on the idea of doing it 'yourself' and 'discovery' of the magical (rock) star/princess inside of the regular girl.

Such representations simultaneously ask girls to question who the 'self' is (ordinary girl or pop star), and gives very little actual information about what it might take to actually achieve notoriety as a musician, and what the consequences of such an outcome might be,[44] failing to provide realistic portrayals of the lives of working professional musicians, most of whom are not 'stars' by any standards, but rather working class or middle class people. With a few significant exceptions, these stars are also all solo singers who generally do not play any instruments.

Additionally, as scholar Diane Pecknold noted in her paper 'The Jonas Brothers Are Dorky and Miley Cyrus Is a Slut: Gender, Power and Money in the Disney Ghetto', presented at the Experience Music Project Pop Conference, 2011:

> 'Girls are, proportionally, a more important target constituency for the music industry in large part because the rest of that constituency has abandoned the industry. In 2006, the RIAA estimated that, between 1995 and 2005, recorded music sales to 10-14 year-olds increased from 7.9% of the overall market to 8.6%, which is not as game-changing as the fact that sales to 15-19 year-olds during the same time dropped more than 5 percentage points, and sales to 20-24 year-olds dropped as well.'

This figure, rather than reflecting the increased buying power of children, reflects the buying habits of their parents or other adults *for* them.

What is the impact of these significant changes on the growth and expansion of rock camps around the world? Like Ladyfest, rock camps became an idea whose structure was rapidly copied by communities of feminist musicians and activists throughout the United States and internationally, a phenomenon made possible in large part because of internet communications. The rock camp model is appealing not just to musicians, but to activists who are interested in gender-segregated educational environments with DIY-values. In 2011, there are more than forty camps worldwide, independent from one another, but affiliated through the Girls Rock Camp Alliance. The camp in Portland serves over 500 girls each year through their camps and after-school programmes. In keeping with the aims for creating mentor relationships between girls and women musicians, only women are allowed to work with girls, and with very few exceptions, the camp environment is all female. The separatist ideas of riot grrrl – the idea of a 'girl gang' – still dominate the ideology of the camp at the same time that staff and volunteers negotiate changes in the knowledge and aesthetics of their campers, as well as the social realities that girls face in their 'real' lives.

Tracing the legacy of riot grrrl, Ladyfest and rock camps for girls

The legacy of these movements can be seen in the ongoing and ever-changing forms of music-related feminist activism available in many communities in the US and the UK, with even more resources available on the internet. According to a recent internet search, 2012 will see Ladyfests happening in Tallinn, Estonia, Boston, MA, and Brighton UK. Others have adapted the grassroots cultural festival in other ways to challenge sexism, homophobia and racism. For instance C.L.I.T Fest (Combating Latent Inequality Together) an annual US-based hardcore punk festival (see chapter 8 on hardcore) aims to combine 'music and education to challenge patriarchal oppression in punk'.[45] Founded in Olympia, WA in 2002, Homo a Go Go took inspiration for its name from the indie rock festival Yoyo a Go Go, which started there in 1994, but also incorporated the non-profit, grassroots organized structure of Ladyfest.

The latest iteration of the festival took place in 2009 in San Francisco, and featured queer-centric music, film, fashion, crafts, spoken word, visual arts and activist-focused workshops. A festival that had its fourth year in 2011 is the FABULOSA festival, which bills itself as a non-profit fundraiser for LGBTQ charities that serve youth in Northern California, and which takes place on a ranch forty-five miles north of San Francisco. An overnight, camping-style event modelled more closely on traditional women's music festivals, attendees can expect 'the time of their lives swimming, canoeing, hiking, attending yoga and other classes and workshops, shopping in the craft market, jamming around the campfire and dancing in the barn.[46] The music at FABULOSA falls more squarely on the queer indie rock spectrum, featuring artists such as Mirah, Phranc, Erase Erata and Gretchen Phillips. Billed as an 'inclusive retreat for all ages and genders,' the majority of attendees are women and identify as lesbian and/or queer.

Rock Camps for Girls have now spread around the world, and are loosely organised by the Girls' Rock Camp Alliance. Holding an annual conference for new as well as seasoned rock camp organisers, the Alliance is made up of camps at all stages of development. Rock camps are not only a place where girls can learn how to play music, but generally offer many opportunities for volunteers to become involved. Sometimes, rock campers graduate into leadership positions of instrument instructor or band coach once they are too old to attend.

The rock camp model is a flexible one and takes on forms unique to the communities they serve. A good resource to see what camp is like is the 2009 documentary, 'Girls Rock! The Movie,' or the book *Rock 'n' Roll Camp for Girls: How to Start a Band, Write Songs, Record an Album and Rock Out!* (ed. Marisa Anderson, 2008).

Finally, in addition to the archival projects that insert riot grrrl into a variety of academic and artistic institutions in the US, a number of other recent riot grrrl-oriented projects are directed at a wider audience. Film-maker Sini Anderson's *The Punk Singer: The Kathleen Hanna Documentary* is scheduled for release in 2012. This film project has a substantial online presence, including a website where fans have posted their own videos about Hanna. Additionally, a Wiki-style blog archive about Bikini Kill at bikinikillarchive.wordpress.com serves to chronicle the band's years and to engage with old and new fans. But beyond the nostalgia surrounding riot grrrl at the moment of writing this, it's important to account for differences both within riot grrrl and between girls (and women) in music. In a 2011 article on Pitchfork.com, 'Not Every Girl Is a Riot Grrrl', Lindsay Zoladz interviewed a number of women musicians about the tendency to conflate women in punk and indie rock into the riot grrrl figure. Zoladz's overarching thesis – that today's women in punk and indie feel constrained by the riot grrrl label – serves to highlight one of the major goals of this chapter and this book. Not every girl *is* a riot grrrl, but that doesn't displace riot grrrl's importance. Rather, it indicates that women – and girls – can make noise in a variety of ways.

Looking forward

Each of these movements – riot grrrl, Ladyfest, and rock camps – gave girls and women new opportunities to be participants and musical creators by drawing on DIY and feminist ideas. Riot grrrl's legacy continues to inspire new generations of grrrls to play music, while Ladyfest and rock camps both give dedicated space to their activities. The sustained efforts by girls and women to make social change happen through musical practice has been profoundly influenced by each of these movements. They each have a unique, on-going significance for participants, who continue to build feminist music communities both in their own towns and cities, and increasingly through connected international networks.

Although it is tempting to view these three movements in a causal relationship to each other (riot grrrl spawned Ladyfest and then rock camps), in part because they share basic ideologies and often personnel, they each evolved with differing goals and in different moments, and they each have a different take on what an 'all-girl band' looks like.

Riot grrrl found its energy primarily in small community formations that were loosely connected and sustained by pen-pal relationships and punk booking networks. Riot grrrl's concept of the 'all-girl band' is situated in a broad context of self expression through a variety of media, and within riot grrrl's origins of resistance within progressive, yet still sexist punk scenes. Ladyfest was a music festival model that depended heavily on the internet as a mechanism for spreading practical planning information and marketing the festival. The broad geographic range, and often very local set of concerns creates a role for the 'all-girl band' within Ladyfest culture that, by necessity, had to remain flexible for each community's needs. The founders of girls' rock camps utilised theories of adolescent girlhood emergent in the early 2000s, and the camps were devised as permanent institutions meant to empower girls using music education, with a heavy reliance on parents and outside funding for support. The sex-segregated learning environment creates a space where the band is *de facto* an all girl band, made up of members who are taught that the music industry and the wider culture do not value their expressive voices.

Riot Grrrl, Ladyfest and Rock Camps for Girls

These phenomena share diverse gestures of self-definition and the goal of activation and expressive personal liberation. The overriding aim is the same: to encourage more women and girls to play more music.

Contributor biographies

Sarah Dougher was active as a musician in the late 1990s and early 2000s in Portland, Oregon and put music out both as a solo artist and in the bands the Lookers, Cadallaca and the Crabs (records were released on K, Kill Rock Stars and Mr. Lady). Although she was not involved with riot grrrl, she helped organise the first Ladyfest in 2000 and was very involved with the development of the Rock Camp for Girls in its first years (she still volunteers at the camp). Her research now is focused on contemporary tween music-making and consumption, and she teaches the history of women and popular music at Portland State University.

Elizabeth K. Keenan first heard about Ladyfest when a band in her master's thesis attended the first Ladyfest in Olympia, and, within a year, she began volunteering for Ladyfest*East in New York City. For her dissertation, she conducted long-term, ethnographic research on Ladyfests in New York, Seattle, and San Francisco, and interviewed organisers from around the world. Since finishing her dissertation, her research has expanded to cover a wide variety of issues, from the historiography of popular music to masculinity in indie rock. Elizabeth plays bass in the NYC indie rock band Faulkner Detectives.

Epilogue: Pussy Riot and the Future

Julia Downes

Women Make Noise offers up a challenge to the argument that the lack of all-girl bands in popular music is because there are simply no 'great' all-girl bands. This book has traced the lived experiences of the all-girl band throughout different genres and environments. Women and girls have found opportunities throughout history to make music together and become skilled musicians, political activists, savvy businesswomen and influential cultural icons. The all-girl band has been and still is a vital strategy for women and girls to claim cultural authority and seize power. However, we have also seen that the all-girl band can provoke contempt particularly if and when women and girls step out of line of the conventional social order. To manage this threat, the all-girl band has been reduced to a novelty, a sex-object, a commercial gesture and a side-note to the 'real' music-making of men. This book has paid particular attention to radical all-girl bands that have used music as a political tool to fight against oppressive actions of dominant regimes and ongoing sexism, racism, classism and homophobia. From the rejection of marriage in pre-feminist 1920s America, punk women's ridicule of British conservative femininities, critiques of patriarchy and militarism in the Women's Liberation Movement, to radical sexualities in queercore, women and girls have a legacy of using music to critically engage with the world around them and fight for social justice.

Women and girls can face punishment for challenging the legitimacy of white masculine elite authorities and interrupting power. One recent example of this continuation of all-girl music collective and social change is Pussy Riot. Pussy Riot formed in Moscow during September 2011 when Vladimir Putin announced his intention to stand for office in the March 2012 presidential elections. The all-woman anonymous feminist punk collective used brightly coloured balaclavas to protect their identities at guerrilla public performances of their punk protest songs. They documented their performances and posted photos and videos online.[1] Pussy Riot performed in various public places around Moscow including metro stations, car showrooms, fashion shows and a detention centre. The political agenda of Pussy Riot fights for freedom from the harmful policies and practices of a Putin-led corporate state dependent on capitalism, patriarchy, conventional morality and social inequalities. As the elections loomed closer Pussy Riot's performances took place in increasingly politically significant public spaces. On January 20th 2012 Pussy Riot performed 'Putin Pissed Himself' on the Lobnoye Mesto in Red Square. This stone platform was used in the Middle Ages to announce the Tsar's laws and to sentence criminals. On February 21st 2012, Pussy Riot performed 'Punk Prayer' in the Orthodox Catholic Christ the Saviour Cathedral. Performing in their trademark brightly coloured clothes and balaclavas the women listed various harmful policies of Putin's government on Russia's citizens, highlighted the use of orthodox religion to bolster Putin's power and appealed to the Virgin Mary to become a feminist and get Putin out:

'Virgin Mary, Mother of God, banish Putin, banish Putin,
Virgin Mary, Mother of God, banish him, we pray thee!
Congregations genuflect,

Black robes brag gilt epaulettes,
Freedom's phantom's gone to heaven,
Gay Pride's chained and in detention.
KGB's chief saint descends
To guide the punks to prison vans.
Don't upset His Saintship, ladies,
Stick to making love and babies.
Crap, crap, this godliness crap!
Crap, crap, this holiness crap!
Virgin Mary, Mother of God.
Be a feminist, we pray thee,
Be a feminist, we pray thee.
Bless our festering bastard-boss.
Let black cars parade the Cross.
The Missionary's in class for cash.
Meet him there, and pay his stash.
Patriarch Gundy believes in Putin.
Better believe in God, you vermin!
Fight for rights, forget the rite –
Join our protest, Holy Virgin.
Virgin Mary, Mother of God, banish Putin, banish Putin,
Virgin Mary, Mother of God, we pray thee, banish him!'[2]

Three members of Pussy Riot, Maria Alyokhina, Nadezhda Tolokonnikova & Yekaterina Samutsevich, were arrested shortly after, and were tried and found guilty of hooliganism motivated by religious hatred on August 17th 2012.[3] Accordingly, Pussy Riot made the song 'Putin Lights Up The Fires' available online that same day.[4] At the time of writing Maria, Nadezhda and Yekaterina are currently serving a two year prison sentence and the Russian authorities are searching for the remaining members.[5] In her final statement Nadsezhda explained why Pussy Riot used punk music as political activism:

Epilogue: Pussy Riot and the Future

'Pussy Riot's performances can either be called dissident
art or political action that engages art forms. Either way,
our performances are a kind of civic activity amidst
the repressions of a corporate political system that
directs its power against basic human rights and civil
and political liberties. The young people who have
been flayed by the systematic eradication of freedoms
perpetrated through the aughts have now risen against
the state. We were searching for real sincerity and
simplicity, and we found these qualities in the *yurodstvo*
[the holy foolishness] of punk.'[6]

The case has provoked an international outcry from artists
including Bjork, Madonna, Patti Smith, Kathleen Hanna,
Peaches and Kate Nash. Identifying the women as fellow
radical performers the slogan 'We are all Pussy Riot' gained
momentum. Numerous petitions, protests, days of solidarity,
fundraising events and provocative actions have taken place
to urge the Russian authorities to Free Pussy Riot. The leader
of the Ukrainian feminist group Femen used a chainsaw to
cut down an Orthodox crucifix in Kiev.[7] The queer feminist
electronic music artist, and outspoken anti-Bush cultural
activist, Peaches created the song 'Free Pussy Riot' and
spearheaded an online petition via Change.org.[8] Others have
developed creative responses to the imprisonment of Pussy
Riot.[9] This has led some to credit Pussy Riot as sparking a
global feminist movement. However, I would argue that Pussy
Riot represent a spectacular moment in the history of women
and girls' use of music to provoke social change and challenge
white masculine authorities. Therefore, questions need to be
asked about why and how Pussy Riot are being made visible
at this particular time. Pussy Riot are not a band – they are a
collective of radical feminist activists, they do not want to be
signed to a major label, release records, go on tour and become
successful musicians. Their radical message runs deeper than

the 'freedom of speech' argument heralded by western popular artists. Is it possible that Pussy Riot is a convenient case used to bolster the legitimacy of western democratic values? As Vadim Nikitin argued:

'Pussy Riot's fans in the West need to understand that their heroes' dissent will not stop at Putin; neither will it stop if and when Russia becomes a "normal" liberal democracy. Because what Pussy Riot wants is something that is equally terrifying, provocative and threatening to the established order in both Russia and the West (and has been from time immemorial): freedom from patriarchy, capitalism, religion, conventional morality, inequality and the entire corporate state system. We should only support these brave women if we, too, are brave enough to go all the way.'[10]

Every generation needs its moment of social and cultural revolution. Women and girls' use of music and culture as protest is often at the centre. Pussy Riot drew upon a legacy of radical feminist cultural resistance that has been recognisable as 'riot grrrl', 'Ladyfest', 'feminist punk' and 'queercore' and many more moments explored in *Women Make Noise*. Maybe we *are all* Pussy Riot but what will we be in the future?

Notes

Introducing the All-girl Band: Finding comfort in Contradiction

1. Maring, Lillian (2011) cited in *Girl Gang zine #2*. Self-published fanzine produced in Berlin by Maren and Kristina. Available to order from http://girlgangzine.com/
2. Tucker, Sherrie (2000) *Swing Shift: "All-Girl" Bands of the 1940s*. Duke University Press, Durham and London, p2.
3. Fast, Susan (2008) 'Girls, Rock Your Boys: The Continuing (non)History of Women in Rock.' Annette Kreutziger-Herr & Katrin Losleben (eds.) *History/Herstory Andere Musikgeschichten*. Köln/Weimar, Böhlau, p156.
4. For instance see Davies, Helen (2004) 'The Great Rock and Roll Swindle: The Representation of Women in the British Rock Music Press', In C. Carter and L. Steiner (eds.) *Critical Readings: Media and Gender*, Open University Press, Maidenhead, p162-78; Holly Kruse (2002) 'Abandoning the Absolute: Transcendence and Gender in Popular Music Discourse'. In, *Pop Music and the Press*, Steve Jones (ed.) Temple University Press, Philadelphia p134-55.
5. Kathleen Hanna lyric from 'Julie Ruin'.
6. Several examples of books that are typical of the 'women in rock' market include: Gaar, Gilian G (1993) *She's a Rebel: The History of Women in Rock & Roll,* Blandford, London; Raphael, Amy (1995) *Nevermind the Bollocks: Women Rewrite Rock*, Virago, London; Reynolds, Simon and Press, Joy (1995) *The Sex Revolts: Gender, Rebellion and Rock n Roll,* Harvard University Press, Cambridge MA; O'Dair, Barbara (1997) (ed.) *Trouble Girls: The Rolling Stone Book of Women in Rock*, Random House, New York; Bayton, Mavis, (1998) *Frock Rock: Women Performing Popular Music*, Oxford University Press, Oxford and New York; Hirshey, Gerri (2001) *We Gotta Get Out of This Place: The True, Tough Story of Women in Rock*, Grove Press, New York; O'Brien, Lucy (2002) *She Bop 2: The Definitive History of Women in Rock, Pop and Soul*, Continuum, London; Raha, Maria (2005) *Cinderella's Big Score: Women of the Punk and Indie Underground,* Seal Press, Emeryville, CA; Leonard, Marion (2007) *Gender in the Music Industry: Rock, Discourse and Girl Power*, Ashgate, Aldershot; Reddington, Helen (2007) *The Lost Women of Rock Music: Female Musicians of the Punk Era*, Ashgate, Aldershot; von Burden, Zora (ed.) 2008 *Women of the Underground: Music. Cultural Innovators Speak for Themselves*, Manic D Press, San Francisco, CA.
7. McClary, Susan (1991) *Feminine Endings: Music, Gender and Sexuality*, University of Minnesota Press, Minneapolis & Oxford; Whiteley, Sheila (2000) *Women and Popular Music: Sexuality, Identity and Subjectivity*, Routledge, London; Burns, Lori and LaFrance, Melissa (2002) *Disruptive Divas: Feminism, Identity and Popular Music*, Routledge, London.
8. Fast, Susan (2008) 'Girls, Rock Your Boys: The Continuing (non)History of Women in Rock.' Annette Kreutziger-Herr & Katrin Losleben (eds.) *History/Herstory: Andere Musikgeschichten*. Köln/Weimar, Böhlau, p154-176; Periano, Judith (2001) Girls with Guitars and other Strange Stories, *Journal of the American Musicological Society* 54:692-709.
9. See studies by Bayton, Mavis (1998) *Frock Rock: Women Performing Popular Music*, Oxford University Press, Oxford and New York. Leonard, Marion (2007) *Gender in the Music Industry: Rock, Discourse and Girl Power.*
10. More information is available on their website http://www.orkidehmusic.com
11. Maring, Lillian (2011) cited in *Girl Gang zine #2*. Self-published fanzine produced in Berlin by Maren and Kristina. Available to order from http://girlgangzine.com

Women Make Noise

1. Female Pioneers of American Old-time and Country Music

1. 'Single Girl, Married Girl', The Carter Family (1927)
2. 'Single Life', Roba Stanley (1925)
3. 'The Wagoner's Lad', The Kossoy Sisters (1956)
4. Sonneborn, Liz (2002), *A-Z of American Women in the Performing Arts,* Infobase Publishing

2. Puppets on a String? Girl Groups of the 50s and 60s

1. Charlotte Greig describes this trajectory in her book, *Will You Love Me Tomorrow?* (1989), and Florence Greenberg's role in shaping the girl group sound deserves more scholarly attention than this chapter can offer.
2. Both Charlotte Greig (as above) and Jacqueline Warwick in *Girl Groups, Girl Culture: Popular Music and Identity in the 1960s* (Routledge, 2007), have described this event as traumatic to The Crystals.
3. In 2011, Darlene Love was inducted into the Rock 'n' Roll Hall of Fame. Many of her interviews at the time specifically cited her struggle with Phil Spector to record under her own name. She told NPR reporter David C. Barnett that, 'I told him, "This is ridiculous. I know you can make hits, and I ain't making no more hits under anybody else's name but my own."' (Barnett, 'Darlene Love: A Prominent Star, Born in the Background', National Public Radio: Morning Edition, February 16th, 2011).
4. Lawyer Beth Wooten has described these legal struggles in her 2011 master's thesis, 'You Don't Own Me: Girl Group Recording Contracts and Copyrights.'
5. Many of the girl groups, including The Ronettes and The Shangri-Las, continued to find success in the mid-1960s.
6. See George Gallup and Evan Hill, 'The American Woman', *Saturday Evening Post* (December 22nd, 1962) p15-32.
7. For more on marriage in the United States and Europe in the 1950s and 1960s, see Stephanie Coontz (2005) *Marriage, a History: How Love Conquered Marriage.*
8. Ibid.
9. For more on the birth control pill in American culture, see Elaine Taylor May's (2011) *America and the Pill: A History of Promise, Peril and Liberation.*
10. In 1964, the Dixie Cups had a hit with 'Chapel of Love' which had also been recorded by The Ronettes and The Blossoms.
11. For more, see Bradby (1988).
12. The song could also be seen as capitalising on the popularity of the 1957 musical *West Side Story*, which had been made into a hit film in 1961.
13. Rather than interpret these sonic differences as markers of 'authenticity', they are more clearly evidence of the ways that racial and class prejudices restricted musical choices and marketing categories for musicians. See Greig (1989) for more on the popular female singing groups that preceded the girl groups.
14. Weller, Sheila (2008) *Girls Like Us: Carole King, Joni Mitchell, Carly Simon – And the Journey of a Generation* (Washington Square Press) p54-55.
15. Weller also describes King's determination to arrange the song's string parts, something she'd never attempted before.
16. Ronnie Spector tells this story in her 1990 memoir, *Be My Baby.*
17. Radio DJ Alan 'Moondog' Freed was notable for popularising the term 'rock 'n'

Notes

roll' in the 1950s and for breaking the colour barrier on the radio.

18. Greig (1989) p17.

19. Warwick opens her discussion of violence in girl group music with a vivid description of fifteen-year-old Elizabeth Eckford's harrowing experience of being a black girl integrating an all-white high school in Little Rock, Arkansas in 1957 (2011) p90.

20. Greig (1989).

21. Early, Gerald (1985) *One Nation Under a Groove* (Ecco) p117-118.

22. Atins, Cholly (2001) *Class Act: The Jazz Life of Choreographer Cholly Atkins*, Columbia University Press, p131

23. For more on femininity and the body, see Susan Bordo's *Unbearable Weight: Feminism, Western Culture and the Body* (2004).

24. Warwick, Jacqueline (2007) *Girl Groups, Girl Culture: Popular Music and Identity in the 1960s* (Routledge, 2007) p56-7.

25. Ibid p185.

26. For more on The Ronettes, see Ronnie Spector's memoir (1990) *Be My Baby: How I Survived Mascara, Miniskirts, and Madness, or My Life as a Fabulous Ronette.*

27. Ortner (2003).

28. Ibid p136.

29. Ibid.

30. Warwick (2007) p190.

31. In an interview with Miriam Linna and Billy Miller, Mary Weiss discussed wearing men's trousers, 'People would look at me like I was gay because I like low-rise pants.' See http://www.nortonrecords.com/maryweiss, accessed July 23rd, 2010.

32. To a New Yorker then, the girls' Long Island/Queens accents would sound middle-class, but to much of America, any 'New York' accent would imply a tough attitude.

33. Barbara Bradby's 1988 article 'Do-Talk and Don't Talk: The Division of the Subject in Girl-Group Music' was among the first to examine the conflicted subjectivities of girl group music. Cynthia Cyrus (2003) explores how the subjectivity of girl group music was reinforced.

34. For an account of girl group fandom see Susan Douglas's 'Why the Shirelles Mattered'(1994) in *Where the Girls Are: Growing Up Female with the Mass Media.*

35. Jacqueline Warwick (2007) describes these boundaries of femininity.

36. Heteronormativity is in full force here, even though some singers of the era, such as Dusty Springfield and Lesley Gore, both later identified as lesbians.

37. Phil Spector's production style is often referred to as the 'Wall of Sound'.

38. In her real life, Ronnie Spector wasn't so confident in her vocal abilities at the time.

39. Coontz, Stephanie (2005) *Marriage, A History: How Love Conquered Marriage,* p237.

40. Collins, Gail (2009) *When Everything Changed: The Amazing Journey of American Women from 1960 to Present,* Brown, p34

41. This 'tell me more, tell me more' scheme would later be used in 'Summer Nights', a song from the musical *Grease.*

42. The Dixie Cups' 'Iko Iko' would use a similar production style a year later, with singers Barbara Ann and Rosa Lee Hawkins and Joan Marie Johnson accompanying themselves with drumsticks in the studio. For more on African-American girls' playground games, see Kyra Gaunt's (2006) *The Games Black Girls Play: Learning the Ropes from Double-Dutch to Hip Hop.*

43. See 'Rock and Sexuality,' Simon Frith and Angela McRobbie's 1978 essay, which is reprinted in *On Record: Rock, Pop, and the Written Word* (1990).

44. Ward (1986), quoted in Douglas (1994).

45. Interview by by Billy Miller and Miriam Linna on March 28th, 2006. (http://www.nortonrecords.com/maryweiss/04.html)

46. Marcus, Griel (1976), *The Rolling Stone Illustrated History of Rock and Roll* (Random House, p160.

47. Ibid.

48. The Go-Go's covered The Shangri-Las' 'Remember (Walking in the Sand)', while Blondie covered their 'Out in the Streets'. The Damned referenced The Shangri-Las' 'Leader of the Pack' in 'New Rose' with the line 'Is she really going out with him?'

49. Dibben, Nicola (1999), *Representations of Femininity in Popular Music,* Cambridge University Press, p343.

50. Fudge, Rachel (2006) *Bitch Magazine* 160.

51. Sisario, Ben. 'Amy Winehouse, British Soul Singer With a Troubled Life, Dies at 22,' *The New York Times*, July 23rd, 2011.

52.http://www.rollingstone.com/music/news/exclusive-ronnie-spector-pays-tribute-to-amy-winehouse-20110727#ixzz1cSsLbMi1

53. See, for example, the group's 2005 interview with Kitty Empire in the *Guardian*: http://www.guardian.co.uk/music/2005/oct/16/10.

54. According to a 2007 interview with Zack Rosen, RiotBecki took her name from riot grrrl (https://thenewgay.net/2007/11/pipettes-riotbecki-talks-sex-girl.html).

55. In an email concerning this book.

3. Truth Gotta Stand: Girls in 60s Garage, Beat and 70s Rock

1. Clawson, Mary Ann, (1999) 'Masculinity and Skill Acquisition in the Adolescent Rock Band', *Popular Music* 18/1, p111.

2. Nevertheless, it must be noted that I *do not* consider the genre to be any more 'masculine' than most other rock styles.

3. Kauppila, Paul (2005) 'The Sound of the Suburbs: A Case Study of Three Garage Bands in San Jose, California during the 1960s'. *Popular Music and Society* 28/3, p391.

4. Bovey, Seth (2006) 'Don't Tread On Me: The Ethos of '60s Garage Punk'. *Popular Music and Society* 29/4, p451.

5. Therefore, bands as different as proto-power popsters The Choir and psychedelic experimentalists The 13th Floor Elevators have been labelled garage music.

6. Various artists (1998) *Nuggets: Original Artyfacts from the First Psychedelic Era 1965-1968*. Rhino: R2 75466. (Rhino is an American record label, founded in the late 1970s, that specialises in reissues.)

7. Cost, Jud and Irwin, Bob (1999) 'Char Vinnedge: A Rare Vintage Indeed'. Sleeve note for *The Luv'd Ones: Truth Gotta Stand*. Sundazed: LP 5033.

8. As above.

9. As above.

10. Quatro, Suzi (2007) *Unzipped*, Hodder and Stoughton, London, p29.

11. 'History – The Debutantes', The Debutantes (Jan McClellan's site), http://www.thedebutantesband.com/historyD.htm (accessed 22nd June 2011)

12. Steil, Mark (2001), 'Remembering the Continental Co-ets', Minnesota Public Radio online, http://news.minnesota.publicradio.org/features/200108/21_steilm_girlband-m/ accessed June 20th 2011.

13. Pomeroy, Debi and Patrick, Mick 'Chicago's Daughters of Eve: the Story of an

Notes

All-girl Band', Spectropop, http://www.spectropop.com/DaughtersOfEve/index. htm (accessed 20th June 2011).

14. 'The Heart Beats Story', Cicadelic Records online, http://www.cicadelic.com/ heartbeats.htm (accessed 20th June 2011).

15. This US-based label had hits with artists such as Eddie Cochran and Bobby Vee in the late 1950s and early 1960s.

16. The group's guitarist Denise Kaufman had written and provided vocals for garage classic 'Boy, What'll You Do Then' prior to joining The Ace of Cups.

17. Hamelman, Steven (2003), 'But Is It Garbage? The Theme of Trash in Rock and Roll Criticism'. *Popular Music and Society* 26/2, p205.

18. Campau, Don (2009) 'Interview with Irwin Chusid'. The Living Archive of Underground Music, see www.doncampau.com/livingarchiveIrwinChusid.htm accessed June 28th 2011.

19. For instance, The Knickerbockers and The Premiers.

20. Steil, 'Remembering the Continental Co-ets' and Pomeroy and Patrick, 'Chicago's Daughters of Eve'.

21. Quatro, *Unzipped*, p34.

22. Gillett, Charlie (3rd ed. 1996) *The Sound of the City: The Rise of Rock & Roll,* Souvenir Press, London p312-24.

23. Montague, Eugene (2006) 'From Garahge to Garidge: The Appropriation of Garage Rock in the Clash's "Garageland" (1977)'. *Popular Music and Society* 29/4, p432.

24. Bovey, 'Don't Tread On Me', p452.

25. However, this was not always the case as the recordings of, for instance, the afore-discussed The Luv'd Ones, She or The Belles demonstrate.

26. Hicks, Michael (1999), *Sixties Rock: Garage, Psychedelic, and Other Satisfactions,* University of Illinois Press, Urbana and Chicago p27.

27. Leonard, Marion (2007) *Gender in the Music Industry: Rock, Discourse and Girl Power*, Ashgate, Aldershot, p6.

28. Palao, Alec (1998), 'Get Me to the World on Time: How the Sound of Nuggets Engulfed the World'. Booklet for *Nuggets: Original Artyfacts from the First Psychedelic Era 1965-1968*. Rhino: R2 75466, p27.

29. Shaw, Greg (1998) 'Sic Transit Gloria…: The Story of Punk Rock in the 60s', see booklet for *Nuggets* as above, p19.

30. This has become apparent researching for my PhD thesis, 'A Musicological Ethnography of Female Musicians in England, 1962 – 1971'.

31. McLagan, Ian (2nd ed. 2000) *All the Rage: A Riotous Romp through Rock & Roll History*, Billboard Books, New York, p37.

32. Ravan, Genya (2004) *Lollipop Lounge: Memoirs of a Rock and Roll Refugee,* Billboard Books, New York, p63.

33. Several variant spellings of the band's name co-exist online: 'the Beat Chics', 'the Beat Chicks' and 'the Beat-Chics'.

34. Outside the beat group context, or perhaps, more accurately, on the fringes of it, She Trinity were a London-based all-girl band that recorded six singles – most of them for Columbia – 1966-1970.

35. 'A Band Called Fanny', *Fanny Rocks,* see http://fannyrocks.com/about-2/a-band-called-fanny (accessed June 23rd 2011).

36. 'A Band Called Fanny'.

37. Young, Charles, M (1976) 'Run-run-run-run Runaways'. *Crawdaddy*, Oct 1976, p34-41.

38. This resurrection was advanced further in 2010 when a biographical film about

the band, simply called *The Runaways*, introduced them to new audiences.

39. Many of the best-known bands of the 1980s revival (The Fuzztones, The Chesterfield Kings and The Cynics) hailed from the US but the phenomenon wasn't exclusively American.

40. The Dirty Water Club was a weekly garage rock night in London. Crittenden now co-runs the Dirty Water empire's record label, see www.dirtywaterrecords.co.uk

41. Interview by email with PJ Crittenden, November 30th 2011.

42. Vibrant pockets of garage may be found, for instance, in several states in the US (with bands such as The Black Lips and The Lords of Altamont), in Latin American countries (Los Peyotes, Los Explosivos), in Spain (Way Y Los Arrghs, The Midnight Shots) and in the UK (any band Billy Childish happens to be with).

43. Perhaps most prominently, the GaragePunk Hideout http://garagepunkning.com

44. The US appears to be leading the pack with festivals such as the Las Vegas Shakedown, Budget Rock in San Francisco and Gonerfest in Memphis.

45. Not to be confused with the 1960s group of the same name.

46. The Donnas started out in the 1990s, albeit only becoming well-known after signing to a major label in the early 2000s.

47. The UK's main contribution in the 1990s came in the form of Thee Headcoatees, protégées of Billy Childish, noted here despite their being essentially a vocal group.

48. Interview by email with Cassie Ramone, December 6th 20122. For more information on the Vivian Girls see www.freewebs.com/viviangirls or www.myspace.com/viviangirlsnyc

49. Some contemporary bands literally wish to reproduce the sounds associated with 1960s garage rock, while some draw influences from other genres and phenomena.

50. For more information on The Nuns, please go to www.myspace.com/itsnunstimes. The Monks were a band made up of American servicemen stationed in Germany in the mid-1960s, whose album *Black Monk Time* has become an outsider classic.

51. Interview by email with Debbie Smith, December 19th 2011, and further quotes.

52. For instance, Ramone mentioned Toody Cole from Dead Moon, while Smith named Poison Ivy from The Cramps.

4. Prog Rock: A Fortress they call the Industry

1. Lowe, D, December 22nd 2008. 1973 was winter of discontent. *The Sun* (online) Accessed October 17th 2011 Available from http://www.thesun.co.uk/sol/homepage/features/2060774/1973-was-real-winter-of-discontent.html

2. Badger, J. 2010. Accessed October 15th 2011. Available from http://jackiebadgersblog.blogspot.com/2010/04/first-gig-of-new-decade-for-us-is.html

3. Mother Superior website. Accessed March 7th 2012 http://www.mother-superior-female-band.moonfruit.com

4. Phone interview with author March 22nd 2011.

5. Mother Superior, 1976. Mother Superior All Girl Band 1976. Accessed 15th October 2011. Available from http://www.youtube.com/watch?v=vyL8WUWv6EU

6. Email conversation with author March 17th 2011.

7. Phone interview with author March 22nd 2011.

8. Email interview with author April 22nd 2011.

9. Email interview with the author March 17th 2011.

10. Mother Superior *Lady Madonna (*1976). Rereleased 1996. Audio Archives

Notes

AACD015. Accessed 17th October 2011. Available from http://www.rockadrome. com/superstore/product_info.php?products_id=1483

11. Email interview with the author 17th March 2011.

12. Phone interview with the author 22nd March 2011.

13. Phone interview with the author 22nd March 2011.

14. Shaarwai, Huda 1924. http://www.womeninworldhistory.com/wisdom.html Accessed March 8th 2012.

15. Martha and the Muffins. 1977. http://www.marthaandthemuffins.com Accessed March 7th 2012.

16. Daphne Oram, http://daphneoram.org Accessed 7th March 2012.

17. Boden Sandstrom, http://www.womanvision.org/radical-harmonies-team.html Accessed March 7th 2012.

18. Interview in person with the author April 30th 2011.

19. Interview in person with the author April 11th 2011.

20. Phone interview with the author April 23rd 2011.

21. Interview in person with the author April 22nd 2011.

22. Interview in person with the author April 7th 2011.

23. Interview in person with the author March 18th 2011.

24. Lee, C. 17th February 1986. Pop Reviews: Silly Sisters. *Los Angeles Times* online. Available from http://articles.latimes.com/1986-02-17/entertainment/ca-9147_1_pop-reviews

25. *The Holy Sisters of the Gaga Dada Let's Get Acquainted* (1986). Bomp! BLP- 4023 vinyl LP. Accessed April 13th 2011. Available from discogs marketplace http://www.discogs.com/holy-sisters-of-the-gaga-dada-Lets-get-acquainted/release/1933886

26. *The Holy Sisters of the Gaga Dada (*1986). 'For Pete's Sake/Shades of Grey' and 'I Won't Breed in Captivity'. Accessed 13th April 2011. Available from http://www.discogs.com/holy-sisters-of-the-gaga-dada-Lets-get-acquainted/release/1933886 and http://www.youtube.com/watch?v=Fw8YjJEBVWs&feature=related

27. Holy Sisters of the Gaga Dada. Accessed 13th April 2011. Available from https://www.facebook.com/pages/HoLY-SIstERs-of-the-GAga-DaDA/110662522327121

28. Purple Rhinestone Eagle. http://lamoustache.org/index.php?/booking-archive/purple-rhinestone-eagle/ Accessed March 7th 2011.

29. Dombal, R. January 13th 2010. Rising: Warpaint.Pitchfork online. Accessed April 16th 2011. Available from http://pitchfork.com/news/37496-rising-warpaint/

30. See www.warpaintwarpaint.com

31. *Rock It to the Moon, The Power Out, Axes* and *No Shouts No Calls* still available from Amazon.com and other outlets. Accessed 18th October 2011 Available from http://www.amazon.com/s/ref=nb_sb_noss?url=search-alias%3Dpopular&field-keywords=electrelane&x=15&y=15

32. Interview in person with the author April 7th 2011.

33. Email interview with author June 7th 2011.

34. Email interview with author June 7th 2011.

35. Interview with www.furious.com Accessed October 16th 2011.

36. Frere-Jones, Sasha. Jan 3rd 2011. Note by Note. *The New Yorker* (online). Accessed 8th March 2011. Available from http://www.newyorker.com/arts/critics/musical/2011/01/03/110103crmu_music_frerejones

37. Email interview with the author June 7th 2011.

38. Phone interview with the author April 23rd 2011.

39. Interview in person with the author April 11th 2011.
40. Email interview with the author June 7th 2011.
41. Email interview with the author June 7th 2011.

5. Feminist Musical Resistance in the 70s and 80s

1. The work of Mavis Bayton is an obvious exception, see (1998) *Frock Rock: Women Performing Popular Music,* Oxford University Press and (1993) 'Feminist Music Practice: Problems and Contradictions' in Bennett, Tony et al eds. *Rock and Popular Music: Politics, Policies, Institutions*, Routledge, p177-193.
2. See http://www.queermusicheritage.us/olivia.html for a fantastic web archive of Olivia Records, one of the most important USA feminist record labels in the 1970s and Morris, Bonnie (1999), *Eden Built By Eves,* Alyson Books.
3. Aune, Kristin and Redfern (2010) *Reclaiming the F-Word,* Zed Books, London; Banyard, Kat (2010) *The Equality Illusion,* Faber, London.
4. Harvey, PJ (2011) 'PJ Harvey performs for David Cameron' on the Andrew Marr Show, October 2nd 2011. See www.twentyfourbit.com/post/10945307260/video-pj-harvey-performs-for-david-cameron-last. Last accessed October 5th 2011.
5. For a full list of all the people who played in Jam Today 1-3 please visit http://womensliberationmusicarchive.wordpress.com/j/
6. Green, Frankie (2010) 'Jam Today 1: Personal Recollections'. Available at http://womensliberationmusicarchive.wordpress.com/j/. Last accessed March 29th 2011.
7. Stroppy Cow (1983) 'Jam Today Lyric Sheet'. See http://womensliberationmusicarchive.wordpress.com/t/. Accessed June 6th 2011.
8. See http://www.youtube.com/user/JamToday3 for YouTube channel and http://www.facebook.com/pages/Jam-Today-3/145754198787220?sk=wall&filter=1.
9. Ibid.
10. Ibid.
11. Schonfeld, Rosemary (2011) 'Postscript'. See http://womensliberationmusicarchive.files.wordpress.com/2010/10/rspostscript.pdf.
12. Now known as Kaffe Matthews.
13. Withers, Jayne (1986) 'If I can't dance to it, it ain't my revolution: An Interview with The Fabulous Dirt Sisters', *Peace News*, 6, p19.
14. Karunavaca (2010), interview with Deborah Withers, May 23rd 2010.
15. 'Women's Liberation Music Project'.
16. Jam Today (1977) 'Benefit for Jam Today'. See http://womensliberationmusicarchive.wordpress.com/j/. Last accessed March 29th 2011.
17. For information about Grunwick, please visit http://www.leeds.ac.uk/strikingwomen.
18. Ibid, p. 28. Available online http://womensliberationmusicarchive.wordpress.com/j/ Last accessed May 12th 2011.
19. Charles, Barbara (1978) 'Jam Today', *Spare Rib*, 66, p26. See http://womensliberationmusicarchive.wordpress.com/j/ Last accessed May 12th 2011.
20. Ibid.
21. Withers, Jayne (1986) 'If I can't dance to it, it ain't my revolution: An Interview with The Fabulous Dirt Sisters', *Peace News*, 6, p19.
22. Ova (1984) *Possibilities*, Stroppy Cow Records.
23. 'Women's Liberation Music Project' (n.d.) Women's Liberation Music'. Available in the Feminist Archive South, Bristol.

Notes

24. Ibid.

25. Jam Today (1977) 'Benefit for Jam Today'. Available online at http://womensliberationmusicarchive.wordpress.com/j/. Last accessed March 29th 2011.

26. David Edwards (1983) 'Interview with Ova on Inside London'. Part of Rosemary Schonfeld's personal collection.

27. Ibid.

28. Stella Patella (2010), Fabulous Dirt Sisters Group Interview with Deborah Withers, May 20th 2010.

29. Karunavaca (2010), Fabulous Dirt Sisters Group Interview with Deborah Withers, May 20th 2010.

30. Withers, Jayne (1986) 'If I can't dance to it, it ain't my revolution: An Interview with The Fabulous Dirt Sisters', *Peace News*, 6, p19.

31. Nicholls, Jill (1977) Spare Rib, n.d. p35. See http://womensliberationmusicarchive.wordpress.com/j/. Last accessed March 29th 2011.

32. Schonfeld, Rosemary (2011), Interview with Deborah Withers, December 17th 2010.

33. Rayner, Alison (2011) Personal correspondence with Deborah Withers.

34. Green, Frankie (2010) 'Jam Today 1: Personal Recollections'. See http://womensliberationmusicarchive.wordpress.com/j/. Last accessed March 29th 2011.

35. Matthews, Kaffe (2010) Interview with Deborah Withers, January 29th 2010.

36. Jam Today (1977) Notice advertising benefit, Spare Rib Available online http://womensliberationmusicarchive.wordpress.com/j/. Last accessed March 29th 2011

37. Ova (1985) 'Making Women's Music Visible'. See http://womensliberationmusicarchive.wordpress.com/o/. Last accessed June 7th 2011.

38. Angele in Charles, Barbara (1978) 'Jam Today', Spare Rib, 66, p26. Available online http://womensliberationmusicarchive.wordpress.com/j/ Last accessed May 12th 2011.

39. Hunt, Teresa (1986) 'Jam Everyday' in Trouble and Strife, Summer 1986, p47.

40. Withers, Jayne (1986) 'If I can't dance to it, it ain't my revolution: An Interview with The Fabulous Dirt Sisters', *Peace News*, 6, p18.

41. Matthews, Kaffe (2010) Interview with Deborah Withers, January 29th 2010.

42. Hunt, Teresa, Personal Correspondence with Deborah Withers, March 24th 2011.

43. Charles, Barbara (1978) 'Jam Today', Spare Rib, Volume 66, January 1978, p27. Available online http://womensliberationmusicarchive.wordpress.com/j/ Last accessed May 12th 2011.

44. David Edwards (1983) 'Interview with Ova on Inside London'. Part of Rosemary Schonfeld's personal collection.

45. Matthews, Kaffe (2010) 'Interview with Deborah Withers,' January 29th 2010.

46. Karunavaca (2010) 'Fabulous Dirt Sisters Group Interview...' May 20th 2010.

47. Holly Near in 'Introduction' in Women's Liberation Music Project Group (n.d.) Sisters in Song, p4.

6. You Create, We Destroy: Punk Women

1. From an interview with the author in 2011.

2. Alexander, E., (2011) 'Vivienne Westwood Red Label Show Report', *British Vogue*. See http://www.vogue.co.uk/fashion/autumn-winter-2011/ready-to-wear/vivienne-westwood-red-label (accessed July 2011).

3. Gedge, D., (2010) 'Reflections of Being Punk For a Day', *Roofs and Rambles* See http://dustygedge.co.uk/roadblog/2010/10/reflections-of-being-a-punk-for-a-day

(accessed July 2011).

4. Blasé, C., 'Writing Women Back Into Punk', *The F-Word*. See http://www.thefword. org.uk/features/ 2010/03/women_in_punk_w (accessed December 17th 2011).

5. Reddington, H., (2011) 'Caroline Coon's SLUT TALK for SLUT WALK London', *Caroline Coon: News*. See//www.carolinecoon.com/news.htm (Accessed July 2011.)

6. Raha, Maria (2005), *Cinderella's Big Score: Women of the Punk and Indie Underground,* p7.

7. 'Chart Archive – 1970s' Singles', *Every Hit* [Online]. See http://www.everyhit.com/ chart3.html (accessed December 2011).

8. (1975) 'The Sex Discrimination Act 1975', *The National Archives*. See http://www. legislation.gov.uk/ukpga/1975/65 (accessed December 2011).

9. Colgrave, S., (2001) Sullivan, C., *Punk,* p12-15.

10. Minx, Zillah, (2007) *She's a Punk Rocker.*

11. Raha, Maria, (2005) *Cinderella's Big Score...* p13.

12. Colgrave, S., Sullivan, C., (2001) *Punk,* p206.

13. Blase, C., 'Women of the Punk Era', *The F-Word*. See www.thefword.org.uk/ features/2010/04/women_of_the_pu (accessed December 2011).

14. Ibid

15. Burkett, E., (2011) 'Women's Movement', *Britannica Online Encyclopaedia*. See http://www.britannica.com/EBchecked/topic/647122/womens-movement (accessed December 2011).

16. From an interview with the author, 2011.

17. Dyson, J., (1999) 'Punk: Out of Bondage', *The Independent*. See www.independent. co.uk/life-style/punk-out-of-bondage-1083239.html (accessed December 2011).

18. Ibid.

19. LeBlanc, Lauraine, (1999) *Pretty In Punk: Girls' Gender Resistance in a Boys' Subculture*, p44.

20. Bell, C., (2005) 'Poly Styrene's Biography', *X-Ray Spex* [Online]. Available at http://www.x-rayspex.com/biography/biography1.html (accessed June 2011).

21. http://feministmusicgeek.com/tag/lora-logic/

22. Savage, J (2002) *England's Dreaming*, p327.

23. Raha, Maria (2005) *Cinderella's Big Score...*p88.

24. Caroline Coon, from an interview with author 2011.

25. Macias, C. (2002) 'In Their Own Words Part 1', *Punk '77*. See www.punk77. co.uk/groups/womeninpunkintheirownwordspart1.htm (accessed July 2011).

26. Colgrave, S., Sullivan, C., (2001) *Punk,* p208.

27. Bradley, S., (2001) 'The Shanne Bradley Interview', *Punk'77*. See www.punk77. co.uk/groups/nippleerectorsshanneinterview.htm (accessed December 2011).

28. McCookerybook, Helen, from an interview with author, 2011.

29. Raha, Maria, (2005) *Cinderella's Big Score...* p79.

30. From an interview with author, 2011.

31. Dyson, J., (1999) 'Punk: Out of Bondage', *The Independent*. See www.independent. co.uk/life-style/punk-out-of-bondage-1083239.html (accessed December 2011).

32. Cooper, L., (2007) 'No Bondage', *The Guardian*. See www.guardian.co.uk/ world/2007/aug/08/gender.arts (accessed August 2011).

33. Crass (1981) 'Poison is a Pretty Little Pill', *P Lyrics*. See www.plyrics.com/c/crass. html (accessed July 2011).

34. Subversa, V., (1984) 'Real Woman', *Lyrics Mania*. See www.lyricsmania.com/ real_woman_lyrics_poison_girls.html (accessed July 2011).

35. Colgrave, S., Sullivan, C., (2001) *Punk,* p207.

Notes

36. McCookerybook, Helen, from an interview with author 2011.
37. Dyson, J., (1999) 'Punk: Out of Bondage', *The Independent*. See www.independent. co.uk/life-style/punk-out-of-bondage-1083239.html (accessed December 2011).
38. Macias, C., (2002) 'In Their Own Words Part 2', *Punk '77*. See www.punk77. co.uk/groups/womeninpunkintheirownwordspart2.htm (accessed July 2011).
39. LeBlanc, Lauraine, (1999) *Pretty In Punk: Girls' Gender Resistance in a Boys' Subculture*, p46.
40. Ibid, p47.
41. Macias, C., (2002) 'In Their Own Words Part 2', *Punk '77*. See www.punk77. co.uk/groups/womeninpunkintheirownwordspart2.htm (accessed July 2011).
42. 'Business Name Search' (2002) *Oregon Secretary Of State Corporate Division*. See http://egov.sos.state.or.us/br/pkg_web_name_srch_inq.login (accessed August 2011).
43. Caroline Coon, from an interview with the author, 2011.
44. Raha, Maria (2005), *Cinderella's Big Score...* p104
45. LeBlanc, Lauraine (1999) *Pretty In Punk...* p45
46. Caroline Coon, from an interview with the author, 2011.
47. Dyson, J., (1999), 'Punk: Out of Bondage' *The Independen*. Available at: http:// www.independent.co.uk/life-style/punk-out-of-bondage-1083239.html (accessed December 2011).
48. 'News', *The Raincoats*. See www.theraincoats.net/news.html (December 2011).
49. *98 Bowery: Punk Years* (2011) 'Punk Years, 1976 – 78', *98 Bowery*. See http://98bowery.com/punkyears/index.php (accessed December 2011.)
50. Sweeting, A., (2011) 'Poly Styrene's Obituary', *The Guardian*. See www.guardian. co.uk/music/2011/apr/26/poly-styrene-obituary (accessed December 2011).
51. Robb, John (2010) 'Ari Up obituary' *The Guardian*. See www.guardian.co.uk/ music/2010/oct/21/ari-up-obituary (accessed March 2012).
52. See www.sister.co.jp/hang_on_the_box/index_e.html
53. See http://wiki.rockinchina.com/w/Hang_On_The_Box
54. See http://sptimes.ru/index.php?action_id=2&story_id=35092
55. Ibid.
56. (2011) 'Sexism in Punk'. Available at: http://punksexism.wordpress.com
57. Caroline Coon, from an interview with author, 2011.

7. Post-punk: Raw, Female Sound

1. Crary, Scott (dir.), (2004) *Kill Your Idols*; Reynolds, Simon, (2005) *Rip It Up and Start Again: post-punk 1978-1984*; Court, Paula, (2007) *New York Noise*; Masters, Marc, *No Wave*; and Moore, Thurston and Coley, Byron (2008) *No Wave: Post-Punk. Underground. New York. 1976-1980*.
2. Howe, Zoe Street (2009) *Typical Girls? The Story of The Slits*.
3. Lunch, Lydia, 'Prologue', in Moore and Coley (2008), p4.
5. Quoted in Savage, Jon, (2009) *The England's Dreaming Tapes*, p138-9.
6. Moore and Coley (2008), p115.
7. Blase, Cazz, 'Women of the Punk Era', published on www.thefword.org.uk (2010)
8. Marcus, Greil, sleevenotes for The Raincoats, *The Kitchen Tapes* (1983).
9. Interview with Delta 5 published at http://www.furious.com/perfect/delta5.html (1996).

10. Interview with Linder, *New Musical Express* (1979).
12. Blase, 'Women of the Punk Era', Ibid.
13. Reddington (2007), p45.
14. Interview, *Warped Reality* magazine, published at http://www.warpedrealitymagazine.com/2006/06/looking_for_edges_an_interview.html (2006)
15. Moore and Coley (2008), p92.
16. Moore and Coley (2008), p61.
17. Howe (2009), p84.
18. Moore and Coley (2008), p116.
19. Dean, Michael W. (dir.), *DIY or Die: How to Survive as an Independent Artist* (2002)
20. Howe (2009), p99-101.
21. Pearson, Deanne, 'Women in Rock', *NME* (1980), p27.
22. Ibid, p27.
23. Reddington (2007), p99-122.
24. Interview, *Warped Reality* magazine (2006).
25. Reynolds (2005), p52.
26. Ibid, p57.
27. Nigg, Heinz, interview with Astrid Spirig translated from the German by Nicole Emmenegger, reprinted at www.killrockstars.com, n.d.
28. Ut, *Warped Reality* magazine (2006), Pollitt, interview with author, May 2011.
29. Bayton, Mavis, 'Feminist Music Practice: Problems and Contradictions', in Bennet, Tony (ed.), (1993) *Rock and Popular Music: Politics, Policies, Institutions*, p177-192
30. Goldman, Vivien, *Melody Maker* (1979). See also O'Meara, Caroline, 'The Raincoats: breaking down punk's masculinities', in *Popular Music* 22 (2003), p299-313.
31. Howe (2009), p57.
32. Ibid, p88.
33. Ibid, p60.
34. Ibid, p57.
35. Reddington (2007), p100.
36. Gregory Mario Whitfield, 'Earthbeat: In the Beginning There Was Rhythm,' *3 AM Magazine*, see www.3ammagazine.com/musicarchives/2003/nov/interview_tessa_pollitt.html (November 14th, 2003).
37. Savage (2009), p304.
38. Reynolds, Simon, http://ripitupfootnotes.blogspot.com/2008/11/footnotes-12-chapter-11-messthetics.html
39. Eltan, Liane, 'Talkin' Bout A Revolution', interview with Ari Up published on www.supersweet.org, (2010); Pollitt, interview with author, May 2011.
40. Quoted in Reynolds (2005), p214, p62.
41. Reynolds (2005), p61.
42. Moore and Coley (2008), p115.
43. Savage (2009), p298; Appelstein, Mike, interview with Palmolive published at http://www.nstop.com/paloma/intervw.html (1995).
44. Interview, *Warped Reality magazine* (2006).
45. Ibid.
46. Quoted in Reynolds, Simon and Press, Joy (1996) *The Sex Revolts: Gender, Rebellion, and Rock'n'roll*, p310.
47. Lyrics from 'Typical Girls' (1979) by The Slits; lyrics from 'Too Many Creeps' (1980) by the Bush Tetras.
48. Quoted in http://bangtheparty.wordpress.com/2008/04/01/au-pairs/ (2008).

Notes

49. Gross, Jason, interview with Marlene Marder, reprinted at http://www.furious.com/perfect/kleenex.html (1998).

50. Nigg (n.d.).

51. Interview with author, June 2011.

52. Quoted in Appelstein (1995).

53. 'Stuff the Good Old Days: Chin Chin', interview published at http://www.neumagazine.co.uk/bands/article/chin-chin-band (2010).

54. Christopher Raymond Brocklebank, 'The Mo-dettes', published at http://www.christopherray.moonfruit.com/#/the-Mo-dettes/4553242032, n.d.

55. Howe (2009), p62.

56. Appelstein (1995).

57. Blase, (2010).

58. Howe (2009), p.211, p5.

59. Moore and Coley (2008) p131.

60. Howe (2009), p51.

61. Moore and Coley (2008), p120.

62. Reynolds (2005), p83.

63. Quoted in Howe (2009), p157, p172.

64. Howe (2009), p172.

65. Savage (2009), p297.

66. Reynolds (2005), p80.

67. Savage (2009), p305.

68. Reynolds (2005), p71.

69. Blase (2010).

70. Quoted in Reynolds (2005), p214.

71. Reynolds (2005), p518-9.

72. Quoted in Goldman, Vivien, 'Poly Styrene, Lost and Found', *Village Voice* (2011), see http://www.villagevoice.com/2011-05-04/music/poly-styrene-lost-found/

73. Reddington (2007), p118.

74. Interview, *Warped Reality* magazine (2006).

75. Reynolds (2005), p57.

76. Blase (2010).

77. Biography from The Bloods MySpace page, see www.myspace.com/thebloodsny.

78. Whitfield, Gregory Mario (2003) 'Earthbeat: In the Beginning There Was Rhythm,' *3 AM Magazine*, see www.3ammagazine.com.

8. Subversive Pleasure: DIY hardcore

1. That's Henry Rollins, singer for perhaps the most well-known hardcore punk band of all time, Black Flag, and Ian Mackaye, his close second Minor Threat, originator of the term 'straight edge.'

2. Mallott (2004), *Punk Rockers' Revolution: A Pedagogy of Class, race and gender,* p24.

3. Peterson (2009) *Burning Fight: The Nineties Hardcore revolution in Ethics, Politics, Spirit and Sound.*

4. Suleiman (1986) *Gender, Politics and the Avant Garde,* pxvii.

5. Klein, 'Duality and Continuity in alternative music communities', in Keetley, D. (1997) *Public Women, Public Words: A documentary history of American Feminism.*

6. Peterson (2009) *Burning Fight: The Nineties Hardcore revolution in Ethics, Politics, Spirit*

and Sound, p36

7. Ibid p37.

8. Julie Burchill - quoted on various blogs online.

9. Anderse (2001) *Dance of Days: Two decades of punk in the nation's capital*, p230.

10. Ibid p73.

11. Peterson (2009), *Burning Fight: The Nineties Hardcore revolution in Ethics, Politics, Spirit and Sound*, p38.

12. Lahickey (1997) *All Ages: Reflections on Straight Edge*, p75.

13. Frith and McRobbie (1978), *Rock and Sexuality*, p372.

14. Blush (2001), *American Hardcore*, p112.

15. Ibid.

16. http://ilivesweat.tumblr.com

17. Peterson, (2009), *Burning Fight: The Nineties Hardcore revolution in Ethics, Politics, Spirit and Sound* , p41.

18. Ibid p43.

19. Ibid, p42.

20. From an interview for this book with Stephie Cristol, 2011.

21. McRobbie (2000)'Girls and Subculture' in *Feminism and Youth Culture* Ed.II, p12.

22. From an interview for this book with Jessica Skolnik, 2011.

23. From an interview for this book with Wick Bambix, 2011.

24. From an interview for this book with Stephie Cristol, 2011.

25. Peterson (2009), *Burning Fight: The Nineties Hardcore revolution in Ethics, Politics, Spirit and Sound*.

26. From an interview for this book with Mish Bondage, 2011.

27. Andersen (2011) *Dance of Days: Two decades of punk in the nation's capital*, p230.

28. From an interview for this book with Adrienne Droogas, 2012.

29. From an interview for this book with Stephie Cristol, 2011.

30. 'Connecting the dots: Riot grrrls, Ladyfest and the international grrrl zine network' in Harris, A. (ed) (2008) *Next Wave Cultures: Feminism, Subcultures, Activism*, p171.

31. From an interview for this book with Jessica Skolnik, 2011.

32. See www.phillyspissed.net

33. Hynes quoted in 'CLITFest:This Weekend' on *Where The Girls Go* Marloff 2011. http://wherethegirls.go.com/2011/07/06/clitfest

34. See www.emancypunx.com

35. From an interview for this book with Layla Gibbon, 2011.

9. Queercore: Fearless Women

1. 'Rise Above' (Black Flag cover) Tribe 8, *Role Models for Amerika*, Alternative Tentacles (1998)

2. Cited in Adam Rathe 2012 'Queer to the Core'. See www.out.com/entertainment/music/2012/04/12/history-queer-core-gay-punk-GB-JONES

3. Harmon, Des (2003) The Culture of AIDS. *Politics & Culture*. See www.politicsandculture.org/2010/08/10/des-harmon-the-culture-of-aids-2

4. Reaction to this protest can be accessed online www.youtube/O6xxMSc0-DM

5. Cited in Adam Rathe 2012 'Queer to the Core'. See www.out.com/entertainment/music/2012/04/12/history-queer-core-gay-punk-GB-JONES

6. For all issues of Homocore, see www.wps.com/HOMOCORE

Notes

7. Cited in Spencer, Amy (2005) *DIY: The Rise of Lo-Fi Culture*, Marion Boyars Publishers, London.

8. Cited in Rathe, Adam (2012) 'Queer to the Core'. See www.out.com/entertainment/music/2012/04/12/history-queer-core-gay-punk-GB-JONES

9. Cited in Spencer, Amy (2005). Ibid.

10. Rathe, Adam (2012). Ibid.

11. Cited in Melanie Maddison (2009) 'GB Jones' *ArtXX*, pg. 27. See http://issuu.com/aorta_magazine/docs/artxx2

12. Tammy Rae Carland cited in *She's Real: Worse Than Queer*. (dir. Lucy Thane, 1997). See http://vimeo.com/12084539.

13. Cited in Ciminelli, David and Knox, Ken (2005) *Homocore: The Loud and Raucous Rise of Queer Rock*. Los Angeles: Alyson Books, p142.

14. Other authors who have made the connection between riot grrrl and lesbianism or focused on queer performers include Cynthia Fuchs (1998), 'If I Had a Dick: Queer, Punks and Alternative Acts,' in, *Mapping the Beat: Popular Music and Contemporary Theory*. Thomas Swiss, John Sloop and Andrew Herman (eds.) Malden, MA: Blackwell, pp 101-17; Mary Celeste Kearney (1997) 'The Missing Links: Riot Grrrl – Feminism – Lesbian Culture,' in, *Sexing the Groove: Popular Music and Gender*. Sheila Whiteley (ed.) London: Routledge, pp207-29.

15. Cited in *It Changed My Life: Bikini Kill in the UK* (dir. Lucy Thane, 1993). See http://vimeo.com/11737681.

16. Cited in *She's Real: Worse Than Queer*. (dir. Lucy Thane, 1997). See http://vimeo.com/12084539.

17. Cited in David Ciminelli and Knox, Ken (2005). Ibid p49.

18. Ibid p142.

19. Ibid p141.

20. Cited in *She's Real: Worse Than Queer*. (dir. Lucy Thane, 1997). See http://vimeo.com/12084539

21. Cited in *How Queer Are You?* Issue #1, p. 2. Date unknown. Independently published fanzine.

22. Personal communication with the author.

23. 'Remember Who You Are'. Team Dresch *Captain My Captain* (1996, Chainsaw Records).

24. Personal communication with the author.

25. Hillary Chute, 221.

26. For instance see Elizabeth Grosz (1994) *Volatile Bodies: Toward a Corporeal Feminism,* Allen & Unwin, London

27. Hillary Chute, 221.

28. Maria Raha (2004) *Cinderella's Big Score...* pg. 186.

29. Personal communication with author.

30. For instance see Michel Foucault (1979) *The History of Sexuality, Vol. 1*. Robert Hurley (trans.); Michel Foucault (1986) *The History of Sexuality, Vol. 2*. Robert Hurley (trans.), Michel Foucault (1988) *The History of Sexuality, Vol. 3*. Robert Hurley (trans.); Gayle Rubin (1984) 'Thinking Sex: Notes for a Radical Theory of the Politics of Sexuality', reprinted in Carole S. Vance (ed.) (1992) *Pleasure and Danger: Exploring Female Sexuality*, pp267-319.

31. Raha, Maria (2004) *Cinderella's Big Score...* p186.

32. Cited in *Rise Above: A Tribe 8 Documentary* (dir. Tracy Flannigan). See www.riseabovethetribe8documentary.com.

33. Raha, Maria (2004) *Cinderella's Big Score:...* p186.

34. Cited in Raha, Maria (2004). Ibid p188-189

35. 'Remember Who You Are'. Team Dresch. Ibid.

36. 'Butch in the Streets' Tribe 8 *Fist City* (Alternative Tentacles, 1995).

37. 'Virus Envy' Sister George *Drag King* (Catcall Records, 1994).

38. 'All Women are Bitches' 7-inch single (K Records, 1992).

39. Cited in *She's Real: Worse Than Queer.* (dir. Lucy Thane, 1997). See http://vimeo.com/12084539

40. Cited in Chick factor #7. Independent self-published fanzine. Date unknown.

41. 'Frat Pig' Tribe 8 *Fist City* (Alternative Tentacles, 1995).

42. 'All I Can Do' Tribe 8 *Fist City* (Alternative Tentacles, 1995).

43. See *Free to Fight* (Candy Ass Records, 1995).

44. Personal communication with author.

45. QZAP is available online: http://www.qzap.org/v6/

46. Judith Halberstam (2007) Keeping Time with Lesbians on Ecstasy. *Women and Music: A Journal of Gender and Culture*, 11: 51-58

10. Riot Grrrl, Ladyfest and Rock Camps for Girls

1. While Fateman was not prominent as a musician during riot grrrl, she collaborated on the zine *Snarla* with Miranda July, and went on to perform in the band Le Tigre.

2. In contrast, Barnard zine library, for example, focuses solely on zines, with special emphasis on personal identity. Additionally, in 2010, the New York Art Book Fair at MoMA's PS1 space in Queens featured Matt Wobensmith's collection of riot grrrl zines in an installation where patrons were able to photocopy whatever they wanted. The NYABF also included a panel discussion about riot grrrl.

3. In summer 2011, Fantagraphics Bookstore and Gallery in Seattle curated an exhibit of riot grrrl visual art, titled *The Quiet Rrriot: Visual Artists from the Riot Grrrl Movement by Megan Kelso, Nikki McClure, Stella Mars*. McClure's work is also featured in a retrospective at the Museum of Contemporary Craft in Portland, OR entitled *Cutting Her Own Path: 1996-2011*.

4. Archivist Lisa Darms described the collection in an interview with Elizabeth K. Keenan on June 28th, 2010; Kathleen Hanna described her contribution in an interview with Keenan on August 17th, 2010.

5. Riot grrrl manifesto (1991).

6. Second Wave feminism's rejection of 'girl' stems from the ways in which it was often used to dismiss grown women's activities. Riot grrrl, and many (though not all) of the subsequent iterations of 'girl power' would focus on youth culture. For a critique of 'girl power,' see Fudge 2006.

7. Hanna, Kathleen, 'Love rock, a girl's perspective.' *Jigsaw* 4, Summer 1991.

8. While the history of punk in the United Kingdom includes such prominent women as Siouxsie Sioux, The Slits and The Raincoats, many of these women did not specifically identify as feminist. For more see O'Meara (2003).

9. For more on how riot grrrl faced these issues in the U.K., see Downes (2007).

10. Japenga, Ann. 'Punk's Girl Groups Are Putting the Self Back in Self-Esteem.' *The New York Times*. November 15th 1992.

11. In 'Revolution Girl-Style Now!,' an article in the September 25th, 1992, *Chicago Reader*, Emily White also compared Hanna to 'Madonna's Boy Toy gone over the

Notes

edge.' Similarly, Farai Chideya's 'Revolution, Girl Style,' which appeared in the November 23rd, 1992 edition of *Newsweek*, mentions Madonna several times.

12. On the other hand, France's article is notable in terms of US accounts of riot grrrl for its acknowledgment of the English riot grrrl movement and Huggy Bear.

13. Matt Wobensmith's *Outpunk* zine in San Francisco, for example, was among the first to chronicle the riot grrrl movement outside the Pacific Northwest.

14. For more on riot grrrl's media blackout, see Marcus, Sara (2010) *Girls to the Front*

15. For a discussion of riot grrrl's connection to the 'angry women in rock' phenomenon, see Schilt (2003).

16. Interviews include Erin Smith, Molly Neuman, Allison Wolfe, Tobi Vail, Rachel Carns, Sharon Cheslow, Jean Smith, Nomy Lamm and Corin Tucker.

17. The women Elizabeth Keenan interviewed in her dissertation research included Teresa Carmody, Erin Donovan, Sarah Dougher, Sasa Foster, Leah Hart-Landsberg, Kathryn Lewis, Jennifer Shafer, Beth Stinson, Maggie Vail, Allison Wolfe and Kanako Wyncoop. Their accounts inform the description of Ladyfest.

18. In 'Olympia Ladystyle,' an August 7th 2000 article about the festival in *Time* magazine, writer Benjamin Nugent waxed effusively: 'Journalists routinely describe them as the world's greatest rock-'n'-roll band, a tag once reserved for the Stones.'

19. Kimberlé Crenshaw's idea of intersectionality – that one's positionality depends not upon just race, or gender, or class, but the ways that these aspects emerge in an individual in different situations – informs Third Wave musicians and activist.

20. Notably, no one I interviewed associated the punk and indie reframing of 'lady' with the use of the word in hip-hop.

21. Kristin Schilt (2004) critiques the universalizing implications of the word 'grrrl'.

22. For more on redefining 'lady' along queer lines – see Kearney (1997).

23. This column serves a similar purpose as William Safire's 'On Language' column in the *New York Times Magazine*, using similar fonts and layouts.

24. Fudge cites numerous iterations of 'lady,' including Baumgardner and Ricards' *Manifesta* (2000), Nomy Lamm, Sleater-Kinney, Mr. Lady, Inga Muscio, Ladies Art Revival, and Kaia Wilson's *Ladyman*.

25. Ladyfest Bay Area 2004 held a 'Trans 202' workshop because organisers felt attendees already had some level of trans awareness; to reach a younger audience and keep all events all-ages, Seattle planned workshops directed at teens.

26. For more on inclusive spaces and black women's separate spaces within those festivals, see Eileen Hayes's *Songs in Black and Lavender* (2010).

27. Often, in Keenan's fieldwork, women would mention that they had read bell hooks (1984; 2000), Gloria Anzaldúa and Cherríe Moraga (2002), and Patricia Hill Collins (1990) as undergraduates. Many Third Wave writers emphasise intersectional identities eg. Daisy Hernández and Bushra Rehman (2002), Rebecca Walker (1995).

28. These examples draw on the longstanding construction of race in the United States, which is often formulated along the black/white division.

29. A pseudonym.

30. From an interview on December 11th 2002.

31. For an expanded discussion of the Michigan Womyn's Music Festival policy, see Hayes (2010).

32. With its highly supportive trans policy, Ladyfest Bay Area 2004 made its support of Mr. Lady Records explicit and invited the Butchies to perform.

33. www.ladyfestbayarea.org (accessed July 2002).

34. www.ladyfestbayarea.org (accessed July 2002).

35. Judith Halberstam has argued that transgender identities are a marker of a more fluid understanding of gender identity (2005).
36. For more on Ladyfest trans policies, see Keenan (2008).
37. While Sleater-Kinney was perceived as a 'Ladyfest band' it had only played the first festival. Other bands, such as Le Tigre and The Gossip, were also perceived as 'Ladyfest bands' despite performing at few Ladyfests. The bands identified as 'Ladyfest bands' in my fieldwork seemed to be the ones most idolised, rather than the ones who had performed at the most festivals.
38. See Leonard, Marion (2007) *Gender in the Music Industry,* p164.
39. Paris, Leslie. 'The Adventures of Peanut and Bo: Summer Camps and Early-20th-Century American Girlhood.' *Journal of Women's History* 12:4(2001), p47-76.
40. Orenstein (1994):xxvii.
41. ed. Anderson (2008) *Rock 'n' Roll Camp for Girls*, p18.
42. The complexity of this environment is explored by Marina Gonik (2006) who investigates the discourses of 'girl power' and 'reviving Ophelia'.
43. The 2011 Portland camp had an overwhelming number of Taylor Swift and Lady Gaga fans, as described in their camp-wide zine, *Why I Rock*.
44. One need only look to the viral video of Rebecca Black, a fourteen year old from Southern California, whose video 'Friday' on Youtube was viewed millions of times and widely condemned. Her resilience (she released a second video in July 2011) was remarkable considering the vitriol hurled her way.
45. See http://clitfestpdx.wordpress.com/2010/01/18/c-l-i-t-fest.
46. See http://fabulosafest.com.

Epilogue: Pussy Riot and the Future

1. Pussy Riot Live Journal available at: http://pussy-riot.livejournal.com/
2. Translated by Carol Rumens, *The Guardian*, Monday August 20th http://www.guardian.co.uk/books/2012/aug/20/pussy-riot-punk-prayer-lyrics?fb=native&CMP=FBCNETTXT9038
3. Information about Pussy Riot is available in several languages at: http://freepussyriot.org/; http://eng-pussy-riot.livejournal.com
4. Guy Grandjean, *The Guardian,* Friday August 17th. Available at: http://www.guardian.co.uk/music/video/2012/aug/17/pussy-riot-release-new-single-video?fb=native&CMP=FBCNETTXT9038
5. Steve Gutterman and Alissa de Carbonnel, *Reuters*, August 20th 2012. Available at: http://www.reuters.com/article/2012/08/20/entertainment-us-russia-pussyriot-idUSBRE87F1E520120820
6. Transcripts of Pussy Riot's closing statements available at: http://nplusonemag.com/pussy-riot-closing-statements
7. Report with photos and video available at: http://rt.com/news/femen-cross-pussy-riot-930/
8. Petition and 'Free Pussy Riot!' video available at: http://www.change.org/freepussyriot
9. http://www.facebook.com/PutOutPutin http://www.facebook.com GlobalWomenandArt
10. Vadim Nikitin, *The New York Times*, Monday August 20th http://www.nytimes.com/2012/08/21/opinion/the-wrong-reasons-to-back-pussy-riot.html?_r=4

Bibliography

American Association of University Women. *Shortchanging Girls, Shortchanging America.* (1991) American Association of University Women

Anderson, M. ed. *Rock 'n' Roll Camp for Girls: How to Start a Band, Write Songs, Record an Album and Rock Out!!* (2008) Chronicle Books

Andersen, A. & Jenkins M. *Dance of Days: Two Decades of Punk in the Nation's Capital* (2001) Akashic Books

Aune, K. *Reclaiming the F-Word* (2010) Zed

Azzerad, M. *Our Band Could Be Your Life, Scenes from the American Indie Underground, 1981-1991,* (2002) Little Brown

Banyard, K. *The Equality Illusion* (2010) Faber

Bayton, M. *Frock Rock: Women Performing Popular* Music (1998) Oxford University Press

Bayton, M. 'Feminist Music Practice: Problems and Contradictions', in Bennet, T. (ed.), *Rock and Popular Music: Politics, Policies, Institutions* (1993) Routledge

Blush, S. *American Hardcore: A Tribal History,* Feral House (2001)

Bordo, S. *Unbearable Weight: Feminism, Western Culture and the Body* (2004) University of California Press

Bovey, S 'Don't Tread On Me: The Ethos of 60's Garage Punk', (2006) *Popular Music and Society v.29 Issue 4*

Bufwack, M.A & Oermann R.K *Finding Her Voice: The Saga of Women in Country Music,* (1993) Crown Publishers

Burns, L. & Lafrance, M. *Disruptive Divas: Feminism, Identity and Popular Music.* (2002) Routledge

Butler, J. *Gender Trouble.* (2006) Routledge

Ciminelli, D. & Knox, K. *Homocore: The Loud and Raucous Rise of Queer Rock.* (2005) Alyson Books

Clawson, M. 'Masculinity and Skill Acquisition in the Adolescent Rock Band'. (1999) *Popular Music v.18 Issue 1*

Collins, G. *When Everything Changed: The Amzing Journey of American Women from 1960 to Present,* (2009) Brown

Collins, P. *Black Feminist Thought: Knowledge, Consciousness, and the Politics of Empowerment.* (2000) Routledge

Coon, C. *1988: The New Wave Punk Rock Explosion.* (1977) Orbach and Chambers Ltd

Coontz, S. *Marriage, a History: How Love Conquered Marriage* (2004) Penguin

Cooper, S. 'Access some areas: pr in the music industry' in *Girls! Girls! Girls!: Essays on Women in Music* (1995) Cassell

Cost, J. & Irwin, B (1999) 'Char Vinnedge: A Rare Vintage Indeed'. Sleeve note for *The Luv'd Ones: Truth Gotta Stand.* Sundazed: LP 5033

Court, P. *New York Noise* (2007) Soul Jazz Records

Crenshaw, K. 'Demarginalizing the Intersection of Race and Sex: A Black Feminist Critique of Antidiscrimination Doctrine, Feminist Theory, and Anti-Racist Practices', (1989) *The University of Chicago Legal Forum*

Davis, J. 'The Future of "No Future": Punk Rock and Postmodern Theory' (1996) *The Journal of Popular Culture v.29/4*

Dawidoff, N. *In the Country of Country,* (1997) Faber and Faber

Women Make Noise

DeChaine, D. Robert. 'We're here, we're queer, let's Rock! Queercore Music's performative Subversion of Sexuality, gender and Identity'. Paper presented at the Organization for the Study of Communication, Language and Gender Annual Conference, Monterey, CA, 1996

De Chaine, D. 'Mapping Subversion: Queercore Music's Playful Discourse of Resistance.' *Popular Music and Society 21*(4): 7-37.

De Laurentis, T. *The Practice of Love: Lesbian Sexuality and Perverse Desire*, (1994) Indiana University Press

Dibben, N. *Representations of Femininity in Popular Music,* (1999) Cambridge University Press

Douglas, S. *Where the Girls Are: Growing Up Female with the Mass Media* (Three Rivers Press, 1995)

Faludi, S. *Backlash: the Undeclared War against Women,* (1991) Vintage

Filene, B. *Romancing the Folk: Public Memory & American Roots Music,* (2000) University of North Carolina Press

Forman-Brunell, M. ed. *Girlhood In America: An Encyclopedia.* (2001) ABC CLIO

Friedan, B. *The Feminine Mystique,* (1963) Penguin Books

Fudge, R. 'Girl, Unreconstructed: Why Girl Power is Bad for Feminism.' In *BITCHfest: Ten Years of Cultural Criticism from the Pages of Bitch Magazine*, edited by Jervis L. & Zeisler, A. (2006) Farrar, Straus, and Giroux

Gaar, G. *She's a Rebel: The History of Women in Rock'n'Roll.* (1992) Seal Press

Gaunt, K. *The Games Black Girls Play: Learning the Ropes, From Double Dutch to Hip Hop* NYU Press (2006)

Giffort, D. 'Show or Tell? Feminist Dilemmas and Implicit Feminism and Girls' Rock Camp' *Gender and Society*, Vol. 25 No. 5, (October 2011)

Gillett, C. *The Sound of the City: The Rise of Rock & Roll.* (1996) London: Souvenir Press

Gonik, M. 'Between 'Girl Power' and 'Reviving Ophelia': Constituting the Neoliberal Girl Subject' *NWSA Journal,* Volume 18, Number 2, (2006)

Greig, C. *Will You Love Me Tomorrow?* (1989) Virago

Griel, M. *The Rolling Stone Illustrated History of Rock and Roll* (1976) Random House

Grosz, E. *Volatile Bodies: Toward a Corporeal Feminism.* (1994) Indiana University Press

Halberstam, J. *In a Queer Time and Place: Transgender Bodies, Subcultural Lives.* (2005) New York University Press

Hamelman, S. 'But Is It Garbage? The Theme of Trash in Rock and Roll Criticism'. (2003) *Popular Music and Society v.26 Issue 2*

Hayes, E. *Songs in Black and Lavender: Race, Sexual Politics, and Women's Music.* (2010) University of Illinois Press

Hernández, D. & Rehman, B. *Colonize This!: Young Women of Color on Today's Feminism.* (2002) Seal Press

Heywood, L. & Drake, J. *Third Wave Agenda: Being Feminist, Doing Feminism.* (1997) University of Minnesota Press

Hicks, M. *Sixties Rock: Garage, Psychedelic, and Other Satisfactions,* (1999) Urbana and Chicago: University of Illinois Press

hooks, b. *Feminist Theory from Margin to Center.* (1984) South End Press

Hooks, b. *Feminism is for Everybody: Passionate Politics.* (2000) South End Press

Jagar, A. & Bordo, S. *Gender/Body/Knowledge: Feminist Reconstructions of Being and Knowing.* (1989) Rutgers University Press 1989

Bibliography

Juno, A. *Angry Women in Rock, Volume 1* (1996) Juno Books

Kauppila, P. 'The Sound of the Suburbs: A Case Study of Three Garage Bands in San Jose, California during the 1960s. (2005) *Popular Music and Society v.28 Issue 3*

Kearney, M. 'The Missing Links: Riot grrrl-feminism-lesbian culture.' *Sexing the Groove: Popular Music and Gender*, edited by Whiteley, S. (1997) Routledge

Keenan, E. *Acting Like a 'Lady': Third Wave Feminism, Popular Music, and the White Middle Class.* (2008) Ph. D. dissertation, Columbia University

Klein, M. (1997) 'Duality and Continuity in alternative music communities' in Keetley, D. *Public Women, Public Words: A documentary history of American Feminism* (1997) Rowman and Littlefield

Lahickey, B. *All Ages: Reflections on Straight Edge (*1997) Revelation Books

LeBlanc, Lauraine, *Pretty In Punk: Girls' Gender Resistance in a Boys' Subculture* (1999) Rutger's University Press

Leonard, M. *Gender in the Music Industry: Rock, Discourse and Girl Power.* (2007) Ashgate.

Lewis, J. *Women in Britain since 1945.* (1992) Wiley-Blackwell

Mallot, C. *Punk Rockers' Revolution: A Pedagogy of Class, race and gender* (2004) Peter Lang Publishing

Marcus, S. *Girls to the Front: The True Story of the Riot Grrrl Revolution.* (2011) Harper Perennial

Masters, M. *No Wave* (2007) Black Dog Publishing

McLagan, I. *All the Rage: A Riotous Romp through Rock & Roll History*, (2000) Billboard Books

McClary, S. 'Same As it Ever Was: Youth Culture and Music'. *Rock She Wrote: Women Write About Rock, Pop, and Rap.* ed. McDonnell, E. & Powers, A. (1995) Delta

McRobbie, A. & Garber, J. 'Girls and Subculture' in *Feminism and Youth Culture* Ed.II (2000) Routledge

McRobbie, A & Frith, S 'Rock and Sexuality' *On Record: Rock, Pop and the Written Word* (1990) Routledge

Mitchell, C & Reid-Walsh, J. *Girl Culture: a Reader* (2008) Greenwood

Monem, N. *Riot Grrrl: Revolution Girl Style Now* (2007) Black Dog Publishing

Montague, E. 'From Garahge to Garidge: The Appropriation of Garage Rock in the Clash's "Garageland" (1977)'. (2006) *Popular Music and Society v.29 Issue 4*

Moore, T. & Coley, B. *No Wave: Post-Punk. Underground. New York. 1976-1980* (2008) Abrams Image

Moraga, C. & Anzaldúa, G. eds. *This Bridge Called My Back: Writings by Radical Women of Color.* (2002) Third Woman Press.

Morris, B. *Eden Built By Eves* (1999) Alyson Books

Nehring, N. *Popular Music, Gender, and Postmodernism: Anger is an Energy* (1997) Sage Publications

Nutter, A. 'Women's Realm and Other Recipes and Patterns' in Dark Star (ed.) *Quiet Rumours: An Anarcha-Feminist Anthology* (2002) AK Press

O'Meara, C. 'The Raincoats: Breaking Down Punk Rock's Masculinities.' *Popular Music.* Volume 22 (2003)

Orenstein, P. *Schoolgirls: Young Women, Self-Esteem and the Confidence Gap.* (1995) Anchor Books

Orenstein. P, *Cinderella Ate My Daughter: Dispatches from the Front Lines of the New Girly-Girl Culture.*(2011) Harper Collins

Paris, L. 'The Adventures of Peanut and Bo: Summer Camps and Early-Twentieth-Century American Girlhood.' *Journal of Women's History* 12:4 (2001)

Paris, L. 'Summer Camps for Girls' in Forman-Brunell,Miriam ed. *Girlhood In America: An Encyclopedia.* (2001) ABC CLIO

Pecknold, D. 'The Jonas Brothers Are Dorky and Miley Cyrus Is a Slut: Gender, Power, and Money in the Disney Ghetto' paper delivered at the Experience Music Project Pop Studies Conference (2011)

Pipher, M. *Reviving Ophelia: Saving the Selves of Adolescent Girls.* (1994) Random House

Peterson, B. *Burning Fight: The Nineties Hardcore revolution in Ethics, Politics, Spirit and Sound* (2009) Revelations Records

Price, J. *Feminist Theory and the Body: A Reader* (1999) Edinburgh University Press

Quatro, S. *Unzipped.* (2007) Hodder and Stoughton

Raha, M. *Cinderella's Big Score: Women of the Punk and Indie Underground* (2005) Avalon

Raphael, A. *Grrrls: Never mind the Bullocks: Women Rewrite Rock* (1995) Virago

Ravan, G. *Lollipop Lounge: Memoirs of a Rock and Roll Refugee.* (2004), Billboard Books.

Reddington, H. *The Lost Women of Rock Music: Female Musicians of the Punk Era* (2007) Ashgate

Reynolds, S. *Rip It Up and Start Again: post-punk 1978-1984* (2005) Faber and Faber

Reynolds, S. & Press J. *The Sex Revolts: Gender, Rebellion and Rock 'n' Roll,* (1995) Serpent's Tail

Rubin, S. 'Thinking Sex: Notes for a Radical Theory of the Politics of Sexuality' *Pleasure and Danger: Exploring Female Sexuality* ed. Vance C. (1984) Routledge and Kegan Paul

Rudden, P. *Singing for Themselves: Essays on Women in Popular Music* (2007) Cambridge Scholars Publishing

Russell, T. *Country Music Originals,* (2007) Oxford University Press

Russell, T. *Country Music Records: A Discography 1921-1942,* (2004) Oxford University Press

Ryzik, M. 'A Feminist Riot That Still Inspires' *New York Times,* (June 5, 2011)

Savage, J. *England's Dreaming* (2002) Faber and Faber

Schilt, Kri. '"A Little Too Ironic": The Appropriation and Packaging of Riot Grrrl Politics by Mainstream Female Musicians.' *Popular Music and Society* 26 (1) (2003)

Schilt, K. '"The Punk White Privilege Scene": Riot Grrrl, White Privilege, and Zines.' In *Different Wavelengths: Studies of the Contemporary Women's Movement,* edited by Reger, J. (2005) Routledge

Schilt, K. & Zobl, E. 'Connecting the dots: Riot grrrls, Ladyfest and the international grrrl zine network' in Harris, A. *Next Wave Cultures: Feminism, Subcultures, Activism* (2007) Routledge

Shaw, G. 'Sic Transit Gloria…: The Story of Punk Rock in the '60s'. Booklet for *Nuggets: Original Artyfacts from the First Psychedelic Era 1965-1968* (1998) Rhino

Smith, V. *Not Just Race, Not Just Gender: Black Feminist Readings.* (1998) Routledge.

Sonneborn, L. *A-Z of American Women in the performing arts,* (2002) Infobase Publishing

Spargo, T. *Foucault and Queer Theory (Postmodern Encounters)* (1995) Totem Books

Spector, R. *Be My Baby: How I Survived Mascara, Miniskirts and Madness, or My Life as a Fabulous Ronette* (1990) Onyx

Spencer, A. 'The Queer Zine' in *DIY: The Rise of Lo-fi Culture* (2005) Marion Boyars Publishers

Bibliography

Stark, J. *Punk '77: An inside look at the San Francisco rock 'n' roll scene in 1977* (1992) Re/Search Publications

Street Howe, Z. *Typical Girls? The Story of the Slits* (2009) Omnibus Press

Suleiman, S. *Subversive Intent: Gender, Politics and the Avant Garde* (1986) Harvard University Press

Sullivan, C. *Punk* (2001) Cassell Illustrated

Vail, T. 'The Jigsaw Manifesto' *Jigsaw* no.4 (Summer 1991)

Walker, R. *To Be Real: Telling the Truth and Changing the Face of Feminism* (1995 Routledge

Ward, G.F *Shout, Sister, Shout! The untold story of Rock n Roll Trailblazer Sister Rosetta Tharpe,* (2007) Beacon Press

Warwick, J. *Girl Groups, Girl Culture: Popular Muisc and Identity in the 1960s* (2009) Routledge

Weller, S. *Girls Like Us: Carole King, Joni Mitchell, Carly Simon – And the Journey of a Generation* (2008) Washington Square Press

Whiteley, S. *Women and Popular Music: Sexuality, Identity and Subjectivity* (2000) Routledge

Whiteley, S. *Sexing the Groove: Popular Music and Gender* (1997) Routledge

Wobensmith, M. *Queercore: a History in Zines* Outpunk #6 (1996) OutPunk

Young, C. M 'Run-run-run-run Runaways'. (October 1976) *Crawdaddy*

Zwonitzer, M. & Hirshberg, C. *Will You Miss Me When I'm Gone?* (2002) Simon & Schuster

If you enjoyed *Women Make Noise* please explore our other books and plays by women writers and editors at:

www.supernovabooks.co.uk

www.aurorametro.com